THE UNTOLD TRUTH OF THE SON OF SAM

A Journal of a Journey

BY PAUL SANTO AGOSTINO

I have tried to recreate events, locales, and conversations from my memories of them. In order to maintain their anonymity in some instances I have changed the names of individuals and places. I may have changed some identifying characteristics and details such as physical properties, occupations, and places of residence.

Printed in the United States of America

ISBN: 978-0-990-51652-1 (hardcover)
ISBN: 979-8-218-31678-5 (paperback)

This journal is dedicated to all the people of New York who lived through and suffered from the "Son of Sam" crimes and its misleading information. A special dedication to Donna Lauria, Christine Freund, Virginia Voskerichian, Alexander Esau, Valentina Suriani, and Stacy Moskowitz. Also to Peter Intervallo, Thomas Chamberlain, Jack and Nann Cassara, Joaquim Neto, Sam Carr, Frances Carr, John Carr, Michael Carr, Craig Glassman, Neysa Moskowitz, and Maury Terry…may you all rest in peace.

Special recognition given to Josh Zeman for his work on his documentary, *The Sons of Sam: A Descent Into Darkness*.

"It becomes difficult for me to understand myself when I can't even understand many of my motives. Unfortunately, too, I wish it were possible for me to list point by point and detail by detail, every single destructive and vandelous act which I committed in my lifetime. I would be overjoyed to show you what one individual could do in his lifetime, how one single man could cause so much chaos. But I never kept a diary."

David Berkowitz

"In the end, is it not more terrifying to accept that there is no grand conspiracy, no structure, no organization, no method to the madness that haunts us all? That there is only rudderless chaos? To me, that is the ultimate evil."

Maury Terry

There are six things the Lord hates, seven that are detestable to him: haughty eyes, a lying tongue, hands that shed innocent blood, a heart that devises wicked schemes, feet that are quick to rush into evil, a false witness who pours out lies and a person who stirs up conflict in the community.

Proverbs 6:16-19

TABLE OF CONTENTS

CHAPTER I

THE DOCUMENTARY

I would like to welcome you to Yonkers, New York...home of the brave. It is a city that is watched and well guarded by its natives. Strong pride runs through the veins of those genuinely born and raised in this place I call home. If you enter this city, I warn you, you will be noticed upon your arrival as an outsider. Like a pack of a thousand wolves ready to defend their kind, the people of Yonkers will never allow their homeland to be disrespected. My name is Paul Santo Agostino...and I am one of those wolves. This is my journal, this is my journey.

In May 2021, the world was suffering from the impact of Covid-19, a deadly virus that changed everyone's way of living in New York. Businesses were shut down and people were confined to their homes for months. During this time, I came across a captivating four-part documentary series on Netflix titled, *The Sons of Sam: A Descent Into Darkness,* by Josh Zeman. To my surprise, many of the individuals featured in this documentary were from Yonkers, which created an intriguing connection for me. I also grew up just a few blocks away from one of the main characters, the most notorious serial killer in New York City history, the "Son of Sam," David Berkowitz.

The "Son of Sam," whose identity was unknown at the time, had all of New York City terrified for a year from his random shooting attacks on innocent people. It all started on July 29, 1976, at 1:00 a.m. Two girls, Donna Lauria, 18, and Jody Valenti, 19, were both shot while sitting in a parked car on Buhre Avenue in the Pelham Bay section of the Bronx. Donna was killed instantly. Jody was wounded in her left leg and lived to give police a description of the killer...a white male in his late thirties wearing a blue striped shirt.

On October 23, 1976, at 2:05 a.m., Carl Denaro, 20, and Rosemary Keenan, 18, sat in a parked car on 159th Street and 33rd Avenue in Flushing, Queens. The couple was attacked out of nowhere as a window to their car began to shatter from a loud boom. Both survived as Carl was shot in the back of the head and Rosemary escaped with some minor injuries...they saw no one.

On November 27, 1976, at 12:40 a.m., Joanne Lomino, 18, and Donna DeMasi, 17, were approached by a white male while they were on the front steps of Joanne's house on 262nd Street in the Bellrose section of Queens. The stranger asked the two girls for directions and then shot them both before fleeing. The victims survived and were able to give police composite sketches of the man they remembered.

On January 30, 1977, at 12:30 a.m., John Diel, 30, and Christine Freund, 26, sat in a parked car on Station Square in Forest Hills, Queens when they were attacked. John was unharmed, but Christine was shot and died instantly. No one witnessed the murder.

On March 8, 1977, at 7:30 p.m., Virginia Voskerichian, 19, was walking home from school alone when she was shot and killed on Dartmouth Street in Forest Hills, Queens...only a half block away from where the last attack occured. A witness saw a single, white male run past him away from the scene of the shooting wearing a ski cap.

This is when the real fear started to set in for the people of New York. Before now, these attacks were considered unrelated, but a few days after this last shooting, law enforcement would have a connection. Ballistic testing to the bullets used in the July 29, 1976 shooting matched the bullets used in the shooting on March 8, 1977. Law enforcement soon realized that a .44 caliber revolver was also being used in the other three unsolved attacks. Now the media had a name for this murderer...the ".44 Caliber Killer."

On April 17, 1977, at 2:50 a.m., Valentina Suriani, 18, and Alexander Esau, 20, were sitting in a parked car near Hutchinson River Parkway in the Bronx when they were both shot and killed by .44 caliber bullets. There were no witnesses, but a letter from the killer was left at this murder scene calling himself the "Son of Sam."

On June 26, 1977, at 3:20 a.m., Judy Placido, 17, and Sal Lupo, 20, sat in a parked car on 211th Street in Bayside, Queens. Both were shot during this attack and survived with injuries. The signature .44 caliber bullets were used once again at this attempted murder. Judy and Sal did not see who shot them, but witnesses at the scene came forward to police with what they saw and another composite sketch was made.

Finally, the last attack would occur on July 31, 1977, at 2:30 a.m., resulting in the death of Stacy Moskowitz, 20, and serious injury to Robert Violante, 20. The couple was sitting in a parked car on Shore Parkway near the Bath Beach Park in Brooklyn. According to a witness, a white male came out from the park entrance and shot into the car Stacy and Robert were in. The man then ran back into the park where he came from. Ten days after this attack, David Berkowitz was arrested and would forever be known as the "Son of Sam."

After his arrest, law enforcement told the public Berkowitz admitted he acted alone committing the shootings and was taking orders to kill from a talking dog. They immediately closed the case, and no information was ever released.

Berkowitz's excuse for shooting these random people was he had been driven by demons and killed out of obedience to his master, Sam Carr. According to Berkowitz, Sam would command him to kill through Sam's dog, a black Labrador Retriever. Sam lived at 316 Warburton Avenue, directly behind David Berkowitz's apartment building at 35 Pine Street in Yonkers and was married to a woman named Frances. They had two sons, John and Michael, and a daughter named Wheat.

The Sons of Sam documentary presented convincing evidence that challenged the narrative of David Berkowitz acting alone while committing the "Son of Sam" shootings. It suggested Berkowitz was aided by a satanic cult that gathered at Untermyer Park located in Yonkers. This theory was based on years of investigative work done by a man named Maury Terry, a Yonkers native who worked as an editor for IBM. In this documentary, Josh Zeman explores Maury Terry's theories as he uses Maury's original groundwork to bring to life Maury's investigation.

In 1977, immediately after Berkowitz's arrest, the media scrambled to get the real story about the "Son of Sam." A *New York Post* editor, Jim Mitteager, was able to visit Berkowitz while he was being held at Kings County Hospital after his arrest. Mitteager saw a letter Berkowitz sent to *New York Post* editor Steve Dunleavy stating, "*There are other 'Son's' out there-God help the world.*" Mitteager showed Maury this letter, and Maury got the urge to find out who those other "*Son's*" were.

Maury then took it upon himself to investigate the "Son of Sam" crimes and soon came across many coincidences which aroused his suspicion to question if David Berkowitz acted alone.

The sketches from the witnesses who saw the shooter at the attacks all seemed to look nothing like David Berkowitz. Maury felt the sketches from each of the witnesses were so different, they couldn't possibly be the same person all of them saw. Two pieces of evidence Maury thought needed more attention were the infamous "Son of Sam" letters.

On April 17, 1977, a letter was left at the Bronx murder scene by the killer. The envelope to the letter was addressed to "*MR. JOE BORELLI QUEENS HOMICIDE.*" Joseph Borrelli was a Queens Detective assigned to the ".44 Caliber Killer" case. The author of this letter called himself the "*SON OF SAM*" and wrote about a mean father named Sam who abused his family. After Maury saw this letter, he was convinced it was written by Sam Carr's son, John.

On June 2, 1977, a second letter was sent from the killer to famed *Daily News* columnist Jimmy Breslin. One of the clues written in the letter was the name "*JOHN WHEATIES*." Maury found a listing in the 1976 Yonkers phone book for John Wheat Carr and believed that "*JOHN WHEATIES*" in this letter was referring to John Carr.

Maury was confident John Carr had written the Borrelli letter, but he didn't think he was the author of the letter sent to Breslin. He stressed there were differences in the handwriting and languages between the two. He thought Michael Carr, who was a graphic designer, wrote the Breslin letter due to the artistic handwriting style.

Michael Carr supposedly belonged to the Church of Scientology in Manhattan, N.Y. From the roots of Scientology, a group of people formed a splinter group called The Process. The Process was an organization that started in London, went to California and Mexico, then split up and relocated in several areas of New York. Maury claimed this was the group David Berkowitz's satanic cult was a part of, calling themselves "The Children," and gathering at Untermyer Park. Maury also connected Charles Manson to The Process Church in California, which painted a way bigger picture than just one crazy guy and a talking dog.

Six months after the arrest of Berkowitz, John Carr allegedly committed suicide and Maury believed it was because of his involvement in the "Son of Sam" shootings. According to the North Dakota Police, they went to question John about trespassing at a housing unit on the Minot Air Force Base, and when they were at the front door of where John was living, they heard a gunshot, then found him dead inside. The North Dakota Police ruled his death a suicide.

A few weeks before his death, John Carr spoke with a psychiatrist in North Dakota, Lee Slagter, who stated John told him he was afraid someone was trying to kill him and he might be in trouble with the law back in New York. Lee Slagter also stated John said he had a connection with David

Berkowitz and information he thought the police in New York would be interested in. Maury heard about this and became more confident of John Carr's involvement with David Berkowitz.

Maury was further intrigued when Michael Carr died in a car accident a year after John's death. Michael was driving home alone late one night on the West Side Highway in N.Y. and crashed into a divider for no apparent reason…he died instantly. These two mysterious deaths after Berkowitz's arrest raised more questions for Maury. Motivated to find answers, he traveled to Minot, North Dakota, where he discovered John Carr's involvement in a satanic cult.

Maury then brought his theories and findings to law enforcement officials, but they continuously dismissed him, and repeatedly told him the case was closed. He believed the police closed the case due to what he thought was sloppy police work, which included an illegal search of Berkowitz's car without a warrant.

Engulfing himself in the case, Maury quit his job as an IBM editor and in 1979, he began publishing articles for *The Gannett Suburban Newspapers* about the "Son of Sam." Soon, his investigation started to gain traction, prompting Queens District Attorney John Santucci to reopen the case and investigate some of Maury's findings. These District Attorney files have never been released.

In 1980, David Berkowitz began to correspond with Maury, and this is when Berkowitz's story started to change. He still took responsibility for the crimes, but claimed he didn't act alone. Berkowitz admitted to being part of a cult and implicated John Carr as another member. He confirmed there were others involved in the "Son of Sam" murders, scattered throughout the United States.

Maury then interviewed Tommy Zaino, a key witness to the last shooting in Brooklyn. Tommy was adamant the person he saw shoot Stacy

Moskowitz and Robert Violante was not David Berkowitz. He told Maury the hair on the man he saw that night did not look like Berkowitz's. He also claimed he saw more than one person in the area during the shooting. To Maury, everything was pointing to Berkowitz having accomplices.

In 1985, Maury met a teenager at Untermyer Park who had witnessed a cult gather there many times late at night to sacrifice animals. During Maury's tour of the park, he saw signs of a satanic cult's presence everywhere. Maury believed he found the cult that David Berkowitz belonged to and showcased his theory in a 1987 episode of *Unsolved Mysteries*, a television show on NBC.

In 1987, Maury became a bestseller, publishing all of his investigative findings on the "Son of Sam" in his book titled, *The Ultimate Evil.*

In 1993, David Berkowitz agreed to meet Maury in person for an interview while incarcerated at the Sullivan Correctional Facility in Fallsburgh, New York. Berkowitz provided Maury with further information and confirmed his theories regarding a satanic cult's involvement in the "Son of Sam" shootings. According to Berkowitz, he made a blood pact with this cult and was forced to hand in pictures of his family. He feared for their safety if he broke the pact. Berkowitz would stunningly admit he only pulled the trigger in two of the shootings, specifically the two in the Bronx. He also confirmed John and Michael Carr were part of the satanic cult, and agreed Michael was killed by the cult because he knew too much.

In 1996, Detective Kevin Murphy of the Yonkers Police Department was assigned to investigate cult activity in Yonkers. Maury and Detective Murphy were friends and began to work together for answers. Their investigation would find many more coincidences surrounding the "Son of Sam" case.

Berkowitz would meet Maury for another interview and confirm Maury's theories were correct once again. During this interview, Berkowitz was able to identify cult members from portraits Maury placed in front of him. These portraits were drawn and given to Maury from a man called Billy the artist.

In 2015, Maury Terry passed away and he left a labyrinth of clues for people still interested in this case to figure out. His work was left in the hands of Josh Zeman, and this amazing documentary he created brought Maury and this case back to life.

While watching *The Sons of Sam*, I realized Maury Terry's sister was my mother's best friend, Kay Terry Amicone. I grew up with Kay's sons, but I don't ever remember hearing anything about Maury when I was younger. I called my mother to ask if Maury's sister had ever told her anything about the "Son of Sam." Kay said her brother came across a lot of bad things that happened in our neighborhoods, so he stopped looking into it. "What do you mean, what did he come across?" I asked. My mother said she did not know, and that is all Kay had ever told her.

CHAPTER II

THE OUTSIDER

I was never a person who was interested in true crime, Yonkers was why I was so attracted to the "Son of Sam" case. I wanted to learn more about it, so I started to search the internet to see what information I could find. I was amazed to see this case was still famous forty-four years later. There were tons of current videos and discussions, most of them debating who was really responsible for the "Son of Sam" shootings.

While searching the internet, I came across a kid named Larry Dunn filming videos on the aqueduct path near Untermyer Park in Yonkers. It was a dirt path that ran straight through all of Yonkers alongside the Hudson River. Larry was discussing Maury Terry's book, *The Ultimate Evil*, as I enjoyed the Yonkers backdrop. He was in agreement with everything Maury had investigated, that there was a bigger picture, a bigger network behind the "Son of Sam" attacks. I could tell immediately Larry was not from Yonkers. He was an outsider, and I could feel it.

With a sense of protectiveness, I checked the date of this video to see when he filmed it. He was just walking around my old neighborhood about a month earlier. The aqueduct path was my backyard, and his video was making me feel at home again.

During this video, Larry brought up an incident that happened while he was working at a synagogue in 2003. He met an usher who was from Yonkers and was convinced the usher knew John Carr. The usher told him John Carr's nickname was "Wheaties," and he was calling David Berkowitz "Berkie." After continuously questioning the usher, the usher became very agitated and started doing stab-like motions at him, yelling "Diablo, Diablo,

Moskowitz." The usher then threatened to shoot him if he continued to bother him.

I could not believe what I was hearing. The usher scared this kid so badly, he never looked at this case again until now. Everything Larry was talking about was new to me. To understand this more, I purchased Maury Terry's book, *The Ultimate Evil.*

A few weeks later, Larry released another video he filmed in the neighborhood of North Broadway in Yonkers. He was now walking on my old paper route from when I was ten years old and claimed this area was heavily populated with doctors who were some how connected to the "Son of Sam."

In this video, Larry stopped at a Baptist Church in Yonkers on Hudson Terrace. I was always around that area when I was young as the houses were vacant. I would often meet my first girlfriend on the front steps of that property where he was filming. Larry explained this church ran an organization called CFLA, Catholics For Latin America. CFLA was set up to help children in need from Latin American countries. Larry claimed this organization was connected to the "Son of Sam" cult and was funneling children from other countries illegally into America to sell for satanic rituals and abuse.

The doctor who was in charge of CFLA was Dr. Robert Onorato. He supposedly lived directly behind the Baptist Church property on North Broadway. I delivered papers to that house in the '80s. This entire North Broadway area Larry was walking around was home to me. I liked the videos, but I wasn't sure if this kid knew what he was talking about. After a few weeks, I started to communicate with Larry through the comment section of his videos. I have never communicated with anyone through the computer before. No email, no Zoom, etc. I know Yonkers, and he won't walk those streets freely...let me welcome this outsider.

Here was my first email to Larry on June 2, 2021.

Paul: I have been watching your videos and don't know if I can help, but I grew up in the area of Hudson Terrace, North Broadway, Warburton, the Aqueduct, etc. I grew up on Jody Lane. I am forty-five years old, and I know it's a little past the events of the Son of Sam, but you never know what you can get leads on. CFLA, the place you are talking about, I hung around those grounds from 1986-1992. The doctor you are talking about, Onorato, I don't remember exactly if it was him, but that house was on my paper route from 1986-1988. Next to that CFLA place, to the left, I think was a nuns' house. Nobody was there much, as I told you we hung out on the grounds a lot. I would also ride my bike on the aqueduct from 1983-1989. I hung out in Untermyer Park from 1982-2000. Went there as a kid and as I got older, we threw keg parties at night, mostly the steps. We also hung out at the Eagle's Nest, or what some called the devil's cliff, which was to the left of the park. I grew up next to Mayor John Spencer, the mayor of Yonkers from 1994-2002, he was like a father to me. I know Kay Amicone, Maury Terry's sister. I grew up with Kay's kids at the Amackassin Club from 1980-1990. I also have worked over twenty years for the City of Yonkers. Lennon Park and the North Yonkers Boys Club is where I grew up playing sports from 1981-1992. Reach out if you want.

Now remember, this was the first email I ever sent to anyone. I didn't even know if I sent it to the right person. Why was I reaching out to an outsider and getting involved in this? For some reason I was drawn to look into this case.

Larry answered my email the next morning.

Larry: Thanks for reaching out Paul.

Paul: I have been asking around the same as you. Just keep me in mind and throw some names at me when you want. Like I said, I knew everyone in this area around the 1980s. I can still get a lot of people in this city to talk. I also work with the police and firemen. I have very close relationships with the detectives in Yonkers, they are my friends. I refurbish the precincts and firehouses in Yonkers, I know just about every one of them. Just looking to help anyway I can, life is good.

Larry emailed me back a few hours later.

Larry: If you come across any information on Boy Scout troops 4 and 12, Karen Wahlstrom, or Brother John, let me know.

Alright, I'm sure I can research these names and come up with something, but before I do, let me see if my mother or father knew Dr. Onorato.

What I found out from my mother was a bit shocking to me at first. I definitely did not expect to hear what I am about to tell you. When I asked if she knew Dr. Onorato, she told me he was the doctor who delivered me at birth. She sent me a photo of my birth certificate and Dr. Robert Onorato was the doctor who brought me into this world.

After speaking to my mother, I called my father who also confirmed Dr. Onorato did deliver me. Both of my parents said he was a good man. I told my father what I was hearing on the internet about Dr. Onorato and he replied that it was all ridiculous.

My father's best friends in Yonkers were doctors, and he said they all used Sam Carr's answering service for their medical calls. This seemed a little strange being that Larry was going around my neighborhoods claiming doctors in Yonkers were part of the beginning of what became the "Son of Sam."

My father did have a Berkowitz story for me. In 1977, my father was training German Shepherds and would often sell them through ads in the newspaper. David Berkowitz responded to one of those ads by calling my house and asking my father how much the dog was. That was the only conversation he ever had with Berkowitz, and he did not come by the house to buy the dog.

After speaking with my parents, I began to research the names Larry emailed me. When it came to Boy Scout troops 4 and 12, I found a name Walter Deyo that stood out to me. Walter Deyo and his extended family were heavily involved in running the Boy Scouts in the Sacred Heart, Yonkers area. What connection did Walter Deyo have with David Berkowitz? I couldn't figure that out. I then researched Brother John and Karen Wahlstrom.

Before I get into these two names, I would like to point out at this time, Larry was making videos I did not agree with. He was walking around my Catholic school and church, Sacred Heart, with some wild accusations. As he walked those concrete sidewalks, sidewalks I knew every single crack of, he was telling his audience it was the breeding grounds for a satanic cult that David Berkowitz was a part of. I knew those neighborhoods extremely well and all the residents who lived there. What was going on in my city that would make this kid say a satanic cult formed there?

In 1961, Paul Ranieri, aka Brother John, was classmates with John Carr at Sacred Heart High School. Maury Terry had the opportunity to personally interview him in 1992. Brother John claimed he was a member of a Westchester cult that gathered at Untermyer Park. He witnessed this cult's early era before he fled New York to save his life in 1973, three years before the ".44 Caliber Killer" shootings began. According to Brother John, this cult was started way back in the early 1950s, was heavily involved in Satanism, and existed long before David Berkowitz came to Yonkers. He said it was John Carr who recruited him and several other adolescents for this cult when they were both freshmen at Sacred Heart. He was raped at Untermyer Park in order to be initiated into this cult. Dogs were also sacrificed at his initiation ritual.

After becoming a member of this cult, Brother John was forced to become a teenage prostitute, and was part of a prostitution ring that operated out of a bar near the Carrs' residence. One story he mentioned in this interview was about when he needed to go to the Carr house to be cared for after he was raped.

Brother John also recalled when he was asked by members of this cult to dig up the bodies of two dead children and re-bury them on the grounds of the Baptist Church on Hudson Terrace. He took a picture so he would remember the exact spot where he re-buried the bodies. The picture showed the front steps of the property. I sat on those steps over a thousand times with my first girlfriend. I spent so many hours there, and this guy Brother John was claiming dead bodies of kidnapped children were buried right beside me the entire time. This next testimony from Brother John leads us into Larry's last person of interest, Karen Wahlstrom.

Karen Wahlstrom was a teacher at Sacred Heart High School in 1961. She taught John Carr and Brother John during their freshman year. According to Brother John, they knew her well and she was asking too many questions about the cult, so she was lured into Van Cortlandt Park in the Bronx and killed. Her death was reported as a suicide.

This interview with Brother John was crucial in Maury Terry's investigation as this information would help him further connect John Carr to a cult at Untermyer Park. This interview also claimed John Carr recruited several kids for a cult when he was a freshman at Sacred Heart High School...in 1961...fifteen years before Berkowitz moved to Yonkers.

On June 23, 2021, I emailed Larry a newspaper article I found about Dr. Robert Onorato.

Paul: Trying to send you an article from the 1970 Gazette. It states Dr. Robert Onorato resigned from the hospital he worked at because he did not agree with the newly passed abortion laws. Dr. Onorato was against killing babies, it went against his religious beliefs. I know you may think it's a diversion, but I don't know, the guy also had seven kids of his own.

Larry: Someone already sent me those articles, thanks.

After I did more research on Dr. Onorato, I realized the Onorato family and the Carr family were related through marriage. Pauline Carr, Sam Carr's sister, was married to Dr. Robert Onorato's brother, John Onorato. I think because of this marriage, Larry assumed the Onoratos were involved with whatever the Carrs were up to.

I found not one negative article about Dr. Onorato. In fact, I found more than one newspaper article stating he was against abortion. That doesn't sound like someone trafficking children to me.

One person who contacted me about Dr. Onorato was a retired detective from the Yonkers Police Department, Detective Hanrahan. He reached out to me by getting my phone number from a mutual friend and told me Larry had things wrong. Dr. Onorato was not a part of what Larry was saying. Dr. Onorato's nieces and nephews were currently living at the house where Larry was filming, and they didn't like the lies he was spreading.

Detective Hanrahan also had a cousin who worked for CFLA, and it was a legit foundation. They were really helping children in other countries have a better life. Dr. Robert Onorato did not have any involvement in child trafficking for a satanic cult.

The next video Larry released was with a man named Bob Cosi. Bob was a parishioner of Sacred Heart Church and grew up around the corner from Sacred Heart High School in the 1960s. He walked with Larry past my church and school, then onto a footpath through Lennon Park, a park that I had walked through hundreds of times growing up.

Bob told a story from when he was twelve years old, the year was 1962. An older teen from the neighborhood used to lure him into abandoned houses and show him pornography. This older teen was connected to the Boy Scout troops Larry was mentioning in his email and videos. The older teen's nickname was "Scout," whose real name was Walter Deyo Jr. Scout was the son of Walter Deyo, the man who I found earlier running the Boy Scouts in the Sacred Heart, Yonkers area.

After going with Scout a few times to these abandoned houses, Scout tried to molest Bob, but he refused and told him to stop. One day, a mother from the neighborhood saw Bob with Scout and called Bob's mother to tell her. When Bob came home later that day, his mother started questioning him about where he had been. She knew he was with Scout and demanded he tell her what was going on. Bob then broke down and told his mother what Scout was doing to him. She immediately called the Yonkers Police Department and had Scout arrested. He was interrogated and admitted to sodomizing six youths in the area. According to Maury, he was told Scout and John Carr hung out together, and were involved in witchcraft.

When I watched Bob's video, it brought back a flood of memories. I hung out in Lennon Park where they were filming so many times. Memories connected to specific places hold significant meanings, and Lennon Park was the backdrop for a lot of events in my life.

I emailed Larry a few days later after I saw a video of him walking right by the house I grew up in.

Paul: Hey, go down a little bit from Hudson Terrace, past Jody Lane, and you have the only historic medieval castle in Yonkers to your left once you turn right on the bend. Your viewers would appreciate it. My parents told me Sammy Davis Jr. almost bought that castle in the 1970s. I checked the graduating classes of Sacred Heart High School in the 1960s and there was a Susan Longbucco Butler who was there. I am very close with her son Dave, and was best friends with her deceased son Danny. Her husband, Arthur Butler, was a detective in Yonkers and is in one of the pictures with David Berkowitz the night he was arrested, I can talk to Dave.

I got another simple reply back from Larry.

Larry: I've seen the castle Paul, it's unbelievably creepy. If I need more info I'll be in touch.

On July 15, 2021, I called an old friend of mine who was now retired from the City of Yonkers to ask him some questions about the Carrs. I was surprised to hear he knew Sam Carr well, as he worked with Sam for five years while working for the city from 1972 to 1977. My friend was Sam's everyday laborer. Coincidentally, Sam did the exact same job that I do now, refurbishing city buildings.

Two weeks before Berkowitz's arrest, Sam told my friend he knew David Berkowitz was the "Son of Sam." I asked my friend, "How did Sam know that?" He didn't remember how he knew, he just remembered Sam telling him David Berkowitz was the "Son of Sam." When I asked if he had ever heard of the Carrs being involved with the "Son of Sam" shootings, he replied, "Never." According to my friend, Sam kept to himself, and didn't bother with many. He got along with him good and said he was an exceptional worker. This was odd, how did Sam know that David Berkowitz was the "Son of Sam" before his arrest?

A few days later, Larry released another video. This time, he had a familiar face with him, my friend Justine. I haven't seen Justine in over ten years, what the hell was she doing with him? In the Bob Cosi video, the woman who tells Bob's mother he was with Scout was Justine's grandmother. Obviously, Justine is watching these videos too. If you connect the dots right, by the end of this journal, you will see what a key piece Justine actually turned out to be.

On July 19, 2021, Justine walked around Untermyer Park with Larry as she recalled in the late '70s how she found a dead German Shepherd in the park and crosses that were carved on the trees. These crosses were supposedly markers for where kidnapped children were buried in the park. She couldn't locate where the crosses were, but she remembered seeing them when she was young. These stories Justine was telling had already been heard by all the people who grew up in Yonkers, but the audience needed to hear them now too.

That night I met with the ex-mayor of Yonkers, my very close friend, John Spencer. He went to Sacred Heart High School with John Carr, was taught by Karen Wahlstrom, and knew Bob Cosi. He mentioned Sam Carr was around the Boys Club a lot in the '80s and I should have known him. He was right, I do remember seeing Sam there when I was young.

Spencer asked Sam in the early '80s what happened to his son John. Sam sadly replied, "John killed himself." Spencer didn't believe that because the rifle John used was not a typical weapon someone would use to commit suicide. When I asked if he knew Maury Terry, I was shocked when he told me they were very good friends. Maury gave him his book personally the first day it was published.

Spencer remembered Karen Wahlstom taught him at Sacred Heart High School during his freshman year and was told she committed suicide. He did not hear anything about any involvement with her and a satanic cult.

The next time I saw Larry on video, he had a co-host with him, Mason Kraft. Mason seemed very educated with video technology, but extremely uneducated with the "Son of Sam" case.

On July 24, 2021, Larry teamed up with my friend Justine again to film another video at Untermyer Park. This time Justine brought up how she would hear beating drums coming from the aqueduct at dusk and thought it was a cult gathering at Untermyer Park. At that moment, something happened to me. The mention of beating drums sparked more vivid memories. I knew I heard those drums before myself.

When Justine brought up hearing those drums, it immediately took me back to my bedroom when I was four years old. My bedroom window overlooked the entire Hudson River, and was one block away from the aqueduct. At dusk, I heard those drums, she made me remember. I didn't think anything of this when I was younger, but was that what it was? Was a satanic cult traveling on the aqueduct to Untermyer Park beating their drums? During this video, Justine also talked about a doctor she was suspicious of who lived next to Untermyer Park. His name was Dr. Albert Laverne.

When I researched Dr. Albert Laverne, thanks to Justine, it opened a few important doors for me when I contacted some good friends who were from Dr. Laverne's neighborhood. One of these friends is extremely essential to this story.

Dr. Laverne was a psychiatrist who specialized in drugging his patients and recording the outcomes. In 1961, Dr. Laverne's wife was shot by one of his patients who complained to him about how he ruined her life. This patient was desperately seeking help from Dr. Laverne, and he would not see her upon her requests. Because Dr. Laverne was refusing to see her, the patient drove to his apartment building and shot his wife in the lobby entrance…killing her in front of her two children.

On September 13, 1979, Dr. Albert Laverne's house caught fire and he was charged with felony arson, reckless endangerment, and grand larceny. The Yonkers Police investigated the arson and found that Dr. Laverne had torched his own home and was attempting to swindle his insurance company by submitting false claims.

Justine said Dr. Laverne had coffins inside his house, recalled his kids were not normal, and said there were always medical supplies littered around his home.

I became skeptical of Dr. Laverne and began to think, he could have been supplying the satanic cult in Untermyer Park with drugs, experimental drugs that could have caused all those devil-worshiping kids to act crazy.

I reached out to a friend who grew up in the area in which Dr. Laverne lived. He did not know Dr. Laverne but knew of him. He remembered when his house burned down, everybody in the neighborhood was outside watching. He used to cut through Dr. Laverne's property, as it was a shortcut to get to the park. He backed up Justine's story by telling me he used to see medical supplies scattered all around his home.

I asked my friend if he ever saw anything around the park pertaining to a satanic cult. Besides all the graffiti, he said he saw dead cats hanging from the trees a few times. He was in the aqueduct's underground pipeline, traveling inside all the way to Hastings, which was a good way from Yonkers. We talked about the famous Devil's Cave, a cement dugout located in the park which was covered with painted satanic symbols. He hung out in the Devil's Cave plenty of times and said he never saw any satanic cults there.

After getting no information about Dr. Laverne, I called another friend of mine, a Yonkers fireman who lived next to the park. He also knew of Dr. Laverne but didn't know him personally. During our conversation, he asked me if I knew Randy Hughes. He heard stories in the '80s that Randy's brother was kidnapped, tied up in Untermyer Park by devil worshipers and forced to watch a dog being sacrificed. With that information, I definitely needed to find Randy Hughes.

I emailed Larry to tell him about Randy Hughes, and asked if he had ever heard of him...I got no response.

The research on this case was extremely overwhelming, and it was clear I was going to need some help. Enter Penny, what a solid go-to researcher she was. Anything that I could not get through, she could. Penny and I decided to look into Scout, Walter Deyo Jr., and after about thirty minutes, we found some people in Yonkers who were related to him. We were stunned, Scout had a cousin who was still living in the area. If this information was correct, I've known Scout's cousin for about 20 years.

On July 27, 2021, Larry released a video and showed two of my emails I had sent him to his audience. It bothered me he showed my emails without first asking me for permission. Why would he do that?

I emailed Larry the next day.

Paul: I'm trying to help you, please do not show my emails again without asking me first. You may think all these contacts are just random people I found, they are not. I happen to love all these people I'm talking to. The last thing I need right now is someone's life getting affected by me doing this. You can't do that to me, to the people I love. Please, just ask me and we can make it right where no one is in danger.

Larry: I apologize for that, it won't happen again.

Paul: Please be careful for all of us, seriously. I know you mean well, you just got to be careful.

That night, I reached out to a lady I've known my entire life, Mrs. Callahan. She was a classmate of John Carr and a student of Karen Wahlstrom at Sacred Heart High School. She provided me with valuable firsthand information about both of these individuals. This lady sat next to John Carr in homeroom class, and when she saw the police sketch of the "Son of Sam," she thought it looked like John because he had squinty eyes, similar to the sketch. She had nothing bad to say about John, she actually said he was very smart. She was told by her teachers that Ms. Wahlstrom was sick and killed herself.

This lady also knew Paul Ranieri, aka Brother John, and said he was a major nut case. She made it clear to me, Paul Ranieri and John Carr were not from the area. They were only at Sacred Heart High School for one year in 1961 before they were kicked out.

Mrs. Callahan also knew Bob Cosi and Scouty Deyo, as she called him. She said Scouty Deyo was a loner who no one hung out with.

I discussed with Mrs. Callahan all the people from our neighborhoods who Larry was associating with this satanic cult. A cult Maury Terry would come to call the twenty-two disciples of hell. In the letter sent to Jimmy Breslin, *"THE TWENTY TWO DISCIPLES OF HELL"* was a clue left by the author. Maury was convinced this clue referred to Berkowitz's twenty-two person cult, "The Children." I went through about ten names with Mrs. Callahan from Larry's videos and she knew every single one of them. Every person I brought up had no connection to David Berkowitz at all and were 100 percent not involved with a satanic cult. This lady also coached Dr. Onorato's two daughters and she didn't see anything wrong with him either, she knew him personally.

When I asked Mrs. Callahan if she ever heard of the twenty-two disciples of hell, she replied, "No." She did hear of Berkowitz being part of a satanic cult, but only after his arrest. She knew no one that was in a cult, and only heard rumors of what went on at Untermyer Park.

Mrs. Callahan owned a yellow Volkswagen bug which was stolen from her in 1976, just a few blocks away from David Berkowitz's apartment. I mention this because Maury had claimed a yellow Volkswagen bug was seen at some of the "Son of Sam" shootings.

I thanked Mrs. Callahan for her time, and told her I missed her. This lady had been like a mother to me, she raised me in a sense. I was blessed this case connected me to her again. I was able to thank her for all she did for me growing up. Our Yonkers community was in great debt to her, she knew and cared for everyone in our neighborhoods. She is an amazing person with a heart of gold, all my love to you Mrs. Callahan.

I walked around every block and called everyone I knew in all the Yonkers neighborhoods from Warburton Avenue to Sacred Heart. No one knew David Berkowitz, and no one heard of a twenty-two person satanic cult that gathered in Yonkers. A lot of people said they had run into Berkowitz, but no one actually hung out with him, or knew him personally. He was an outsider and was treated like one.

On July 30, 2021, I emailed Larry for more information about a suspect from one of his videos.

Paul: Send me what you have on Robert "Tocco" Grady.

Larry: Robert "Tocco" Grady was supposedly David Berkowitz's handler in this twenty-two disciples of hell cult. Maury Terry looked into Tocco and insinuated he was with Michael Carr and David Berkowitz at the Candlelight Inn in Scarsdale the night a lady was shot in the leg while inside the restaurant. Maury heard they had an argument while inside the bar area and left. That same night, a lady was shot in the leg by someone from outside the establishment. Maury claimed it was Berkowitz or someone from his group who shot the lady. Maury also said on a different night, Wheat Carr shot the clock out above the bar.

In 1996, while I was home from college, I visited my neighborhood bar Olde Tymes on Lake Avenue to catch up with a few friends. I remember this big, burly guy walked in all drunk and wobbly. The entire bar started screaming, "Tocco." This guy had to be about fifty-five years old at the time, and everyone in the bar was messing around with him. I remembered this once Larry mentioned Tocco's name. Could this possibly be the same Tocco this kid was talking about in his videos? The first thing I noticed after I began to research Robert "Tocco" Grady was his arrest in 2014 for being a sex offender to underage children.

That evening, I was introduced to the horrible things that can occur on the internet. I went on Twitter for the first time in my life and saw Larry was fighting with people, exchanging insults. I was a bit puzzled by the way he was acting as he always came across on video as being calm and accepting. What I was now seeing on Larry's Twitter was a lot of nasty comments he was sending to people. What was he thinking? He was sure to turn people away when they saw his negativity and insults.

I emailed Larry that night to give him some confidence.

Paul: I kind of thought you might feel like you are losing steam, content is getting low, keep your head up, don't forget Berkowitz. Justine just opened up Laverne, hang in there and stop answering those Twitter clowns, stay focused.

Larry: That's exactly how I'm feeling, thanks. Do you think you can get the file on Walter Deyo Jr., aka Scout, that Bob Cosi saw in 1967? I'm curious to see if Maury's name is on it. I won't publicize any of the names from the report unless one of them is Maury Terry.

The file Larry was asking for had the names of the six boys Scout, Walter Deyo Jr., had sodomized in 1962. The interrogation report was put into the Yonkers Police files, which Bob Cosi saw when he was employed as a Yonkers Police Officer at the evidence department in 1967. Bob left the force soon after he found this report and said finding it factored into him quitting. This proves, without doubt, a report was taken and entered into Yonkers evidence.

Larry said he would only publicize Maury's name if it was on the report. What was that all about? Did Larry have something personal against Maury Terry? Why would he want to shame him?

That night, I made some phone calls to a few Yonkers Detectives and street cops to ask about the records on Scout. I was told all records from 1984 and down were thrown out, destroyed, or lost.

On August 2, 2021, I emailed Larry.

Paul: Can we Zoom later tonight so we can talk in private?

Larry: Tonight I won't be available, I will get a hold of you next week.

Larry then announced on Twitter he was only releasing his videos on a paid website going forward. The paid website to follow him cost ten dollars a month.

I emailed Larry after I read this.

Paul: I'm in, I'm sending you some cash tomorrow, I'll get it to Justine.

I wanted to help this kid, so I gave Justine's sister three hundred dollars for Justine to give to Larry. Justine's sister knew nothing about what her sister was doing at all. I gave her the money, and didn't hear from Larry for three days.

On August 5, 2021, I emailed Larry about the money.

Paul: Did the cash reach you that I sent the other day?

Larry: I appreciate it, but I'm not accepting it, thanks though.

Paul: I see you stressing out, I'm just trying to help, no problem.

This kid didn't want my help. I knew everyone in this city, and he didn't want to trust me. I thought it was time I took a hint. At the least, I'm glad I was able to get this kid away from my church.

All these people Larry discussed in his videos had nothing to do with the "Son of Sam." His leads on the many people from Yonkers I vindicated for him were not adding up, and I couldn't sit there and watch an outsider come into my city, around my church, and tell an audience of people, this was where the "Son of Sam" cult started. He even had me vindicate a well known priest from my neighborhood, a man I looked up to my entire life. I spoke to numerous people from Yonkers about this case, and no one knew Berkowitz or anyone who was associated with him.

It was mid-August 2021, and Larry had not quit. He was still releasing videos of doctors he thought were involved with a child trafficking ring in Yonkers, still accusing people of being involved with the "Son of Sam." I wasn't too concerned with most of the doctors Larry was reporting about. I just didn't see any real connections to David Berkowitz with these doctors he was trying to include. Dr. Laverne was the only doctor I thought was suspect. He lived right next to the park and was known for experimenting with mind-altering drugs. If you look into Dr. Laverne more, you will see several shady incidents he was involved with.

After a couple of dead videos of Larry walking around Untermyer Park, I was getting bored. At this time, Penny and I reached a point of frustration and disappointment with Larry's shows. We were discouraged by his lack of interest in the information we were giving him. I had all intentions of just walking away from this case, but that was not God's plan.

CHAPTER III

THE YELLOW BRICK ROAD

September 4, 2021, it had been a week or so since I last looked at any research, and Larry was still walking in circles at Untermyer Park. He had nothing going on, and it seemed no content was coming in. I had no hard feelings against Larry, I just couldn't understand why he wasn't taking my help. I had no agenda and didn't need to get involved in this.

The next morning, I awoke to a call from my job to come in for work. There was a storm the night before and one of the precincts in Yonkers had been majorly flooded. There were about eight of us removing tons of files and paperwork into a dumpster. I normally didn't do this kind of work so I was with some guys I was usually not around.

When the job was done, we were all hanging out, passing time until the shift was over. I got a call from Penny asking me about Tocco Grady. She obviously had not stopped researching and we began to talk about Tocco while I was in front of some of the other workers. I said Tocco Grady's name to Penny and one of the workers looked at me funny and asked, "You know Tocco Grady? My friend Billy hates that guy." I hung up the phone with Penny and started to question my co-worker. He had a friend named Billy Quinn who told him Tocco had done some horrible things to him and his friends when they were young. I gave my co-worker my number to give to Billy, and later that evening, Billy called me. The stories he told me about Tocco were disturbing. In 1972, when he was eleven, Tocco used to give him and his friends drugs and alcohol for free. When they became impaired, Tocco would try to sexually molest them. Unfortunately, some of Billy's friends ended up being victims of Tocco.

Billy told me a lot about Tocco, but there was no association with David Berkowitz, and he knew of no connection with Tocco and a satanic cult either.

I finished my conversation with Billy and immediately called Penny to tell her what he had said. She couldn't believe I found someone who knew Robert "Tocco" Grady. I explained to Penny I really didn't want to bother with Larry again and had no intentions on contacting him. Penny said, "Are you serious? You have to tell him this information about Tocco, come on." Penny, of course, talked me into contacting Larry.

I emailed Larry the next day, after a month of no contact, the information I had on Tocco.

Paul: Got a confession from a person who Tocco Grady tried to molest. He and his friends were all drugged and some were molested by him. This guy said the first car he ever drove was Tocco's, he knew him very well. They wanted to kill Tocco for what he did to them. He knew no connection of Tocco with a satanic cult, Berkowitz or the Carrs. This guy will talk to you, this is 100%, he is eager to put Tocco's stuff out there. This will verify everything about Tocco, and this guy will be a good character for your show, he is Yonkers.

Larry immediately emailed me back.

Larry: Where have you been, sorry about the money issue. I would love to meet this guy, hook it up!

Paul: Is tomorrow good around 12 p.m.? I will call the guy and set up a time and place for us to meet. I'll even pay'em if he wants. People should be compensated when they are brave, Mr. Larry Dunn.

I called Billy and asked if I could treat him to lunch at my favorite Portuguese restaurant in Yonkers, Lusitania, so Larry could interview him. Billy agreed and we made plans to meet at noon the next day.

I emailed Larry to set up the interview.

Paul: 12 p.m. tomorrow, meet me at Lusitania, a Portuguese restaurant on Lockwood Avenue. The guy will meet us there. I am very good friends with the owner. When you get there, go to the back room.

I eat lunch at this Portuguese restaurant Lusitania at least three times a week. The owner lets me sit in the back room alone so I can make my phone calls and meet people for the day. The food is outstanding and the owner Joe is a true gentleman, an honest business owner.

I did not hear back from Larry, so a few hours later, I emailed him again.

Paul: Do you have plans on filming this guy tomorrow? He sounds like he is all in unlike many other people who just want to stay away. You should bring your equipment. To me, he sounds like he will go on film. He said he went to Catch A Predator TV series on Tocco, and they denied him.

Again, no response, and Billy was meeting me tomorrow for lunch at noon. At this point, I didn't even know if Larry was going to show.

The next morning I emailed Larry again.

Paul: Are you good for 12 p.m.?

Larry: I don't want to meet in the back room of a restaurant, I don't feel comfortable doing that. Sounds like a scene out of a mafia movie to me.

Paul: I eat at this restaurant all the time, I know the owner. You are making me laugh.

Billy was meeting me at noon, and I couldn't even get this kid to meet us now. I was trying to help him, and he continues to not want it. Why did I listen to Penny?

Paul: Really? I'm tired of emails. You are the first person I ever communicated like this with and I hate it. Like I asked you months ago, can we talk for a second. Only thing I can get by helping you is in trouble. Call me around 9:45, if you do not, I will call this guy and cancel. I'm telling you right now you would be making a big mistake, he is willing to talk.

Larry: Can we meet at Untermyer Park? I'm not going to a back room of a restaurant and I'm willing to lose the story over it.

Paul: Is the marina ok, I can meet you there at 12:30.

Larry: Yes, I can do the marina, but I'm in the middle of doing laundry so I can't meet until 1.

This kid was something else. I wanted to have lunch with Billy, you connect with people better while breaking bread. What Billy was going to discuss with us really wasn't a conversation anyone else needed to hear. Lusitania was very private, no one would be in the back room.

I met Billy Quinn that day at Lusitania, introduced myself, and got "Yonkersly" acquainted with him by playing the "Do you know this guy" game. It was a very common game played whenever two Yonkers people ran into each other. I knew exactly who Billy was when I saw him. I had a job a few years back at the Yonkers city dump refurbishing the office and Billy was stationed in that department at the time. I broke the news to him there was no time for lunch and we had to meet Larry at the marina.

Billy and I hung out at the marina discussing this case while we waited for Larry. We both had no idea who this kid was, nobody knew him from Yonkers. I explained to Billy, I only knew Larry through email, and probably knew him better than I knew Larry.

It was now 1:15 p.m. and Larry sent me a text he would be at the marina in five minutes. Ten minutes later, Larry drove down the ramp in a red, beat-up station wagon. He parked next to where we were standing and asked if I was Paul. I replied, "Yes, what's going on Larry?" We shook hands and Larry said, "I thought you were some old crazy guy. You're young, how old are you?" "Forty-five," I answered.

I introduced him to Billy and we conversed for about three minutes until Larry didn't want to hear anymore, he wanted it fresh for the camera. Larry asked me if I wanted to be in the video and I declined, "Nope, but thanks. I'll be by the docks out of the way. I'll wait until you guys are finished to make sure everyone is cool, and then I'm out."

Larry started filming and Billy began talking about his experience's with Tocco as I walked away. In this video, Billy remembered one time, Tocco gave him alcohol and he passed out on Tocco's couch in his apartment. When he woke up, Tocco was trying to molest him. One of his good friends became an alcoholic and was hellbent on getting Tocco back for what he did to him. Billy angrily described how Tocco would leave money in a wooden box for kids in the neighborhood to easily steal so he could lure them into his apartment. Billy was describing a real dirtbag. Who knows how many kids this guy Tocco actually got a hold of. Billy would say again for the audience that he knew of no connection between Tocco and David Berkowitz.

They finished the video and we all met back up at our cars. I asked them, "Everything good?" "Yeah, great stuff," Larry replied. It was very important for me to make sure everyone was good at all times.

Before Billy left, Larry asked him, "Do you want to be part.of the team now?" Billy thanked us and said, "I'm okay, I just wanted to expose that shit bag." I spoke with Larry briefly as he was in a rush to leave.

I got home that evening and there was an email waiting for me from Larry.

Larry: Thanks for coming through Paul, and my apologies for not making friends earlier. I am fully on team Paul Agostino. I'm looking forward to hooking up again soon. Billy Quinn was amazing.

Finally, this kid opened his eyes.

Paul: I'm going to watch the video now. I will reach out to Billy later, tell him thank you, and to use my number if I can do anything for him.

Billy did a great job coloring in Tocco. This was the first interview with someone who knew a suspect that was supposedly part of Maury's twenty-two disciples of hell cult. During the interview, Billy described how Tocco looked…a big guy, burly…and then it hit me. This son of a bitch Tocco was the guy in the '90s at my neighborhood bar Olde Tymes. I mentioned this earlier to Larry. I thought it might have been Tocco's father because he was so old. I never bothered to follow up.

On September 8, 2021, I sent out a picture of Mr. Robert "Tocco" Grady to over forty people on my phone. About thirty of them got back to me…it was him at Olde Tymes bar for sure.

I received a phone call that afternoon from a bartender who worked at Olde Tymes, whose mother just happened to be the cousin of Valentina Suriani, a "Son of Sam" victim. This bartender knew Tocco very well. Tocco was a known cocaine dealer, yet there was never any buying of cocaine from him, he was always giving it away for free. This bartender laughed at me during this entire conversation. He knew Tocco for over twenty years and said there was no way Tocco was involved with David Berkowitz.

When I talked to a few people from my neighborhood who knew Tocco, they all said the same thing…he gave out cocaine to everyone at the bar for free. They were not threatened by him and said he never carried a weapon. One of my friends remembered asking Tocco if he gets laid. Tocco replied, "I take it any way I can get it." My friend awkwardly walked away. When I asked if Tocco had anything to do with Berkowitz, they all adamantly said, "No way." You have no idea how many people from my neighborhood knew this guy.

Later on that day, Larry emailed me. He wanted to have a Zoom meeting at 1:00 p.m. on Sunday and asked me to look into a woman named Susan Conway.

Susan Conway was a female who Maury suspected was part of the twenty-two disciples of hell. There was supposedly a woman that was a part of this cult who was a shooter at some of these attacks, and Susan Conway was one of a few females who Maury looked into to fill that void.

Susan Conway lived at 50 Mulford Gardens in the '60s. I was sent a burglary arrest with her and Priscilla Morrissey from 1965. Her common-law husband was Ed DeMaria and they lived at 236th Street, Mount Vernon, in 1970. She was also arrested one time with a man named Venerio, who was killed in a mob hit. I saw a name I recognized who was involved with that and he is for sure a connected guy in Yonkers. Susan was abused as a child according to a few newspaper articles I found.

On September 11, 2021, my friend Ryan, a Yonkers Detective, brought me to a social club on Lockwood Avenue for a raffle party. The members were all people from the north area of Yonkers, the area Tocco roamed in. As soon as I walked in, I was greeted by faces I hadn't seen in decades. Most of the people at this party I grew up with and were from the Lake Avenue, Sacred Heart area. Just about everyone in there knew Robert "Tocco" Grady.

Many of the people I questioned about Tocco had partied with him at several bars in the Yonkers and Bronx areas. One thing that made them uncomfortable about Tocco was he always had teenagers around him. Some told me he gave free cocaine to these teenagers for sexual favors in return. All these people assured me Tocco had nothing to do with the "Son of Sam." I also met Detective Hanrahan's cousin who grew up with Tocco. He confidently told me, Tocco had no connection with David Berkowitz.

I found out a lot about Robert "Tocco" Grady, more than I needed to know. He never stopped luring in young boys with drugs for sexual favors since the '70s, when he was doing it to Billy Quinn and his friends. The more I found out about Tocco, the more I wanted to get away from him. He had absolutely nothing to do with David Berkowitz.

The next day I had a Zoom meeting with Larry and went through all the information on Tocco, he was speechless with what I was telling him. He asked me about Susan Conway, and if I knew anyone who lived in Mulford Gardens in the '60s and '70s. I immediately thought of two people I could speak with, Mrs. Callahan, the lady who was taught by Karen Wahlstrom, and a very good friend of mine who was a Vietnam veteran.

Larry then repeated the incident about the usher who scared him at a synagogue in 2003. The usher who was screaming, "Diablo, Diablo" at him, the usher he said supposedly knew John Carr. Larry was convinced the usher was the shooter at the Moskowitz/Violante attack, the last "Son of Sam" shooting in Brooklyn. He also claimed the usher told him John Carr was alive and living in New Hampshire. When I asked Larry to tell me the usher's name, he said, "Albert Chevone." I just put my head down and squeezed my forehead. The usher Larry was talking about was my good friend Albie, the Vietnam veteran I knew from Mulford Gardens. I was stunned once again with what this kid was telling me. I knew Albie extremely well, this was crazy. We ended the Zoom meeting and I did not like what this kid was assuming about my friend. I definitely had to hide my real name on the internet from now on because I couldn't take a chance on anyone seeing me involved in this. After the zoom meeting, I called the usher, my good friend, and asked him about the incident with Larry.

Here was my conversation with Albert Chevone.

Paul: Albie, what is good my brother?

Albie: Paulie, where the hell have you been?

Paul: Me, where the hell have you been? I miss you man, you haven't stopped by in a while.

Albie: My cancer has come back and I have just been enjoying my grandson.

Paul: Hate hearing that Alb, hope you are ok. How is Mark doing? You should be proud of him, good guy your son.

Albie: He's doing great, just became a lieutenant. He has eighteen years now Paulie.

Paul: Wow, time flies Albanooch. I'm happy to hear he is doing well. Hey Snappy, I ran into someone the other day who told me that you threatened him back in 2003 at a synagogue. Do you remember anything like that?

Albie began laughing, which led into coughing from his years of smoking.

Albie: That kid, I remember that kid. He wouldn't leave me the fuck alone Paulie. He found out I was from Yonkers and kept bothering me about Son of Sam stuff.

Paul: Did you threaten him? He told me you were screaming Diablo at him, and Moskowitz.

Albie: Moskowitz, what is Moskowitz? What the hell are you talking about? I told the kid after about a week of him harassing me, that if he didn't leave me alone, I was going to handle him. The fucking guy wouldn't stop Paulie, he kept insisting that I knew John Carr. I didn't threaten anybody, that kid was crazy.

Paul: Did you tell him John Carr was alive and living in New Hampshire?

Albie: Now how the hell would I know that?

Paul: What was he saying to you?

Albie: He kept asking me questions about the Carr family and David Berkowitz, insisting I knew them.

Paul: Did you know the Carrs?

Albie: I knew who they were, but I didn't know them. I had a cousin who lived across the street from them on Warburton. We used to hang out a lot at this tree swing on the aqueduct behind the Carr house. I saw Sam a lot, but I never really saw John or Michael, maybe once or twice.

Paul: How about Wheat?

Albie: Wheat was friends with my cousin, I would see her from time to time.

Paul: Did you know David Berkowitz?

Albie: No, but I used to see him driving that ugly yellow car a lot. I'll never forget that car. He had a 4:00 p.m.-12:30 a.m. post office shift in the Bronx and everyday around 3:30 p.m. we would see him driving down to Warburton in that ugly car. I'll never forget that car.

Paul: Did you ever see John Carr and David Berkowitz together?

Albie: I did, down at the marina. A group of them untied a boat from the dock and it drifted out into the Hudson River. The cops had to come get it back in.

Paul: So John Carr and David Berkowitz knew each other?

Albie: I don't know, I just remember seeing the two of them down there that night. I didn't know either of them personally, just by face.

Paul: How did you know that "Wheaties" and "Berkie" were their nicknames?

Albie: Everybody in the neighborhood talked about this when it went on. The newspapers all day had information on this stuff. The Post, Daily, Gannett, for years kept printing information on this case and I read the paper everyday before work. Everything I know is from those newspapers.

Paul: Did you know anyone who knew John Carr or David Berkowitz?

Albie: No, nobody I knew, knew those guys. You are starting to sound like that kid now.

Paul: Did you know Maury Terry?

Albie: No

Paul: Did you ever read The Ultimate Evil?

Albie: No, I didn't need to. It was all in the newspapers.

Paul: Do you think Berkowitz acted alone?

Albie: I don't know. Everyone in the neighborhood and the newspapers didn't think so. I heard that gun, the .44 was passed around. I read that in a Gannett article.

Paul: Was that Maury's article?

Albie: I'm not sure.

I got off the phone with Albie after we made plans to see each other soon. I knew Albie for over twenty years, I also grew up with his two sons. If he knew anything about any of this, he would have told me.

After my conversation with Albie, I emailed Larry.

Paul: I reached out to my friend who you had problems with at the synagogue. I would take him off your suspect list, I've known this guy for a long time and you are mistaken. He may have seen these people around the neighborhood, but he did not know them personally or hang out with them. He told me you wouldn't leave him alone and were insisting he had something to do with the Son of Sam because he was from Yonkers.

Larry: Got to get me that Scout report. It's a bigger deal than you think.

The next day, Larry sent a joint email to me and Justine. He was asking us if we could get Detective Kevin Murphy's reports on the "Son of Sam" from the Yonkers Records Department.

As soon as I received this message, I walked into the Yonkers Records Department and asked for all files pertaining to David Berkowitz, "Son of Sam," Kevin Murphy, and Walter Deyo Jr. I was told again all records before 1984 were no longer in existence. I left the records department and went to speak with the Yonkers Chief of Police, Joe Monaco. He assured me there were no files on the "Son of Sam" and Kevin Murphy had left nothing of the work he did when he investigated in 1996. Chief Monaco and a few of his colleagues were still interested in this case and said he would give me a few contacts who could help me.

I was going to do whatever it took to get the answers I needed, and people were going to be the key to this. The more information I found, the more people would come on board.

Larry emailed me the next morning he was meeting Justine and John Spencer for lunch on Lockwood Avenue.

John Spencer was like a father to me, and I was going to get him to talk to Larry soon. I previously told Larry I needed some time before I brought him to Spencer. Spencer knew what I was doing and he would never agree to meet Larry without me there. I called Spencer that day and he knew nothing about meeting Larry.

I emailed Larry back letting him know I would be on Lockwood Avenue at Lusitania if he and Justine wanted to stop by. I did not hear from him for the rest of the day.

Larry was an outsider without a pass, reporting things about Yonkers people that were not true. I had to vouch for the outsider as many wolves were not happy.

The next day Larry emailed me a picture of a guy named Alfonso Carozza, the alleged Wicked King Wicker.

Larry: This is a picture of the Wicked King Wicker, a clue from the Breslin letter. Maury claimed he was a member of the twenty-two disciples of hell.

Paul: I know a Carozza family in Yonkers. I am going to have to go see Frank Carozza who owns a construction company across the street from my family's pizzeria. I did find something that had Alfonso living at 22 Wicker Street in 1976. That house is right behind Berkowitz's apartment at Pine Street.

CHAPTER IV

THE CAVEMAN

On September 22, 2021, I woke up to my phone alarm like every other morning and did my daily commute to work. I signed in, hopped in my work van, and headed to my work garage for my job supplies. Upon leaving the garage, I noticed my wallet was missing. I know I used it ten minutes earlier to key myself out of the courthouse. Where the hell was it? I had it on my lap when I arrived at the garage and it must've fallen off my lap onto the sidewalk when I got out of my van. I asked everyone around, but nobody saw it. That "I lost my wallet" feeling started to settle in.

It was around ten o'clock when I came to terms my wallet was gone. A few hours later, I got a phone call from a City of Yonkers Supervisor telling me to call a lady named Sue because she knew where my wallet was. I immediately called this lady who told me a neighborhood bum named Ray had my wallet and was showing it to people. She saw my city ID when Ray was bragging about his find and called the City of Yonkers to notify them. I knew exactly who Ray was, so four of my friends and I took two cars to go bum hunting.

We went through every street in Yonkers looking for Ray. The drug dealers probably thought we were undercover cops because we circled the blocks so many times. I stopped at a park where these three people were hanging out and one of them, coincidentally, was the lady Sue who called the city to report my wallet found. I thanked Sue for what she did and told her we were looking for Ray. She said, "Look for a guy named Caveman who lives in a trailer on Worth Street, he will know where Ray is."

Before I left, I had to ask, "Did any of you know David Berkowitz?" One of the guys replied, "I used to play pool with him at a bar on Ashburton called Edgars." I said, "Really, do you know of any satanic cults in the area that Berkowitz belonged to?" He never saw Berkowitz with anyone, but told me there was some satanic stuff going on at the carriage house on the bottom of Odell Avenue. A little info never hurt, and off we went to Worth Street to go see Caveman.

I never in my life heard of this guy Caveman before, and I could only imagine what a guy named Caveman looked like. My friend and I drove down Lockwood Avenue, made a right on Saw Mill River Road, and a quick left onto Worth Street. We continued down this block and on the right was an old beat-up trailer, inside a gated fenced-up area. I parked in front of the trailer and my friend yelled for Caveman…no one came out. I couldn't wait to see what this guy looked like, but I had to find Ray and get my wallet. After about five minutes of yelling "Caveman," we got no answer and left to continue our bum hunting. It was getting late in the day, and I had to start heading back home so I figured if I couldn't stick around any longer, I might as well have the cops look for Ray.

I called the 4th Precinct in Yonkers, told them what happened, and asked if they could meet me at the bottom of Lake Avenue. Two officers arrived and I explained how the neighborhood bum Ray had my wallet. They knew Ray as well and quickly displayed his mug shot on their cruiser computer. Just then, I got a photo on my phone. It was a picture of Ray passed out on a set of steps at the bottom of Lockwood Avenue. I told the cops where Ray was and they offered me a ride. I declined and told them I would meet them there.

Two minutes later, four of my friends and I were emptying out Ray's pockets…and out fell my wallet. I asked the cops not to bother Ray as it was my fault I dropped it, but I still had some choice words for Ray. He knew all of us city workers, he could have easily got my wallet back to me by stopping any city vehicle and handing it to them.

I visited the 4th Precinct the next day and bought the entire precinct pizza. I appreciate Yonkers and its people…no good deed should ever go unnoticed. I was very thankful the police helped me when I called. Buying them a few pizzas was showing my gratitude. I got my wallet back with nothing missing…I was lucky.

On September 25, 2021, I was researching on the internet and came across an ex-Satan worshiper turned preacher named John Ramirez from the Bronx, N.Y. John talked about how he would constantly ask for the devil to enter him and take over his soul. Well, the devil finally did just that, and John swore whole-heartedly he had been possessed.

After watching John's video, I came to understand that maybe David Berkowitz was really possessed by the devil. John said this was something he went through, and it was possible to be possessed. If you can fill yourself with love from Jesus, I guess you can do the same by filling yourself with evil from the devil. After watching *The Sons of Sam*, and reading *The Ultimate Evil*, I believe David Berkowitz was worshiping the devil, asking for the devil to enter him.

We all do things in honor of who we follow, possession is just a word. Am I possessed by Jesus for following His ways? If you believe in God, you have to believe in Satan. Satan was introduced to us through the Bible. He is just as real as God. So, the possibility of committing these murders for satanic purposes was there.

That day Larry emailed me asking if I had spoken to Justine. Justine went silent and was not answering his emails.

I emailed Larry back.

Paul: I have not spoken to Justine, but I can reach out to her if you want. Have you been to Pelham Bay Park in the Bronx. That is where Berkowitz says his first meeting with these devil freaks was. I emailed John Ramirez, see where that goes.

Larry: Whose John Ramirez? I need Billy Quinn's number again. I want to talk to him about Tocco.

Paul: Billy Quinn would love to go on video again. John Ramirez is a guy I found online. He claims he was a warlock from the Bronx and was the devil's son. He said he was possessed by the devil and is now a follower of Christ. I sent you his video this morning. Also sent you a journal writing from Berkowitz. He states, "*unfortunately, the reporters from those early interviews got it wrong, naive, trusting and just plain dumb. I allowed them to lead me along.*"

On September 28, 2021, I had a conversation with Larry before one of his shows about how Carl Denaro, a living victim from one of the "Son of Sam" attacks, and a few members from his Maury Terry group on Facebook, did not like he was working with Mason Kraft, Larry's co-host.

After Maury's death in 2015, Carl Denaro continued to administer Maury Terry's Facebook page called the Official Maury Terry Facebook Group. This group consisted of over 800 people who were seeking the truth behind what Maury had investigated. Carl and some of his researchers were previously helping Larry with the case, but they did not like the direction he was going in with Mason. This caused Larry to start arguing with all of Carl's group and he refused to work with any of them. Larry went on his show that night and released information Carl and his group gave to him under the agreement he wouldn't report it on his show. In this video, Larry also insulted Maury Terry and his work.

In order for this to work, there should be no enemies. A positive attitude and positive atmosphere will bring positive results. Positive results will bring forth more people with information. There was more information, I needed this kid to be positive.

I emailed Larry, again trying to counsel.

Paul: I know you don't want to hear this, but I'm on the outside with reason. I don't believe in insulting Maury Terry in public. The guy made mistakes, but in no way do I think bashing him in public is a positive move.

As I ripped through my city like a pitbull, vindicating many names for this outsider, it seemed he was starting to doubt Maury's work. Larry was now more into proving Maury wrong than proving Maury right. I just wanted the names, the numbers, and the addresses of people so I could get information. What went on in Yonkers with David Berkowitz is what I needed to focus on. Maury claimed an organization that split from The Process Church came to Yonkers and formed the twenty-two disciples of hell. He also said the twenty-two disciples of hell practiced their cult rituals in Untermyer Park, and that is why Berkowitz moved to Yonkers, to get closer to the center of activity, to get closer to Untermyer Park.

On September 30, 2021, Larry emailed me after speaking with Billy Quinn.

Larry: I'm going to Yonkers later to film another video with Billy Quinn. I am getting emails that Carl Denaro and Josh Zeman are not happy with my videos.

I didn't respond to Larry's email. In my opinion, Larry disrespected Carl, Josh, and Maury in his last video. I felt he was causing a negative atmosphere that was sure to cause problems.

I got home from work and began to watch Larry's new video with Billy Quinn. They were walking around the streets Billy and Tocco were from, giving me my dosage of the beautiful Yonkers backdrop. Billy talked about the old times in his neighborhood, Tocco stories, and other Yonkers tales. It was classic Yonkers once again, thanks to Billy Quinn.

During this video, Billy mentioned he visited a friend of his the night before, and his friend told him to look for a guy named Cavemen. Caveman lived in Untermyer Park in the '80s and would know what was going on in the park back then. Caveman? Was Billy talking about the guy I was told to go see at the trailer on Worth Street when I lost my wallet? I just heard of this guy Caveman a couple of days earlier for the first time in my life, and now Billy was saying Caveman would know about things that went on in Untermyer Park…unbelievable.

The next morning, I drove straight to Worth Street, where I was told I could find Caveman. I parked right in front of the gated trailer and yelled out "Caveman" a few times…nothing. I stayed there a few minutes, and suddenly I saw the curtains move in the trailer window. I yelled again, "Caveman." I then heard a door slam shut and out walked this round, covered-in-oil, bearded guy. He unlocked the front gate and started walking toward my van. I rolled down my window a little and said, "Are you Caveman?" He grunted, "Yes." I asked, "Can I talk to you for a second?" Holy shit, it's him!

Here was my first conversation with Caveman.

Paul: What's going on man? I don't want you to feel uncomfortable. Don't worry about anything, I'm not a cop. I'm doing a movie, a documentary type of movie on Yonkers and someone passed your name around that you used to be around Untermyer Park a lot so I thought you would be interesting to talk to.

Caveman: Why you plan on filming up there?

Paul: Ummm…there's been some stuff going on there about the Son of Sam. Did you know David Berkowitz?

Caveman: I knew him when I was a kid. I used to sell him THC. What's really fucked up, one day, I'm sitting on the wall out front. I'm like ya know, talking about Son of Sam, saying he ain't from New York 'cause you don't shit in your backyard. I'm sitting there and I remember, not too far from me sitting over there was Berkie.

Caveman went on to tell me, on the same night he went home after hanging out with Berkowitz, two people got shot in front of the Saw Mill Diner in Yonkers. I questioned, "Was it Berkowitz?" He answered, "No, it was a mob hit." Caveman remembered hanging out with Berkowitz the night this incident happened.

I would later check the newspaper about this mob hit at the Saw Mill Diner and it happened 100 percent. I knew someone who knew all the parties involved. The best part of Caveman's story was it fit in the sixteen-month timespan for when Berkowitz was living in Yonkers.

Paul: How long did you know Berkowitz?

Caveman: I just knew him from selling him drugs. You know what it is? I was friends with all the devil worshipers and the founding members.

Paul: Where was the LSD coming from?

Caveman: It was THC.

Paul: You were selling him marijuana?

Caveman: No, it was like little tiny pills. I think they called it monkey tranquilizers.

I researched this drug THC, the monkey tranquilizer pills Caveman was selling to Berkowitz. It was THC, telazol hydrochloride, which was utilized in veterinary medicine as a small animal anesthetic. This drug was comparable to ketamine, also known as "K" in the streets of New York.

Paul: They were really doing devil worship shit in there, huh?

Caveman: The devil worshipers were different then Berkowitz. All the devil worshipers were like one group and Berkowitz and his friends, say this is the wall right here, Berkowitz and his friends would hang there.

Paul: Who would Berkowitz hang out with?

Caveman: Ahhh...the Carrs and all them. Then I heard from one of my friends, that one of our friends, was one of their friends. This kid Kurt Weitzman, I think, was one of the kids supposedly hooked up with Berkowitz and their group. He is about the only one I can think of from that group that was part of our group.

I would like to point out, Caveman did not know me before these first three minutes. I asked Caveman who Berkowitz hung out with, and Caveman said without hesitation, the Carrs. I did not ask him if Berkowitz hung out with the Carrs. I hadn't mentioned the Carrs yet at all. He brought up Berkowitz with the Carrs after I asked him who Berkowitz hung out with.

Paul: That's what I think. He was in Untermyer Park, but was not a part of what was going on down there. No one knew him.

Caveman: He wasn't, that was all the devil worshipers. They were just a bunch of people that fucked around. A small group of people that just did it for the hell of it. Like this one kid Dwight used to carry a Bible around and say, "never know when you need one to burn." Our main spot, we called it the hot spot, was at the top of the stairs.

Paul: I have had many keg parties there at the stairs.

The top of the "thousand stairs," as called at Untermyer Park, was famous in the '90s for keg parties. At times, there would be fifty of us or more at these parties, all people from Yonkers. None of us ever saw or ran from any devil worshipers.

Paul: You know what puzzles me the most is, what is Sam Carr to all of this?

Caveman: The old man?

Paul: Yes.

Caveman: It was his kids, they hung out with Berkowitz, and supposedly if you looked out Berkie's window, you could see the Carr house.

Paul: I'm sure you have seen too all the dead animals in the park.

Caveman: At Warburton Avenue when your dog died, instead of burying it or whatever, you just threw it out on the wall there by Warburton and we used to hang the dead animals at the devil's cave. Do you know where the devil's cave was?

Paul: Yeah, you seen a lot of shit, huh?

Caveman: I lived at the park for eight years in the 1980s, hung out there from the mid-1970s and lived there most of the 1980s.

Paul: So, you knew John Carr like you knew Berk?

Caveman: I knew the Carr boys, you know, just enough to say hello. They were just a different group.

Paul: How was John?

Caveman: He was alright. The old man was a prick. I know everybody used to say Carr was just a pain in the ass and used to always call the cops on their vehicles parked near his house.

Paul: Who shot Sam's dog?

Caveman: I don't know. Maybe could've been one of his kids. His kids were assholes.

Paul: That is what I thought, 'cause a witness seen a blond-haired man running after the shooting on the aqueduct with a shotgun.

Caveman: Well, Kurt Weitzman, I don't know how much he was involved. I just heard from someone that he was connected with all that. He was blondish, white-colored hair. They all got what they wanted. If you ever notice, all the police drawings never looked like Berkowitz. They wanted to be the Zodiac killers of the east.

Paul: Did you know what was going on with them while it was going on?

Caveman: No, I just figured it had something to do with someone who was not from NYC.

Paul: What do you think is the reason Berkowitz doesn't tell on anyone? Who is he afraid of?

Caveman: People in the group. Supposedly there is film of those people being shot.

Paul: And you heard that from people?

Caveman: People, there was film.

Paul: Do you mind walking around Untermyer Park with me and my friend so you can tell us more?

Caveman: Sure, but I don't want to be on no video.

Paul: No problem, I got you, thanks.

Again, I mentioned nothing of a film and Caveman brought this up without me asking. Maury claimed the Moskowitz/Violante shooting was filmed. Could this be the same film Caveman was talking about?

Caveman confirmed Berkowitz hung out at the park, yes, but the satanic practices that were going on there was not being done by him. There were people devil worshiping in the park, but according to Caveman, it wasn't Berkowitz and his friends.

I emailed Larry I found Caveman and to meet us at Untermyer Park at 9:00 a.m. on Saturday to interview him. He emailed me back he would check his schedule and get back to me.

One thing to realize when you are trying to get information is you have to take whatever you can get at all times, every time, at any time. Never let anyone go a second longer if they are willing to talk to you. You always have to get what you can from the person before they have any time to change their mind.

Larry then called and asked if Mason could join us. I had no problem with that at all.

On October 2, 2021, I drove down to Yonkers and picked up Caveman. He hopped in my car with a half-lit cigar in his mouth which made my car reek for weeks. As we traveled to the now luxurious Untermyer Park, he told me a bunch of crazy stories that happened around Yonkers. When I arrived at the park, Larry and Mason were waiting for us with their equipment out. We got out of the car and I introduced Caveman to Larry and Mason...Caveman just grunted. I could tell right from the beginning he didn't like these guys. When you are not from Yonkers, we can feel it. Plus, I think, with all the video equipment Larry and Mason had, he didn't feel comfortable. They promised Caveman they wouldn't show him, or use his real voice on video, and he was okay with that. Before Caveman could say any more, Mason clipped a mic on him and they started to walk around the park to film.

During the video, Caveman insisted Berkowitz was not a part of the devil worshiping in the park. The locals did not know him, and thought he was a cop. With that statement, Caveman gave me more reason to believe what he was saying, it made too much sense. The local kids at the park thought Berkowitz was a cop because he was not a familiar face to them. If the local kids knew who he was, and hung out with him, they wouldn't have suspected he was a cop. This also explains why a twenty-three year old David Berkowitz was buying his drugs from a fifteen year old Caveman. The regulars at the park wouldn't deal with Berkowitz, as they thought he was a cop, but a fifteen year old Caveman didn't care. I have a feeling Caveman would get the money from Berkowitz, see his friends in the park, make a little side money for himself, and then give Berkowitz what he paid for. Caveman then told us without asking, Berkowitz and the Carrs were part of a different religion which was based in Manhattan.

Maury said Michael Carr was a part of Scientology in Manhattan, so I could only assume Caveman was talking about that. Whatever Berkowitz was a part of, it had nothing to do with what was going on at Untermyer Park.

We walked around the entire park with Caveman leading us. I stayed off camera once again because I didn't need anyone to see me. I still didn't know who exactly was involved in all this and was always at ground zero... safety first.

I could tell during the interview Caveman was not as comfortable talking to Larry and Mason as he was with me. Larry was getting noticeably frustrated because Caveman would not answer most of his questions. He was very vague in his answers to them and was basically just glad to be walking around his home again.

At the end of our tour, Caveman pulled me away from Larry and Mason, walked me over to a section in the park, took off his mic, then pointed and said, "That is where the bodies are buried." I waved over Larry and Mason, but they were too late, they got none of it on video. I told them both what he said, but I didn't know what to make of it. As soon as Larry was done getting what he needed, he rushed out with Mason, leaving me in the park with Caveman, my new buddy.

Before I left the park to drive Caveman home, we stopped at a tent near the entrance of the park where they were selling books about Untermyer Park. The book cost twenty dollars and I only had a hundred-dollar bill on me. The men at the tent didn't have change for a hundred so Caveman whipped out a knot of money and told me he got me. He gave me five twenties for my hundred-dollar bill. The Caveman was not as broke as I thought.

I emailed Larry a summary of Caveman later that day.

Paul: You got some stuff there, but I expected more. Point out to the audience that Maury couldn't find this guy who lived in the park. The cops even had Caveman's address as Untermyer Park. Caveman also said he never heard of Billy the artist or the twenty-two disciples of hell. Berkowitz wasn't a devil worshiper at the park, and they really thought he was a cop. It makes sense being that he stepped on the scene in 1976 out of nowhere. Don't forget to tell the audience Caveman never read The Ultimate Evil or saw The Sons of Sam. He knew about one of the shootings being on film and said some had seen it. You are right, he was holding back a bit on you. I'll be visiting him again, I'm sure. Also told us Berkowitz and the Carrs were together. Caveman swore to me the locals in the park were faking sacrifices of animals to mess with the cops and tourists. Maybe the cops were right and Maury was just trying to make something out of nothing. By the way, my car stinks.

Billy the artist was a guy Maury met who had drawn portraits of the twenty-two disciples of hell after hanging out with them at Untermyer Park. Maury showed these portraits to David Berkowitz during an interview and

Berkowitz confirmed these people were part of his cult. I asked Caveman, whom was basically at the park every day and night from 1975 to 1987, if he had ever heard of Billy the artist, or a twenty-two disciples of hell cult that hung out in the park. His answer was, "I ain't ever heard of those people."

CHAPTER V

INTERESTING INFORMATION

The day after filming the Caveman video, Larry emailed me some very interesting information.

Larry: I've been in contact with Wheat Carr for weeks now. She tells me her parents were well liked in Yonkers, and her brothers, John and Michael, didn't know Berkowitz. There is one story she told me I do find strange. She said Maury Terry was physically thrown out of her house by her father for acting inappropriately inside their home. Maury was supposedly disrespecting John's girlfriend and Sam didn't like it.

Let's take a moment to talk about Wheat Carr, the daughter of Sam Carr, and sister to John and Michael. According to newspaper articles, Wheat, a civilian working as a Yonkers Police Dispatcher, was the person who spoke to the NYPD when they called the YPD about David Berkowitz and a parking ticket he received at the last shooting in Brooklyn. Wheat told the NYPD about David Berkowitz, and how she knew he was the "Son of Sam." How did she know Berkowitz was the "Son of Sam" before his arrest? Her father was saying the same. Wheat, knowing this information and giving up Berkowitz to the NYPD did look very suspect. It seemed as though she was trying to throw Berkowitz under the bus and make him the fall guy.

The Sons of Sam documentary portrays John Carr as being the real "Son of Sam" and an accomplice to the shootings, with all the evidence coming from Maury Terry. The Carr family hired a lawyer after Berkowitz's arrest and were charging $15,000 to anyone who wanted to speak with them about the case. I'm puzzled why the police didn't interrogate the Carrs. Why wouldn't Wheat speak to Maury? Larry told me Maury thought Wheat was a shooter in at least two of the attacks. Supposedly she was also the driver of a yellow Volkswagen bug at the Moskowitz/Violante shooting, the last shooting in Brooklyn.

Paul: Don't let that go.

Larry: Here is my latest email exchange with her.

Larry: I met a guy recently who lived in Untermyer Park in the 1970s and 1980s. He told me he saw your brothers and David Berkowitz together in Untermyer Park, but they were not part of what was going on there.

Wheat: We will skip the part about the 1980s because if he is telling you that that is when he saw them, well there goes that story. Back in the 1970s a teenager living homeless in Untermyer—possible at that time, not really likely—today it would be more plausible. The 1970s again, somewhat questionable—just based on verifiable facts—like David Berkowitz had repeatedly, until Maury Terry started visiting, denied anyone else was involved. David Berkowitz was not the most reliable source, but still—other than his threats to destroy our family, he did not name any names other than those in his delusions, until prompted to do so after their deaths, when both would have been protected from slander and defamation because they were dead. After his marriage, John almost never came home to visit. If we wanted to see him, we went wherever he happened to be stationed. Again, how do people literally miles away "hang out"—more than one DA exhaustively tracked, with the assistance of the Air Force, John's movements, airline tickets, dated family photos, and message slips manually time stamped in Michael's handwriting showing he had been "working the night shift" because our night operator could no longer stand the stress of the hate calls that came in at night. I am well aware that for a variety of reasons, mostly to protect the privacy of others who were guilty of nothing more than living in Yonkers and knowing us, I cannot prove my own "story," and yes, that is something I have more or less accepted most of the time. There are still people out there who deserve to be protected from lurid curiosity and speculation.

Unbelievable...having contact with Wheat Carr was extremely important.

Paul: What would be her reason for speaking to you? All she has to do is watch and enjoy. Doesn't make sense, why would she not talk to the police or Maury, but she will talk to you? Crazy, there has to be a reason.

Larry: I haven't the slightest idea. I think she likes me.

I had been communicating with Larry now over the phone, and in a conversation we had, he told me Wheat used to date David Berkowitz. He said in Maury's notes, Berkowitz complained about having sex with Wheat. Why was Wheat reaching out to him now? It has been forty-four years, and to my knowledge, no one has ever interrogated her. She is the only one alive who can tell you exactly what happened besides David Berkowitz. She was crucial to keep in contact with.

With all these allegations against Wheat and her family, why hadn't she defended her family before like she did in this email? There were questions to ask, and Larry had her ear.

Paul: Ask her about the interview which is recorded, when she says she would be lying if she said her brother wasn't in the occult, she admitted that. Ask her why John Wheaties is in the letter? What went on in North Dakota? Why would the police in North Dakota make up those cult stories? Why was Wicker Street mentioned and not Pine Street? Who told her Berkowitz was the Son of Sam?

Larry: Here are your answers in an email from Wheat.

Wheat: As I previously stated, the one time Maury visited our home he was verbally abusive and physically aggressive towards a girl. When my brother

John stepped between them, he started saying obscene things to me and the girl (I was at most thirteen in an adjoining room, so I could hear it all) when my father walked in and also heard. Maury was given the opportunity to apologize and leave quietly to go home and sober up. He continued to mouth off and behave aggressively, wrong thinking that just because he had a few inches and maybe twenty pounds on my father he could bully him, he thought wrong. He was physically removed and was told never to come back. My father did not stand for that kind of language in front of "ladies" and certainly not used against his own daughter and that of our neighbors. Let's start with the name listed in the only non-business listing in the telephone directory (you know those big books with thousands of pages published by Ruben and Donnally) and was the phone number where most of the first years harassment came in. It was set up around the time I started first grade, with both mine and John's name combined because it was thought that would make it easier for our grade school friends to find us. We both would tell people to look for that listing so as not to tie up trunk lines that went through the switchboard. So far, I cannot find anyone who knew us who ever heard John go by the name "John Wheaties." I am talking about asking every person he "hung out with" from eighth grade up. People he spent all his time with up until he left for one semester of college and then almost immediately to Air Force basics. It is just one of the many Berkowitz/ Maury Terry fabrications. As to the letter you seem to be referring to, well I'm pretty convinced that there were people (including ones we paid for) who analyzed that letter along with the several psychologists who gave their opinions—might know what they're talking about. (Breslin hired an independent criminal psychologist, and we provided him as well, with various police departments, handwriting samples from letters as such) The Wicker Street reference? Well, it was/is the street that ran behind us down the side. We are talking about a paranoid schizophrenic with serious delusions, have you ever studied the photos from inside his apartment? There is no making sense unless he wanted what he got, which was notoriety and glamour. I am told that Berkowitz approached me in a dance club in Riverdale. Apparently, I said I was waiting for my fiancé, but thanked him for his compliment. I did not remember the incident until the bartender told me about it after the arrest. Other than that, the only time I ever actually remember seeing him "not on TV" was watching him from the fourth floor as he was brought in by YPD to headquarters and taken to the DD on the first floor. Others have told me that someone at least resembling Berkowitz showed up in other places asking about me. Rumors to the contrary, there just were not enough hours in the day for me to do all these things I have been accused of.

That was it...that was why Wheat was speaking to Larry. He was going against Maury, and no one had ever done that before.

Here is a letter I found online that was sent to Sam Carr from David Berkowitz after his arrest while he was being held at Kings County Hospital:

Dear Mr. Carr,

You are the man who should be in prison not Mr. B. What did you do to him? Mr. B. did not get into this situation by himself. You and your family have a good life while you ruin someone else's. It must make you and your daughter feel proud to do this. Mr. B. was a decent person never having been in trouble with the law until he moved in your neighborhood. How do you account for that? Why would Mr. B. lie about you? You must be the evil that most people can't see. We all know there is evil here, but few come face to face with it.

The letter is then cut off.

In this letter, David Berkowitz was blaming the Carr family for getting him into trouble, specifically Sam and his daughter Wheat. Why doesn't he mention John or Michael? He says, "*you and your daughter*." He singles them out from the rest of the family. Why was Berkowitz only blaming Sam and Wheat?

On October 4, 2021, I met with John Spencer again and asked if Maury would have known John Carr. He said they may have crossed paths at Sacred Heart, but Maury wouldn't have hung out with him. Maury was an exceptional athlete and very popular, where John was a skinny nerd who couldn't even throw a baseball. Spencer never heard Maury was thrown out of the Carr house, but he didn't know for sure. At the time this incident supposedly occured, Wheat was thirteen, and John was seventeen. That would make John a senior at Gorton while Maury was a three-star athlete at Sacred Heart. I just can't see them hanging out. Everyone in Yonkers knows students from Gorton did not hang out with the students from Sacred Heart. If Maury was at the Carr house, that would mean he knew John Carr. Why would Maury never mention this in *The Ultimate Evil*?

On October 6, 2021, I decided to look for Randy Hughes, the person my fireman friend told me about a while back whose brother was kidnapped by devil worshipers in Untermyer Park. After Penny and I researched the Hughes family, we found where Randy worked, and again, unbelievable. Randy just happened to be working in the same building I was working in that week. I left my number with a co-worker of his and asked that he give it to Randy. He did, and it turned out, Randy knew Maury Terry pretty well.

In 1985, Maury decided to visit Untermyer Park and came across a few teenagers playing in the woods. He began questioning these teenagers, asking them if they ever saw any satanic cult activity in the area. Randy Hughes was one of those teenagers. He was the one who told Maury he had witnessed over forty animal sacrifices that took place at certain areas in the park. Maury was astonished, he felt what Randy had witnessed was what he was looking for and included it all in his 1987 *Unsolved Mysteries* episode. The re-enactment scene from *Unsolved Mysteries*, when the satanic cult was in robes chanting, was everything Randy had witnessed and relayed to Maury. In the early '80s, he and his friends would see older men in robes gather in the park late at night carrying candles and chanting as they sacrificed everything from chickens to cows, never mind dogs.

I asked Randy if he ever saw any human sacrifices or any sexual ceremonies being held by these people. He replied, "No, I never saw any human sacrifices, or anything sexual go on with them in the park, it was always just animals. When we saw the headlights of their cars enter the park, we would hide in the bushes, and they would just kill the animal and leave." I asked Randy if he ever heard of David Berkowitz being a part of any cult activity that went on in the park, his answer was, "I never heard David Berkowitz was anywhere around this area until Maury showed up in 1985." Randy's opinion…Maury was trying to connect David Berkowitz to the cult he had witnessed. I asked Randy if he would walk around Untermyer Park and show me everything he showed Maury. "Not a problem" he said, and we made plans to meet at the park later that week.

Before we ended our conversation, I asked him about the incident with his brother being kidnapped by devil worshipers. He confirmed that was true and said, "Whoever kidnapped my brother were not the same people who gathered in the park at night. Local delinquents that hung out in the park held my brother down and forced him to watch a dog being killed." His brother was rushed to the hospital with trauma and that's all he had to say about the incident.

So I basically just found the kid who helped make the *Unsolved Mysteries* episode with Maury Terry in the '80s. This find was so unbelievable, when I told Larry, he thought I was setting him up with false information. He questioned me as if I was trying to play a prank on him. I laughed and told him to get his equipment ready. I was going to give him and his audience the same tour through Untermyer Park that Maury had in 1985.

Meeting Randy helped me realize there could have been a misunderstanding with what Maury reported. There was devil worshiping going on at Untermyer Park, but in Randy's many years there, he never heard of David Berkowitz being involved. These cultists Randy saw seemed like an older crowd, people who were born into this culture for whatever reasons. There were no kidnappings of kids, no sexual abuse, and no human sacrifices according to Randy. I do believe Berkowitz was at Untermyer Park, but not a part of this older organized crowd.

I already heard Caveman tell me Berkowitz was not a part of the local kids who hung out at the park. Now I was hearing of another group I thought also had nothing to do with David Berkowitz. It seems to me, what Randy had witnessed helped Maury connect his cult theory to Untermyer Park. Who else did Maury talk to from the park? Personally, I have spoken to a lot of people who hung out there in the '70s and '80s, and none of them had spoken to Maury Terry.

On October 10, 2021, *Sons of Sam* producer Josh Zeman displayed an interesting police report online. The report was taken a day after Berkowitz's arrest on August 11, 1977, at 9:46 a.m. by Yonkers Police Officer Steven E. Kogan:

On August 11, 1977, while on post I was approached by one Ruben Anthony, male, black, 256 Woodworth Avenue, who is a maintenance man at 10 Burbank Street (Bryn Mawr Knolls) who stated to me, David Berkowitz, male, white, 24, 35 Pine Street was at a motorcycle club on Point Street on August 6, 1977 and he was carrying a gun in the small of his back. He further states Berkowitz was wearing a wig. Anthony states Berkowitz had frequented the area on previous occasions. On this date (8-6-77) he asked if Mickey Carr was around as he wanted to see her.

With this report, there was a lot to check on. First, I could see the paper the report was written on was real. I've worked in the police department buildings for the past twenty-two years and I have seen these paper reports a lot. This was a real Yonkers Police paper report.

The reporting police officer was Steven E. Kogan. I made some phone calls to a few cops and confirmed, Steven E. Kogan was a Yonkers Police Officer who was stationed at the 4th Precinct in 1977, Berkowitz's area.

Now to find Ruben Anthony. I noticed he worked as a maintenance man at 10 Burbank Street. I used to live right around the corner at 8 Stokes

Road, Bryn Mawr Knolls, from 1999 to 2008. Those maintenance men were the same maintenance men from my building…maybe I knew him?

I started to look for Ruben Anthony using his address, 256 Woodworth Avenue, a bad neighborhood located near Warburton Avenue. After an hour of searching the internet, I found a man named Ruben Anthony who lived in Wisconsin. This Ruben Anthony was fifty-eight years old, so he would have been thirteen or fourteen in 1977…that did not fit. The officer would have said in the report it was a youth he spoke to. Plus, the man who gave this report had a maintenance job, and I don't think a fourteen year old was working at that age.

I kept looking into this Ruben Anthony and came across a speech he had given. He was a deacon, and mentioned in this speech, he had grown up in the bad neighborhoods of Yonkers. Maybe this Ruben Anthony was related to the Ruben Anthony I needed to confirm this report with? I called Penny for contacts on him, and within a few hours, I was talking to Ruben Anthony…the son of the man who had given the report.

Ruben told me his father passed away, but he assured me the report his father gave was real. His father told him about the incident a few times, but he couldn't quite confirm all the details in the report. As far as Berkowitz wearing a wig and carrying a gun, he could not confirm those details, but he could confirm his father had run into Berkowitz, and whatever his father said in the report happened.

This was six days after the Moskowitz/Violante shooting, and four days before Berkowitz's arrest. It happened, this report was real, but how did Berkowitz know Wheat Carr's nickname? Wheat Carr also went by the name Mickey. Mickey referred to Wheat's middle name, Wheat Micheline Carr. Why was he looking for her, and how did he know her nickname was Mickey?

On October 13, 2021, I paid Caveman a visit with a fresh box of cigars. I wanted to make sure he was okay with everything, and nobody was bothering him for speaking with me. I met Caveman this time around the block from his trailer. He had a garage filled to the brim with everything and anything for sale. I watched him dive into a heap of junk, then reappeared with a bunch of photos and negatives of Untermyer Park from the '80s. He also had a few newspaper articles about the park from the late '70s. On this visit, Caveman said again, the group David Berkowitz was hanging around with were into a religion of their own, and it had to do with people from Manhattan.

CHAPTER VI

NEO YES THE ONE

A lot of things had been happening to me since I watched Josh Zeman's documentary, so I reached out to Josh with an email. He started this "Son of Sam" wave I was on and I wanted to discuss some of the people I had found with him. Josh did a lot for this case by showing the world Maury Terry's theories and I respected that.

I've done a lot of groundwork in Yonkers so far, and it was the only groundwork anyone had done since Maury. If I was going to keep looking into this, I felt Josh could help my success with all of his information. Josh Zeman had more files and documents on this case than anyone alive.

When I told Larry I reached out to Josh, he was against me contacting him because he was having problems with Josh behind the scenes. Now what was I supposed to do? Larry seemed to panic, and stressed I shouldn't talk to Josh, but I had already emailed him.

A few days later, Josh emailed me back with his phone number to call him. Since I really didn't know what was going on between him and Larry, I decided to wait to speak with him because I didn't want to cause any problems.

Besides Larry trashing Maury in his videos, some of the problems he had with people were because of his decision to work with Mason. I respected he backed Mason, but that had nothing to do with me.

On October 31, 2021, I met with Larry and he handed me a piece of paper with about fifty names on it. He claimed David Berkowitz told Maury the people listed on this paper were all some how involved in the "Son of Sam" crimes. I did not know where Larry got this list, but now I had some names to look into.

After Larry left, I thought to myself as I looked at this long list of names, there was no way this many people could have been involved, no way. You have a hard time with one person knowing your business, never mind fifty, and I definitely didn't think these devil worshipers would be able to hide the truth of what happened for forty-four years among fifty people.

That night during Larry's show, for the first time, he told his audience about me. He called me Neo, and said I was equipped with a ton of Yonkers connections. I was using the name NEO YES THE ONE on the internet since the situation with Albie, but before that, I was using my real name. Larry brought up how I found Caveman, but he didn't explain the story correctly. I'm certain I gave him all the details of everything that happened and how I found Caveman. Why did he not tell the story right?

In Larry's video, Mason brought up a stone underground room in Untermyer Park that Caveman had slept in. Maury claimed this stone underground room was the hole David Berkowitz was referring to when he wrote "*Hi My Name Is Mr. Williams And I Live IN this hole*" on his apartment wall at 35 Pine Street. Mason was implying that Berkowitz may have been referring to Caveman as Mr. Williams, as this was the hole Caveman had slept in. Sounded good, but Caveman started sleeping in the park in the '80s and Berkowitz wrote that on his wall in the '70s.

I emailed Larry after the show.

Paul: OK, I guess I'm Neo. Mason messed up with his Mr. Williams theory, but besides that, good stuff. I'm not going to lie either, I really thought Mason had something there. It did make sense and looked like he finally pulled one out, but the dates didn't match. Caveman was not living in the park in 1977...and then you crushed his entire thought by mentioning this.

As soon as you mentioned the dates didn't add up, I hit the floor. I was laughing my ass off. It sounded good, I really thought he may have caught something and then it was like he got slimed...like on that old TV show, You Can't Do That On Television. The poor guy, funny shit.

On November 4, 2021, I reached out to a friend from my old neighborhood, Dave Butler. Dave used to work for a man named Jim Faulkner who was very good friends with Wheat Carr. Jim was a former New York City Police Officer who bought the Carr house at 316 Warburton Avenue when they sold it. I asked Dave if he could get in touch with Jim and ask if he would speak with me. I was extremely eager to see if Jim was willing to share any information he had about the Carr family since he knew them so intimately.

I called John Spencer that night to ask about Kevin Murphy and his investigation. He didn't know Detective Murphy personally, he just remembered some Irish detective asked him if he could investigate the case and he allowed him to do just that. Spencer said nothing came out of the work Detective Murphy did.

John Spencer was a Vietnam veteran I have known my entire life. I have seen firsthand how being a part of a war can affect you. This man was forced to live a life that was not chosen by him, but by our government. The Vietnam War was a mistake, and we have had to live with the damaged human products of that mistake...it breaks my heart. David Berkowitz was one of those damaged human products from the Vietnam War who was returned to our society...you will read about this later.

On November 8, 2021, I went to see Chief Monaco to ask again about the Yonkers files on the "Son of Sam." He was a very close friend of my family. My brother Chris, who passed away, was best friends with him growing up. Chief Monaco would do anything for me, in honor of my brother. He confirmed again that all the Yonkers files on the "Son of Sam" case were ruined in a flood, stolen, or turned over to the NYPD. He gave me his card and told me whatever I needed he would help me with.

Chief Monaco got the word out that I was looking for information about the "Son of Sam," and in just a few hours, I received a phone call from one of his detectives who sent me a letter that was written by retired Yonkers Detective William Powers.

Detective Powers sent a letter to *New York Post* editor Steve Dunleavy in the 1980s. The letter stated Yonkers Police passed along information to the NYPD, and they never followed up on their reports. He wrote this letter to vindicate the YPD of not doing their job and blamed the NYPD for not following their leads. Detective Powers was stationed around Pine Street and knew of the crimes in the area by Berkowitz. He claimed they went back to Sergeant Novotny, their supervisor, with their information on David Berkowitz, and their instructions were to contact the New York City Omega Task Force...they did, and were ignored. Nothing happened when they relayed their information to the NYPD.

RIP Detective William Powers. Detective Powers had just passed away a few weeks before I received his letter.

This was the first time I heard anything about what happened back then from Yonkers law enforcement. Maury had painted a picture that the police would not share any information or cooperate with his investigation. As far as I knew from watching *The Sons of Sam* and reading *The Ultimate Evil*, law enforcement closed the case, Berkowitz did it, that was it. They would not entertain anyone with conspiracy theories, never released any records, never shared what they knew, and would never discuss the case with anyone. What crimes were committed in the Pine Street area by Berkowitz that the YPD knew about? Only thing I can remember reading about was the Carrs' dog being shot.

On November 10, 2021, Larry emailed me something I found odd.

Larry: I exchanged emails with a former YPD Detective who said there may be more of Kevin Murphy's files. This was his email.

On a side note, has your guy in Yonkers given you more of Kevin Murphy's reports because I know there was more than just one. There were at least a couple of case files that contained file folders on numerous individuals. If your guy has access to that report on William Powers, he should have access to all the files. If that's the case, Kevin Murphy would not be needed as much if you had his files.

Paul: I got that Powers letter from a detective friend, not records. I went to records and talked to the Chief, he told me there was nothing in records for the Son of Sam. I specifically asked for Murphy's files, he said he would try calling him. Everything was destroyed, lost or given to the NYPD. Who is this guy? Let me talk to him. Tell him to call me so he can tell me where to go. Tell the cop my name, Spencer probably hired him and I will know him. Ask him if he ever worked with Monaco or Wynne?

Larry: Let's not start throwing your name around too much, you never know.

Paul: All the cops here know what I'm doing, don't worry. If he is a good guy, I will know him. I don't need him at all, if those files were there, I would've had them already. Just want to make him feel comfortable, chances are he knows me or Spencer.

Larry: The guy seems to be good. I've worked with him almost since the beginning, his name is Mike Perez.

Paul: Then what is he afraid of, tell him to get the files. Can I meet him?

Larry: He doesn't want to get involved too much, but he will meet you in person, let me know. He said he knew both of the cops you mentioned.

Paul: I have already asked for the files, there are none. Let's see if this guy knows something I don't.

I called Larry and made plans to meet Mike Perez on Tuesday at 3:30 p.m. at Gianna's Restaurant in Yonkers. I looked up Mike Perez on the internet and found nothing. I would know this guy or he would know me. I knew just about every cop who worked for the City of Yonkers since the '90s, and I have never heard of Mike Perez.

On November 15, 2021, I emailed Larry some news I received about Detective Murphy.

Paul: One of my buddies got back to me about Kevin Murphy, he wants to put this all behind him, he doesn't want to talk about it anymore.

At 3:30 p.m. the next day, I met Larry at Gianna's restaurant. Before I went to meet Larry, I stopped at the Yonkers Detective Division to ask about Mike Perez. No one knew or ever heard of him. I waited with Larry for thirty minutes...Mike Perez was a no-show. Larry said he got stuck at work and would have to meet me on a later date. Something was odd about this, and I could tell from the start. I left Larry that day a little puzzled. What was this really all about?

I emailed Larry later that night.

Paul: You told me this guy Mike Perez worked with Joe Monaco for a number of years. I asked Joe today if he knew Mike Perez, he did not. I asked three other cops if they knew Mike Perez and they did not. Are you sure you have the right person? What happened to Justine?

Larry: Justine has gone ghost. I haven't spoken to her in a while.

Justine was nowhere to be found? What happened? When I first saw Justine, I thought to myself, this is great, she will help him gain attention with their videos. I could give Justine the information I found, and she could represent Yonkers...what happened? It's been about five months now and I never got to speak with her. We could have done a lot of good work together in Yonkers. I just wished Larry would have Zoomed with us all together so I could have spoken to her. She has no idea how much she helped me, and how important she was in all this.

As for Mike Perez, there was no Mike Perez. No cop in Yonkers knew Mike Perez. I felt Larry made him up to get me to do things for him.

When I found Randy Hughes, Larry questioned me if I was telling him the truth. He asked me, "Are you setting me up?" It took me ten minutes to convince him I was not lying. It was an insult, Randy was real. Now there was this Mike Perez insult.

That evening, I got a phone call from a very important person who was crucially essential to all this. Enter one of Yonkers' finest, Cold Case Detective John Geiss. He was a decorated detective for the City of Yonkers for forty years. Chief Monaco gave him my number and he had a lot to offer. Detective Geiss was very interested in what I was doing, and had contacts that would prove to be a big part of the progression in this investigation. He told me stories about his friends who knew Berkowitz growing up and gave me contact numbers to reach out to them. These contacts grew up with David Berkowitz in Co-Op City, the Bronx. One of the contacts Detective Geiss gave me was retired Yonkers Police Officer John Rinciari. John Rinciari worked with Berkowitz at the Co-Op City fire auxiliary in the '60s. I gave Larry John Rinciari's contact number and told him to call when he got a chance. Larry did, and got no answer, but left a message on his voicemail.

Larry called me later that night, he found files on Randy Hughes. In these files it stated Randy's brother Jimmy was caught by cultists in Untermyer Park and forced to watch a dog being sacrificed. He was taken to St. John's Hospital in trauma after the incident. I told Larry those files were correct. That was what I heard first about Randy, it was that story which led me to him. I reminded Larry it was one of the last things I emailed him about before he sent my money back to me in July.

On November 25, 2021, Thanksgiving Day, I emailed Larry for his friends and family to have a Happy Thanksgiving.

Larry: You beat me to it, was just about to email you the same thing, thanks bro. You have become my ally in this thing, and when the history is written, it's you and not me that will go down as one of the most important investigators in the Son of Sam case.

We both had our roles to play, and it was our different roles that would make this work. I could handle the groundwork, I just needed him to keep making videos. As long as he kept putting out content, people would come forward. As long as I kept bringing in information, he would have content.

That afternoon I got a call from Dave Butler who asked his mother about the "Son of Sam." She and his dad used to drink with Berkowitz at a bar near the marina in Yonkers. They weren't friends, but they knew him from hanging out in the bar. I three-wayed Larry into our phone conversation and Dave told us Berkowitz used to tell his parents he was sort of a cop. His mom said Berkowitz would try to talk cop talk with her husband, who was a Yonkers Detective. Before our conversation ended, Dave said he would get back to me when he had some answers from Jim Faulkner.

Larry emailed me later that night.

Larry: After speaking to your friend Dave, I think Berkie was a cop put in Yonkers to infiltrate the satanic cult. He knew too many power players in Yonkers, it makes too much sense. Berkie was NYPD auxiliary, and now we have him admitting he's a cop. Caveman also said all the locals thought he was a cop. What if he was placed in Yonkers, got caught up, and then was set up?

I think Larry took what we heard from Dave and talked this over a little too much with his conspirator friends. There was no way David Berkowitz, the biggest serial killer in New York history, was a cop sent in to infiltrate this satanic cult we were looking for. I'll leave that way of thinking to him. I don't think Berkowitz knew any power players. Caveman and his friends only thought Berkowitz was a cop because he was not a regular local. He was a clean-cut outsider at the park that no one knew. That is always a red flag to locals, especially drug dealers.

CHAPTER VII

KEITH AND THE CROSS ON THE TREE

That Thanksgiving night, Mason got an email from a fan of the show. Larry forwarded the email to me.

Hi my name is Keith. I'm trying to get in touch with Larry Dunn. Can you forward him my contact information. I lived in Yonkers and was born in 1965, I know a lot about the Son of Sam case having lived very close to many so called cult members. I would like to set a couple of things straight because there is a lot of mis-information out there. I know more about this case than most and there's probably only a handful of people that know as much about this case as I do. My story is beyond fascinating and I don't talk to just anybody about this stuff. I chased for the truth with this case for a long time and I knew Maury Terry personally. You can contact me by email or call my cell phone. Thanks, Keith.

I messaged Larry after I read Keith's email.

Paul: See, stay positive, I told you a few weeks ago this hasn't peaked yet, there's a lot more coming. This is working, the seal is broken.

That week, Larry met up with Keith at Untermyer Park and was told some very, very disturbing information. When Keith was ten, he was kidnapped by three kids who were sixteen years old. These kids took him behind a school in Yonkers and sexually abused him. When Keith was nineteen, he found Maury Terry and explained to him what happened. He thought these kids who did this to him may have been part of the satanic cult in Yonkers Maury was seeking. Maury took him in as a member of his team and had him help with his investigation.

See, Keith had seen Robert "Tocco" Grady get exposed in Larry's videos, and he wanted to do the same to his attackers. I could not get involved in this exposure. I was already not minding my business enough, but of course, I did look into this matter. I can assure you, it had nothing at all to do with Berkowitz or a satanic cult.

Keith had a lot to offer as he was on Pine Street the night Berkowitz was arrested. I read a newspaper article where Keith was bragging about taking pictures of the inside of Berkowitz's apartment the day of his arrest and selling the photos. Keith knew a lot about Maury, and could help with knowledge of Maury's investigation.

On November 30, 2021, Larry and Keith found something in Untermyer Park, something Justine had talked about in her previous videos. It was a carved cross on a tree, which was supposedly a marker for where kidnapped kids were buried. The tree was in the same area Caveman pointed to when he pulled me away from Larry and Mason the day we filmed his video.

I have to be honest, this cross on the tree did nothing for me. It was from pre-Berkowitz, and I wasn't interested in what was going on before Berkowitz came to Yonkers. Justine had previously mentioned in her videos the carved cross on the tree, and finding it was all part of the plan.

Any attention to this case was good. I needed more people to come forward with information, and the cross on the tree did just that. It was a golden key for me to use that would open more doors. Larry thought this was a big deal and asked to have a Zoom meeting to discuss the situation.

That night I met Larry and Mason for a Zoom meeting. They both wanted to rent a ground-penetrating radar machine to check the area of the park where the cross was for dead bodies. I asked them if they ever used a ground-penetrating radar machine and neither of them had. I then asked if they were to find any detection of bodies, who was going to dig them up?

Mason said he could handle renting the machine and we would worry about the digging later, if necessary.

On December 1, 2021, I woke up to my phone alarm, drove to work, and had coffee at the Yonkers courthouse. Upon leaving, I ran into a good friend of mine, a Yonkers Police Officer, Albert Buddy. I grew up with Albert, I have known him for over thirty-five years. I did not mention anything to him about Untermyer Park or the cross on the tree, but I did ask him if it was legal to use a ground-penetrating radar machine on public property. He told me I could use the machine anywhere, but wanted to know what the hell I was up to. He suggested I let the police do the work, it was their job.

I immediately called Larry and asked if he wanted me to bring him to the Yonkers Police Department and have them help us. I didn't really care about this cross on the tree, but if this was going to be the open door I had to connect him to the Yonkers Detectives, I needed to take advantage of this. Larry had information on this case, and who better to research his leads than the detectives. It was Larry's decision, I would stick to the plan we had agreed on with Mason, but recommend he take the help. He first needed to talk to Mason and would call me back.

After speaking with Mason, Larry told me Mason was unhappy I had spoken to the police about our plan. I assured Larry I ran into this cop by chance, and I didn't bring up Untermyer Park or anything we were going to do. All I did was ask my friend about using the machine in public places. Was I not allowed to ask if using the machine was legal? Yes, my friend was a cop, but this was all off record. I didn't go into the police department, he was a friend I ran into.

I asked Larry, "Am I not allowed to talk to my friends who are cops? I was making sure we would be okay. I did not talk to the police about what our plans were." I didn't understand this, I was giving Larry an opportunity to connect with the Yonkers Police...and this was a bad thing? This was an opportunity I was not sure of until this morning. Besides Detective Murphy, law enforcement never cooperated with anyone looking into this case. This was supposed to be a home run, but instead, I was left at the plate waiting for the pitch.

Larry called me that afternoon and decided to take me up on the offer from the Yonkers Detectives. I stressed to Larry, I didn't want any problems with Mason and was willing to speak with him about the situation…Mason declined.

That evening I called Larry on three-way with Chief Monaco and discussed the alleged dead bodies buried in the park. Caveman did mention dead bodies in that area, and the carved cross carried some stories with it. The conversation went well, and Chief Monaco agreed to help.

When I called Larry after our three-way conversation with Chief Monaco, I told him I wanted to connect Carl Denaro with some of these detectives. Carl was a victim and I wanted him to have some law enforcement to work with. Larry didn't want that, he did not want to help Carl. Carl wanted to know who shot him, and giving him some law enforcement help was the right thing to do. After about twenty minutes, I got Larry to agree with me, so I called Carl and was able to put him together with some Yonkers Detectives. Also, my detective friend Ryan did me a favor and spoke to Carl and Josh as well. To me, there were no teams, just Berkowitz.

I emailed Larry after our phone conversation.

Paul: You made the right decision. These are friends before cops, remember that.

Larry: Amazing! Mason is on board. He wants to film the dig. I told him I didn't really know if that would be possible.

Paul: It is possible. I see this is what Mason likes. I asked one of the detectives, he can film it.

Larry: Mason is still a little miffed about everything.

Paul: I did nothing wrong. I think we are on the up by using these detectives expertise. Now more cops will have no problem talking to you when you tell them you are in contact with Chief Monaco. You may even get some cops to come on your show now thanks to him. Chief Monaco is family, you can 100% trust him. Just wait until you talk to Detective Geiss, the guy knows his stuff.

First off, I owed Mason nothing, and this was not my decision. I was doing all the groundwork on my own, since when did I have to ask Mason for permission to do anything? This bond with the police was a positive move, and Mason was mad at me for doing this? I was helping this case in a way that was progressive for answers. I was forming alliances and molding a new era of trust to this case. What did I do wrong?

On December 3, 2021, I got an early morning email from Larry, Mason was still upset.

Larry: Mason thinks you are a social engineer sent in to harm the investigation. When he gets like this it's hard to convince him to think differently.

I just hooked this kid up with some detectives to work with, and this is what I get? I'm a social engineer? I don't even know what a social engineer is. I kept my word, and this argument was wasting my time.

Paul: He's not here at ground zero, things happen and things change. You get what you can, when you can get it, or you might lose it. I always talk to the cops, they are my friends. Trust me, give these cops a chance. If they fail us it's on me, then I'll fess to a mistake. Always judge people by their intent not the outcome...I don't fail. Don't let anyone cloud your mind with conspiracy bullshit, live life and deal with it as you breathe. Now can I continue what I was doing?

Larry: A retired Yonkers cop who grew up with Berkowitz called me, John Rinciari. This was the guy you told me to call, remember? I left him a message and he called me back. Like you said, knowing the YPD will open new doors.

Paul: John Rinciari is the cop Detective Geiss had call me a few weeks ago. These cops are all near retirement or retired. This was a good move.

On December 5, 2021, Larry and I met Yonkers Detectives John Geiss and Pat McCormick at Untermyer Park to show them the cross on the tree. Larry was ecstatic about his find, I myself didn't think they would be to impressed. I did this to get the detectives involved, and it was already proving to be beneficial. After seeing the tree, the detectives told us there wasn't much they could do with just a carved cross. They needed more evidence to assume there were dead bodies buried there.

I emailed Larry after we left the park.

Paul: I know you're upset about the detective's lack of interest in the cross. If we have to do things ourselves, they will let us. I have friends who work at Untermyer Park that can help us. I just talked to Geiss, he wants to meet up soon. I told you, Chief Monaco has made all these cops comfortable, here they come. You can get farther with them than without.

Larry: I might not be working with Mason for too much longer. He hasn't returned my emails since our last show.

Paul: Mr. Spencer called me asking about Scout, he wanted to know his real name. When I told him Walter Deyo Jr., he knew him. Everyone in the neighborhood used to call him "Blowjob Deyo," no one went near him, never mind hung out with him. Scout was a loner, a skell. Mr. Spencer will meet you now, it's time this thing starts taking off...stay positive.

CHAPTER VIII

JOHN SPENCER

On December 7, 2021, I brought Larry to meet John Spencer at a restaurant on Midland Avenue in Yonkers. Spencer had some rough years recently, which is why I needed to wait to bring Larry to him. His ex-wife passed away about two years earlier and he was having a hard time coping with it. Spencer lived in Yonkers his entire life and there is no one that knows this city better than he does.

I introduced Spencer to Larry, and we began to talk about Yonkers, Maury, and the "Son of Sam." Spencer did not know David Berkowitz and he never saw him in our neighborhoods. He didn't know anyone who knew him besides Maury.

John Carr was in his freshman class at Sacred Heart High School, but left after freshman year and never saw him again. He didn't know John well and described him as a quiet loner. He remembered the rumors of people sacrificing animals in Untermyer Park, but never heard of The Process or a twenty-two disciples of hell cult. Spencer also knew my good friend Albie from the Vietnam veterans posts and tried to help Larry accept that Albie had nothing to do with Berkowitz.

I then had Spencer clear several of the names for Larry I had already vindicated for him from his videos, validating my word. David Berkowitz did not hang out with anyone from the north in Yonkers...my church was not the breeding grounds for a satanic cult.

One thing Spencer mentioned was he heard the search and seizure the day of Berkowitz's arrest was not done properly. All of the evidence was obtained without a search warrant and could have been contested in court. He heard the warrant was issued after they searched Berkowitz's car.

When I asked Spencer about Maury Terry and David Berkowitz's relationship, he said they were very good friends. He would hang out with Maury at times, and out of nowhere Maury would say, "I got to go see David, I'll see you later." Maury visited David Berkowitz a lot in prison and they became very close. Spencer liked Maury's book but said some of the stuff in it was a little off. He didn't like the Charles Manson connection.

What Spencer said next confirmed one of Maury's interview's with Berkowitz. Maury told him Berkowitz admitted John Carr was the "Son of Sam." We ended the interview and Spencer asked for his name not to be mentioned, he didn't want to upset anyone.

On December 11, 2021, while Larry was preparing the Spencer interview, I emailed him.

Paul: Remember, say the ex-mayor of Yonkers, I don't think he will mind that. Make sure you stress the point he told us, that Maury was good friends with Berkowitz, he visited him in prison a lot more than we were told. Spencer said Maury told him Berkowitz admitted John Carr was the Son of Sam.

Ten minutes later, Larry posted the Spencer interview on his website using John Spencer's name all over it. I could only hope Spencer didn't get upset because I was not ready to have another argument with someone over helping this kid. Why didn't Larry respect Spencer's request? I know he got my email before he posted the interview, so why did he continue to do this? He didn't even call me to discuss it, he ignored me.

Paul: I saw the interview, I would have rather you didn't mention his name.

The next day, Larry did his show solo and announced to his audience that Mason would not be working with him anymore. Whatever choices Larry made for his show were all his, I could only give him advice.

I was able to connect Larry, Carl, and Josh with detectives to work with, everyone had information to offer and receive. Carl had plans to visit Berkowitz in prison soon, and to show unity, I talked him into doing an interview with Larry after his visit. This had Larry talking to Carl and Josh again, everyone was now involved. Fighting was not the way. All doors must always be open, and contacts should never be discarded.

On December 16, 2021, I spoke with Albie again. I knew no matter what I said to Larry, he would still be in doubt about Albie. After our conversation, I emailed Larry.

Paul: I'm hanging out with your buddy Albie later, cheers!

Larry: I still don't believe him. There's no way Albie didn't know "Berkie" and "Wheaties" intimately but whatever. We're never going to agree on this. If Carl doesn't do this interview with me soon, I hope it makes you realize he's not a good guy.

Paul: I can have Albie talk to you if you like, in fact, my friend Ryan also knows him well, do you want to talk to him about Albie? I'm not easily fooled Larry. I told you from day one with him, no way. I've been tight with him for about twenty years now, he would have told me. He is stopping by later, and you are welcome to join. He would never disrespect me or do anything to you. He is not even mad about this, he is laughing.

Larry: I'll pass, I won't mention Albie again. You just gave Carl and Josh detectives to work with, what do we get in return?

Paul: We get peace, no negativity...and good information.

All I wanted was to include everybody for the ride, especially a victim and the people who came before me. I asked Carl that night to call Larry, keeping him involved was important to me. He agreed, and would also write a post for his website apologizing for the mishaps. Excellent...olive branches were falling from the sky.

Larry then emailed me something very odd again.

Larry: A fan of the show got this guy John to get in touch with me, he knew Berkowitz from Co-Op City.

I knew the John he was talking about, John Comparetto. He was sent to Larry by John Rinciari and Detective Geiss, not by a fan of his show. They both spoke with John Comparetto and asked him to get a hold of Larry for an interview. Why was Larry acting like a fan made this happen when he knew Comparetto was sent from the YPD?

John Comparetto, like John Rinciari, was friends with Berkowitz in the late '60s. They were all part of a fire auxiliary for Co-Op City in the Bronx. He was a New York City Police Officer for over forty years. Now retired, he was willing to share his experiences he had growing up with David Berkowitz.

On December 19, 2021, Detective Geiss called and said we could do whatever we wanted with the cross on the tree. He was told Kevin Murphy had already found the cross in the '90s and checked the park for dead bodies. They were not interested in digging.

I emailed Larry after my conversation with Detective Geiss.

Paul: I've been thinking about the dig, and I think you are better off not digging. If you do decide to dig and nothing is found, you look nuts. If you just show everything you have to the audience, you can't lose. Let them just assume you are right rather than take a chance and be wrong.

Larry: I agree.

The next morning, Larry emailed me Carl was mad at him for allowing negative posts on his website. I didn't respond, and got another email from Larry an hour later saying he talked to Carl and everything was good. It was becoming obvious to me I was going to have to ignore all of Larry's nonsense behind the scenes. Where is David Berkowitz? I have wasted a lot of time looking for a satanic cult that no one but Maury knew about. I needed to start looking into what I knew for sure was connected to Berkowitz. I needed to find the beginning to all this.

CHAPTER IX

STRIP AND REBUILD

Sometimes to get the right end results, you need to go back to the beginning and start over. I realized I was going to have to strip this case down and rebuild it. So far, I've spoken to a lot of people in Yonkers, and no one heard of, or knew of, a satanic cult called the twenty-two disciples of hell. This cult of twenty-two people which supposedly included Berkowitz, was nowhere to be found. How could twenty-two people be involved with these crimes and not one person in forty-four years be positively connected? Maury's theory of a twenty-two-person cult originated from reading the Breslin letter. One of the clues in the letter was "*THE TWENTY TWO DISCIPLES OF HELL*" and Maury felt this clue was referring to Berkowitz's cult of twenty-two people. I don't think that is what the clue meant. I don't think twenty-two people were involved.

I still had doubts Berkowitz acted alone. With all of Maury's evidence, John Carr looked to be the real "Son of Sam." I think John and Michael Carr were a part of a satanic cult with David Berkowitz, but there couldn't be more than a handful of people involved with these crimes. In an interview Berkowitz had with Maury, he said he met Michael Carr first and John Carr was involved. He also claimed a police officer was a member of this cult. Another person to add, Wheat Carr, who according to Maury, was possibly a shooter in some of these attacks.

When it came to John Carr, I could not find anyone who knew him personally. The only connections I had to John with this case was the letter he supposedly wrote to Queens Detective Joseph Borrelli and the name "*JOHN WHEATIES*" in the Breslin letter. According to what Maury heard,

Sam Carr was a bad child abuser and didn't get along with his kids, so John seemed to fit as the author of the Borrelli letter.

Here is the famous Borrelli letter that was left at the Bronx murder scene on April 17, 1977:

I AM DEEPLY HURT BY YOUR CALLING ME A WEMON HATER. I AM NOT. BUT I AM A MONSTER.

I AM THE "SON OF SAM." I AM A LITTLE "BRAT."

WHEN FATHER SAM GETS DRUNK HE GETS MEAN. HE BEATS HIS FAMILY. SOMETIMES HE TIES ME UP TO THE BACK OF THE HOUSE. OTHER TIMES HE LOCKS ME IN THE GARAGE. SAM LOVES TO DRINK BLoOD.

"GO OUT AND KILL" COMMANDS FATHER SAM.

BEHIND OUR HOUSE SOME REST. MOSTLY YOUNG-RAPED AND SLAUGHTERED-THEIR BLOOD DRAINED-JUST BONES NOW.

PAPA SAM KEEPS ME LOCKED IN THE ATTIC TOO. I CAN'T GET OUT BUT I LOOK OUT THE ATTIC WINDOW AND WATCH THE WORLD GO BY.

I FEEL LIKE AN OUTSIDER. I AM ON A DIFFERENT WAVE LENGTH THEN EVERYBODY ELSE-PROGRAMMED TOO KILL.

HOWEVER, TO STOP ME YOU MUST KILL ME. ATTENTION ALL POLICE: SHOOT ME FIRST-SHOOT TO KILL OR ELSE. KEEP OUT OF MY WAY OR YOU WILL DIE!

PAPA SAM IS OLD NOW. HE NEEDS SOME BLOOD TO PRESERVE HIS YOUTH. HE HAS HAD TOO MANY HEART ATTACKS. TOO MANY HEART ATTACKS. "UGH, ME HOOT IT URTS SONNY BOY."

I MISS MY PRETTY PRINCESS MOST OF ALL. SHE'S RESTING IN OUR LADIES HOUSE BUT I'LL SHE HER SOON.

I AM THE "MONSTER"-"BEELZEBUB"- THE "CHUBBY BEHEMOUTH."

I LOVE TO HUNT. PROWLING THE STREETS LOOKING FOR FAIR GAME-TASTY MEAT. THE WEMON OF QUEENS ARE Z PRETTYIST OF ALL. I MUST BE THE WATER THEY DRINK. I LIVE FOR THE HUNT-MY LIFE. BLOOD FOR PAPA.

MR. BORELLI, SIR, I DON'T WANT TO KILL ANYMORE. NO SIR, NO MORE BUT I MUST, "HONOUR THY FATHER."

I WANT TO MAKE LOVE TO THE WORLD. I LOVE PEOPLE. I DON'T BELONG ON EARTH. RETURN ME TO YAHOOS.

TO THE PEOPLE OF QUEENS, I LOVE YOU. AND I WANT TO WISH ALL OF YOU A HAPPY EASTER. MAY GOD BLESS YOU IN THIS LIFE AND IN THE NEXT. AND FOR NOW I SAY GOODBYE AND GOODNIGHT.

POLICE: LET ME HAUNT YOU WITH THESE WORDS;

I'LL BE BACK!

I'LL BE BACK!

TO BE INTERPRETED AS-BANG, BANG, BANG, BANK, BANG-UGH!!

YOURS IN MURDER MR. MONSTER

Sam Carr was the Sam this letter was referring to and it looks like it was written by his son, John Carr. Berkowitz confirmed to Maury on numerous occasions that John was involved, so I too felt this had to be John who was the author of this letter.

My theory with this letter was John Carr had written it to get back at his father and may not have told Berkowitz he was leaving it at the murder scene. The second letter, which was sent to *Daily News* columnist Jimmy Breslin, I don't think John wrote.

Here is the second letter which was received by Jimmy Breslin on June 2, 1977:

DEAR MR. JIMMY BRESLIN,

HELLO FROM THE GUTTERS OF N.Y.C. WHICH ARE FILLED WITH DOG MANURE, VOMIT, STALE WINE, URINE, AND BLOOD. HELLO FROM THE SEWERS OF N.Y.C. WHICH SWALLOW UP THESE DELICACIES WHEN THEY ARE WASHED AWAY BY THE SWEEPER TRUCKS. HELLO FROM THE CRACKS IN THE SIDEWALKS OF N.Y.C. AND FROM THE ANTS THAT DWELL IN THESE CRACKS AND FEED ON THE DRIED BLOOD OF THE DEAD THAT HAS SEEPED INTO THESE CRACKS.

J.B., I'M JUST DROPPING YOU A LINE TO LET YOU KNOW THAT I APPRECIATE YOUR INTEREST IN THOSE RECENT AND HORRENDOUS .44 KILLINGS. I ALSO WANT

TO TELL YOU THAT I READ YOUR COLUMN DAILY AND I FIND IT QUITE INFORMATIVE.

TELL ME JIM, WHAT WILL YOU HAVE FOR JULY TWENTY-NINTH? YOU CAN FORGET ABOUT ME IF YOU LIKE BECAUSE I DON'T CARE FOR PUBLICITY. HOWEVER, YOU MUST NOT FORGET DONNA LAURIA AND YOU CANNOT LET THE PEOPLE FORGET HER EITHER. SHE WAS A VERY, VERY SWEET GIRL BUT SAM'S A THIRSTY LAD AND HE WON'T LET ME STOP KILLING UNTIL HE GETS HIS FILL OF BLOOD.

MR. BRESLIN, SIR, DON'T THINK THAT BECAUSE YOU HAVEN'T HEARD FROM FOR A WHILE THAT I WENT TO SLEEP. NO, RATHER, I AM STILL HERE. LIKE A SPIRIT ROAMING THE NIGHT. THIRSTY, HUNGRY, SELDOM STOPPING TO REST; ANXIOUS TO PLEASE SAM. I LOVE MY WORK. NOW, THE VOID HAS BEEN FILLED.

PERHAPS WE SHALL MEET FACE TO FACE SOMEDAY OR PERHAPS I WILL BE BLOWN AWAY BY COPS WITH SMOKING .38'S. WHATEVER, IF I SHALL BE FORTUNATE ENOUGH TO MEET YOU I WILL TELL YOU ALL ABOUT SAM IF YOU LIKE AND I WILL INTRODUCE YOU TO HIM. HIS NAME IS "SAM THE TERRIBLE."

NOT KNOWING WHAT THE FUTURE HOLDS I SHALL SAY FAREWELL AND I WILL SEE YOU AT THE NEXT JOB. OR SHOULD I SAY YOU WILL SEE MY HANDIWORK AT THE NEXT JOB? REMEMBER MS. LAURIA. THANK YOU.

IN THEIR BLOOD AND FROM THE GUTTER "SAM'S CREATION" .44

HERE ARE SOME NAMES TO HELP YOU ALONG. FORWARD THEM TO THE INSPECTOR FOR USE BY N.C.I.C.:

"THE DUKE OF DEATH"

"THE WICKED KING WICKER"

"THE TWENTY TWO DISCIPLES OF HELL"

"JOHN 'WHEATIES'- RAPIST AND SUFFOCATER OF YOUNG GIRLS.

PS: J.B., PLEASE INFORM ALL THE DETECTIVES WORKING THE SLAYINGS TO REMAIN.

PS: J.B., PLEASE INFORM ALL THE DETECTIVES WORKING THE CASE THAT I WISH THEM THE BEST OF LUCK. "KEEP EM DIGGING, DRIVE ON, THINK POSITIVE, GET OFF YOUR BUTTS, KNOCK ON COFFINS, ETC."

UPON MY CAPTURE I PROMISE TO BUY ALL THE GUYS WORKING ON THE CASE A NEW PAIR OF SHOES IF I CAN GET UP THE MONEY.

SON OF SAM (with a satanic like symbol underneath Son of Sam)

These two letters, all in capital letters, looked to be in totally different handwriting. Maury's theory was John Carr wrote the first one, and because Michael Carr was a graphic designer, he must've written the second one as the lettering was very artistic. The second letter had a different feel than the first. In the first letter, the author has Sam as the father. In the second letter, Sam is more of a person the author knew. I believe John Carr had written the Borrelli letter, but I think Berkowitz sent the letter to Breslin. The Breslin letter read, *"JOHN 'WHEATIES'-RAPIST AND SUFFOCATER OF YOUNG GIRLS"* and I doubt John or anyone from the Carr family would have written that. Maybe Berkowitz didn't like John left the Borrelli letter at the crime scene and decided to write his own to Jimmy Breslin.

On December 23, 2021, I had a funeral to attend. I entered the church, took my holy water, and closed my eyes as I kneeled to pray. A lot of things go through your mind while praying. I'm extremely grateful for my life.

I emailed Larry after the funeral.

Paul: Have you spoken to Keith?

Larry: No, I had to stop talking to him. He kept saying Wheat was innocent, he is insane. Something is not right with him. I'm going to leave him alone.

That night I sat and thought about this case, and who the main characters of this "Son of Sam" story were. I needed the real characters, not vampires and witches. I was not getting anywhere looking for this satanic cult. I would have 100 percent been able to find some kind of a connection to this cult...but, there was nothing. I was going to have to start educating myself by reading every book possible about the "Son of Sam." Penny could handle the newspaper articles, no more relying on anyone else's leads.

I AM DEEPLY HURT BY YOUR CALLING ME A WEMON HATER. I AM NOT. BUT I AM A MONSTER.
I AM THE "SON OF SAM." I AM A LITTLE "BRAT."

WHEN FATHER SAM GETS DRUNK HE GETS MEAN. HE BEATS HIS FAMILY. SOMETIMES HE TIES ME UP TO THE BACK OF THE HOUSE. OTHER TIMES HE LOCKS ME IN THE GARAGE. SAM LOVES TO DRINK BLOOD.

"GO OUT AND KILL" COMMANDS FATHER SAM.

BEHIND OUR HOUSE SOME REST. MOSTLY YOUNG - RAPED AND SLAUGHTERED - THEIR BLOOD DRAINED - JUST BONES NOW.

PAPA SAM KEEPS ME LOCKED IN THE ATTIC TOO. I CAN'T GET OUT BUT I LOOK OUT THE ATTIC WINDOW AND WATCH THE WORLD GO BY.

I FEEL LIKE AN OUTSIDER. I AM ON A DIFFERENT WAVE LENGTH THEN EVERYBODY

ELSE - PROGRAMMED TOO KILL.

HOWEVER, TO STOP ME YOU MUST KILL ME. ATTENTION ALL POLICE: SHOOT ME FIRST SHOOT TO KILL OR ELSE. KEEP OUT OF MY WAY OR YOU WILL DIE!

PAPA SAM IS OLD NOW. HE NEEDS SOME BLOOD TO PRESERVE HIS YOUTH. HE HAS HAD TOO MANY HEART ATTACKS. TOO MANY HEART ATTACKS. "UGH ME HOOT IT URTS SONNY BOY."

I MISS MY PRETTY PRINCESS MOST OF ALL. SHE'S RESTING IN OUR LADIES HOUSE BUT I'LL SEE HER SOON.

I AM THE "MONSTER" - "BEELZEBUB" - THE "CHUBBY BEHEMOUTH".

I LOVE TO HUNT. PROWLING THE STREETS LOOKING FOR FAIR GAME - TASTY MEAT. THE WEMON OF QUEENS ARE Z PRETTYIST OF ALL. I MUST BE THE WATER THEY DRINK. I LIVE FOR THE HUNT - MY LIFE. BLOOD FOR PAPA.

MR. BORELLI, SIR, I DONT WANT TO KILL ANYMORE NO SIR, NO MORE BUT I MUST, "HONOUR THY FATHER."

I WANT TO MAKE LOVE TO THE WORLD. I LOVE PEOPLE. I DONT BELONG ON EARTH. RETURN ME TO YAHOOS.

TO THE PEOPLE OF QUEENS, I LOVE YOU. AND I ~~WA~~ WANT TO WISH ALL OF YOU A HAPPY EASTER. MAY GOD BLESS YOU IN THIS LIFE AND IN THE NEXT. AND FOR NOW

I SAY GOODBYE AND GOODNIGHT.

POLICE: LET ME HAUNT YOU WITH THESE WORDS;

I'LL BE BACK!

I'LL BE BACK!

TO BE INTERRPRETED AS- BANG, BANG, BANG, BANK, BANG – 'UGH!!'

YOURS IN MURDER

MR. MONSTER

DEAR MR. JIMMY BRESLIN,

HELLO FROM THE GUTTERS OF N.Y.C. WHICH ARE FILLED WITH DOG MANURE, VOMIT, STALE WINE, URINE, AND BLOOD. HELLO FROM THE SEWERS OF N.Y.C. WHICH SWALLOW UP THESE DELICACIES WHEN THEY ARE WASHED AWAY BY THE SWEEPER TRUCKS. HELLO FROM THE CRACKS IN THE SIDEWALKS OF N.Y.C. AND FROM THE ANTS THAT DWELL IN THESE CRACKS AND FEED ON THE DRIED BLOOD OF THE DEAD THAT HAS SEEPED INTO THESE CRACKS.

J.B., I'M JUST DROPPING YOU A LINE TO LET YOU KNOW THAT I APPRECIATE YOUR INTEREST IN THOSE RECENT AND HORRENDOUS .44 KILLINGS. I ALSO WANT TO TELL YOU THAT I READ YOUR COLUMN DAILY AND I FIND IT QUITE INFORMATIVE.

TELL ME JIM, WHAT WILL YOU HAVE FOR JULY TWENTY-NINTH? YOU CAN FORGET ABOUT ME IF YOU LIKE BECAUSE I DON'T CARE FOR PUBLICITY. HOWEVER YOU MUST NOT FORGET DONNA LAURIA AND

YOU CANNOT LET THE PEOPLE FORGET HER EITHER. SHE WAS A VERY, VERY SWEET GIRL BUT SAM'S A THIRSTY LAD AND HE WON'T LET ME STOP KILLING UNTIL HE GETS HIS FILL OF BLOOD.

MR. BRESLIN, SIR, DON'T THINK THAT BECAUSE YOU HAVEN'T HEARD FROM FOR A WHILE THAT I WENT TO SLEEP. NO, RATHER, I AM STILL HERE. LIKE A SPIRIT ROAMING THE NIGHT. THIRSTY, HUNGRY, SELDOM STOPPING TO REST; ANXIOUS TO PLEASE SAM. I LOVE MY WORK. NOW, THE VOID HAS BEEN FILLED.

PERHAPS WE SHALL MEET FACE TO FACE SOMEDAY OR PERHAPS I WILL BE BLOWN AWAY BY COPS WITH SMOKING .38'S. WHATEVER, IF I SHALL BE FORTUNATE ENOUGH TO MEET YOU I WILL TELL YOU ALL ABOUT SAM IF YOU LIKE AND I WILL INTRODUCE YOU TO HIM. HIS NAME IS "SAM THE TERRIBLE."

NOT KNOWING WHAT THE FUTURE HOLDS I SHALL SAY FAREWELL AND I WILL SEE YOU AT THE NEXT JOB. OR SHOULD I SAY YOU WILL SEE MY HANDIWORK AT THE NEXT JOB? REMEMBER MS. LAURIA. THANK YOU.

IN THEIR BLOOD
AND
FROM THE GUTTER

"SAM'S CREATION" .44

HERE ARE SOME NAMES TO HELP YOU ALONG. FORWARD THEM TO THE INSPECTOR FOR USE BY N.C.I.C. :

"THE DUKE OF DEATH"
"THE WICKED KING WICKER"
"THE TWENTY TWO DISCIPLES OF HELL"
"JOHN 'WHEATIES' - RAPIST AND SUFFOCATER OF YOUNG GIRLS.

PS: J.B. PLEASE INFORM ALL THE DETECTIVES WORKING THE SLAYINGS TO REMAIN

PS: J.B., PLEASE INFORM ALL THE DETECTIVES WORKING THE CASE THAT I WISH THEM THE BEST OF LUCK. "KEEP EM DIGGING, DRIVE ON, THINK POSITIVE, GET OFF YOUR BUTTS, KNOCK ON COFFINS, ETC."

UPON MY CAPTURE I PROMISE TO BUY ALL THE GUYS WORKING ON THE CASE A NEW PAIR OF SHOES IF I CAN GET UP THE MONEY.

SON OF SAM

CHAPTER X

WICKER STREET AND THE NETOS

The first book I read was *Son of Sam* by Dr. Lawrence D. Klausner which was published in 1981. He was the first doctor to write a book about what David Berkowitz claimed had happened. In this book, Berkowitz believed Sam Carr was a duality. There was the visible person Sam Carr, but within him also lived another creature named Sam who was the high official of a devil's legion. The demonic Sam worked under "*General Jack Cosmo*," Jack Cassara, who to Berkowitz, was commander of an army of demon dogs. Berkowitz would receive his orders to kill from Sam, through Sam's dog.

Berkowitz also believed there were demons living at 316 Warburton Avenue (Sam Carr's house), 18 and 22 Wicker Street, which were all located directly behind his 35 Pine Street apartment in Yonkers. He explained when the souls of a victim he shot left their body, these demons would be there. They would snatch the souls of the victims and take them to the attic of 316 Warburton Avenue, or to the attics at 18 and 22 Wicker Street to rape and molest forever. "*It's messy. It's brutal. There's no sleep for the victim's souls. No resting, no peace,*" said Berkowitz.

The Cassara family were main characters in this "Son of Sam" story. Jack and Nann Cassara, along with their son Steven, lived at 174 Coligni Avenue in New Rochelle and rented a room to Berkowitz in February of 1976, right before he moved to 35 Pine Street in Yonkers. Berkowitz claimed Jack Cassara and Sam Carr were Satan themselves and were out to get him unless he killed for innocent blood. According to Berkowitz, killing was the only way to stop the demons around him from tormenting his life.

Another character in the Klausner book I was introduced to was Craig Glassman. Craig moved to 35 Pine Street, apartment 6E, right beneath Berkowitz on March 15, 1977. Berkowitz thought Craig was put there by Jack Cassara and Sam Carr to torment him. Craig would play his television set loud at night which Berkowitz said caused him to go out and kill.

This is odd, Berkowitz admits to Dr. Klausner that he stabbed two young girls on December 24, 1975, but did not kill them. I can't see how Jack Cassara, Sam Carr, or Craig Glassman had anything to do with those attempted murders as Berkowitz did not know them until after February of 1976.

Also in this book, Sam and Wheat Carr went to the police and tried to get them to question Berkowitz before his arrest. If they were involved, again it looked like the family was trying to throw Berkowitz under the bus, which is why I think Berkowitz wrote the Breslin letter. He may have been trying to frame the Carrs. Either Berkowitz was with John against his father Sam, or Berkowitz had a fall-out with the Carrs and it was all about the blame game.

The Klausner book brought up so much more, read it. It is an important book to read in order to understand Berkowitz. What I also needed from it were the real characters to this story. There was no mention in the entire book of Untermyer Park or a twenty-two person satanic cult. Berkowitz talked about demons at Wicker Street, I'll check out Wicker Street.

I started to do research on the residents who lived on Wicker Street during the shootings and I came across some articles about a Portuguese family named the Netos who lived at 18 Wicker Street. Berkowitz mentioned in the Klausner book that Robert Neto, "*Joaquin the Joker*" lived there who was also taking orders from "*General Jack Cosmo,*" Jack Cassara. I called Larry and asked if he had ever spoken to the Netos because I noticed some of the family was still alive, he had not. I asked him if he knew anything about that family, he did not. I hadn't heard much about this family myself. Something went on there at Wicker Street and I needed to find this Neto family.

I was starting to see, and soon felt, it was all still out there, the untold truth. There was no cover-up. The plain truth was just never found, nobody looked.

Within a few hours, I found the Neto family from Wicker Street... Sylvia, Joaquim, and Maria. Sylvia was alive, she was twelve years old in 1976. Joaquim, Sylvia's father, passed away in 2018. Maria, Joaquim's wife, Sylvia's mother, was eighty-seven now and still alive. I don't think Maury got the opportunity to talk to the right people about this case, plain and simple.

On December 27, 2021, I discussed with Carl some information I was researching and he suggested I speak with his friend Max to get answers to some of the questions I had. Max was Carl's right-hand man when it came to files and articles, he knew more about this case than anyone. Larry did a show that night and Max reached out to me through the show's live chat to get a hold of him. I said in the chat I would, and the next morning I got this email from Larry.

Larry: I see Max is playing nice with you in the chat. Before you speak to him or start a phone conversation, speak to me first. I do not trust the guy and I want to just warn you about his tendencies to cause trouble and play people against each other. He is close with Carl, but not to be trusted. Be careful what you share with him.

I thought Larry made peace with Carl and his group? Why should I not trust this guy? What could he do that was so bad? Carl said Max had been researching this case for a while now and he was the man to talk to for information. How bad could this guy be?

I had to stop letting Larry's personal issues with people interfere with who I wanted to speak with. Max was extremely up-to-date with this case.

Talking to him proved to be very beneficial as we went back and forth with documents and articles. He was a diehard Maury Terry follower, and was loyal to Maury's work. I want to believe Maury, but some of the information I got after speaking to the people of Yonkers didn't make sense. *The Ultimate Evil* was a great book I recently just finished reading and rumors of Maury having to spice his book up for the publisher's acceptance was talked about. Maybe some of it was off, but Berkowitz having accomplices seemed undeniable.

On December 28, 2021, I was enjoying my lunch at Lusitania in the back room while talking to the owner of the restaurant Joe, when I remembered the Neto family was Portuguese. Joe was from Portugal, and the Portuguese community in Yonkers was very close. I took a shot and asked Joe if he knew the Netos...he did! His best friend was married to Sylvia Neto. Joe told me Joaquim Neto had passed away, but Maria Neto was still alive and living in Yonkers. He didn't want to give me their contact numbers just yet, not until he talked to them first, but he would get back to me. During our conversation, Joe told me Sylvia used to play in a band called Blackout 77...thank you Joe.

All I needed was the band name, Blackout 77. Twenty minutes later, I found Sylvia. She was very hesitant to talk to me at first until I told her I was good friends with Joe, her husband's best friend. I also told her I had spoken to a few people who knew her father. There was a club in Yonkers all of the Portuguese people belonged to, and her father Joaquim was this club's president at one time. He was a hard-working immigrant, a man for his people.

This was my conversation with Sylvia Neto.

Paul: Thank you so much for speaking with me Sylvia.

Sylvia: Joe called me earlier and said you were looking for me.

Paul: Yeah, I eat at the restaurant all the time.

Sylvia: He told me, he asked me if I would talk to you about some of the things that went on at my home in the '70s.

Paul: Do you mind?

Sylvia: I don't like talking about this, but I guess if your friends with Joe your're ok.

Paul: Thanks Sylvia, I really apprieciate that.

Sylvia: Sure, what would you like to know?

Paul: Did David Berkowitz do anything to your home on Wicker Street?

Sylvia: He shot and killed my dog Rocket on Christmas Eve in 1976.

Paul: I thought I read something like that.

Sylvia: Yeah, we had a German Shepherd named Rocket and on Christmas Eve in 1976, while my family was having a party in our basement, he shot our dog.

Paul: Did you see who it was? How do you know it was Berkowitz?

Sylvia: I was playing the piano in the front room when I heard two gun shots come from outside. When I went outside, Rocket had been shot. We didn't see anyone and didn't know who did it at the time.

Paul: How did you find out it was him?

Sylvia: A New York City detective named Zigo came to our house three days after Berkowitz was arrested and told my father Berkowitz admitted to shooting a dog on our property.

Paul: Whoa, ok, geez Sylvia. Did anything else happen?

Sylvia: Oh, it was horrible. For two years, just about every other month something would happen. We would have family memebrs sit at the front window at night so we could sleep in peace.

Paul: When did this start?

Sylvia: In 1975, somewhere at the end of 1975. It started with rocks getting thrown through the front window. Then a letter came.

Paul: What did the letter say? Do you have it?

Sylvia: No, my grandmother burned it. It said something about a queen living in our attic and that they were going to burn our house down. We were even getting phone calls to our house.

Paul: What were the phone calls saying?

Sylvia: It was a man and he would ask my mother to speak with me.

Paul: Speak with you? How old were you at the time?

Sylvia: I was twelve, yeah, and the caller would want to speak with me. He told my mother one time over the phone that a queen was living in our attic just like in the letter. Then came the Molotov cocktail.

Paul: Sylvia, this is crazy.

Sylvia: Oh yeah, they tried to burn the house down. On May 13, 1976 while I was sleeping in a bedroom on the second floor with my grandmother, someone threw a Molotov cocktail at the window.

Paul: My God Sylvia, did you guys see who threw the cocktail?

Sylvia: No, the fire started outside the house. Luckily, it bounced off the window screen and dropped down in front of the house.

Paul: Oh my God, seriously. If that bottle would have went through your screen it would have been bad.

Sylvia: Yeah, I know. I was sleeping in that room. It was around three in the morning.

Paul: You're very lucky Sylvia.

Sylvia: I know, thank God the screen didn't rip. Then, if I remember correctly, there was a SWAT called to our home.

Paul: A what?

Sylvia: A SWAT, someone called the Yonkers Police and told them that my father Joaquim had gone crazy and was killing everyone in the house.

Paul: What the hell was that all about?

Sylvia: We didn't know what was going on. One day the cops showed up at our home banging on our front door. When my father opened the door, all the cops had their guns out pointed at him. My father was a hunter so thank God he didn't open the door with his shotgun. We were going through a lot with the harassments so I'm just glad he didn't open the door armed. The police rushed in and began searching our entire house. They told us they received a call that Joaquim was killing everyone in the house. We told them we don't know what you're talking about. My mother was so upset. After about ten minutes the police knew it was a false call.

Paul: They could have shot your father.

Sylvia: I know, it was bad. Then the last thing I can remember happening was when Rocket was shot. Nothing happened after that.

Paul: Did Berkowitz admit to doing all this?

Sylvia: The only thing I know he admitted to was shooting my dog.

Paul: Insane Sylvia. Did Maury Terry ever speak to you guys?

Sylvia: My father wouldn't talk to him. My father wouldn't talk to anybody about this. I know Maury came to the house and tried to talk to my father, but my father told him to get lost.

Paul: Your father Joaquim, did anyone ever call him Joaquin the Joker?

Sylvia: I have never heard anyone call him that. Where did you get that from?

Paul: Berkowitz says in the Klausner book that a Robert Neto lived at 18 Wicker Street and he called him Joaquin the Joker.

Sylvia: There was no Robert Neto living there. The only Netos who lived there were me and my parents.

Sylvia and I spoke for a while about how crazy Wicker Street was, and before we finished our conversation, she agreed to do an interview for me with Larry. Even better, she was going to ask her mother Maria to join us. This was big, I don't think anyone has heard their entire story. I arranged to do an interview with Maria and Sylvia the next day at 6 p.m. at 18 Wicker Street, where Maria still resided...the home of the demons.

I emailed Larry as soon as I hung up the phone with Sylvia.

Paul: Charge your equipment for tomorrow at 6 p.m., I'll meet you at Wicker Street. I got the Netos to do an interview.

Larry: Holy Shit! I'll be there.

The next day around 5 p.m., I stopped by Lusitania to thank Joe for his help in connecting me with the Netos. Joe laughed as I told him he slipped with Sylvia's band name. Sylvia's husband was also there so I was glad I got to meet him and let him know what I was doing. We discussed the situation and I made him very comfortable with what was going on.

I bought the two best bottles of Portuguese wine the restaurant had so I didn't show up to the Neto house empty-handed. The main question I wanted answered was, why did David Berkowitz bother this house at 18 Wicker Street?

I left the restaurant and went to meet Larry on Grove Street, which was right around the corner from the Neto home. We walked down to 18 Wicker Street, and all I could picture in my mind as we got closer to the house was Sylvia's dog being shot. The bullet holes in the aluminum siding of the house were still there from 1976. I opened the gate to their fence, proceeded to the front door, and rang the bell. Maria answered with Sylvia behind her and invited us in, both ladies were very welcoming. The inside of their home was an immediate time warp for me as it reminded me of being in my aunts' and uncles' houses in the '80s…I felt so much at home. We sat down in their dining room and began discussing what happened to their family.

In 1975, the Neto family had rocks thrown through their front window, followed by a threatening letter and phone calls asking for Sylvia, telling them a queen was living in their attic. Maria said on one phone call, a man threatened to burn their house down to the ground. The Netos then had a Molotov cocktail thrown at their second-floor window on May 13, 1976. A little after the Molotov cocktail, they recalled the police were sent to their house because someone called the YPD and told them Joaquim was killing his family.

Then on December 24, 1976, the Netos' dog Rocket was shot dead in front of their house. They saw no one to accuse for any of these crimes. After their dog was shot, the Netos were not bothered again, but still lived in fear until Detective Ed Zigo from New York City came to their house three days after David Berkowitz's arrest to notify them Berkowitz admitted to shooting a dog on their property. None of the other crimes done to the Netos were discussed, and some of them, according to this timeline given by the Netos, could have been done before Berkowitz moved to Pine Street in Yonkers.

Was Berkowitz harassing this family prior to living in Yonkers, or was someone else committing these crimes before he moved there? Berkowitz did not live in the Wicker area until April of 1976. Who threw the rocks through their window, sent them a threatening letter, and called their house? These three incidents all occurred before the Molotov cocktail on May 13, 1976, according to how the Netos explained the incidents. Maybe the letter and phone calls came in when Berkowitz was living at 35 Pine Street, but the rocks that were thrown through their window occurred in 1975. Also, the calls were asking for Sylvia. Asking for a twelve-year-old girl did not seem to fit Berkowitz's terror schemes.

While still at the Neto home, during our interview, I looked at Larry and said, "So why did Berkowitz bother this family?" "Sylvia, someone was stalking Sylvia," Larry replied.

Just then it clicked, Larry was right, the phone calls were for Sylvia. Sylvia even mentioned the caller knew what school she attended. John Carr was living across the street, and according to Maury's reports, John Carr liked young girls. According to the Breslin letter, John Carr was a "*RAPIST AND SUFFOCATER OF YOUNG GIRLS.*"

The Carr backyard was the aqueduct path, and the way the aqueduct was set up, you could walk along the path and look right into people's homes. In fact, the way 22 and 18 Wicker Street houses were, you could see right into both of their backyards clearly just by standing on the aqueduct. To me, it looked like John Carr was stalking Sylvia, and when Berkowitz came to town, the terror started to escalate.

After the interview, I began some small talk with the Netos. During this conversation, I was able to catch the name of a lady who resided at 22 Wicker Street during the shootings. There was also a cousin of the Netos who was there the night their dog was shot that I could speak with, Teresa Ramos.

As I was leaving, I closed the gate to the fence behind me and looked at the Netos home. My heart sank because Maria now lived on her own, and the family life she once had was gone. I know this house had a lot of family around through the years, and now she was alone, it hurt me to leave her. Maria remained in the same house all these years, even kept the same telephone number. She will never let go of the love this house has brought to her no matter those terrible times. This is where her husband's heart is. Maria was a warrior...warriors motivate me.

The aftermath of that interview caused me a bit of depression. I started to think about how easy it was to walk that aqueduct path and pry into people's lives. Maria remembered hearing dogs scream in pain one night, how many animals were killed on that trail? How many girls were being stalked? I then thought to myself, what can I look at from this case that is connected to John Carr?

As I mentioned before, the only things I had to look at from this case on John Carr were the Borrelli and Breslin letters, and I must have read those letters about a thousand times. For some reason, new information can often make things look different to you, so I read the Borrelli letter again. I reached the part of the letter where it says, "*I MISS MY PRETTY PRINCESS*

MOST OF ALL. SHE IS RESTING IN OUR LADIES HOUSE BUT I WILL SHE HER SOON," and the letter started to look different to me. "*I MISS MY PRETTY PRINCESS,*" Princess? Didn't the harassment calls and letter to the Netos talk about a queen living in their house? Could Sylvia be the princess John Carr missed?

This letter was dropped on April 17, 1977. The Netos hadn't been bothered since December 24, 1976, almost four months earlier. Did John Carr stop stalking Sylvia when the shootings started getting more attention? John's involvement with the shootings could have kept him out of town, and he may have missed stalking Sylvia.

"*SHE IS RESTING IN OUR LADIES HOUSE,*" our ladies house? The queen's house? Could Sylvia be the princess resting in the queen's house?

"*BUT I WILL SHE HER SOON.*" John Carr was getting ready to stalk Sylvia again, as soon as he was done with their terror campaign.

Was this it? Was this what the letter meant? Could Sylvia really be the pretty princess this letter was referring to? I emailed Larry what I found and got no response. I was filled with curiosity and needed to talk to someone about this. I wanted to hear someone's opinion on what I thought. I wanted someone to tell me I was wrong.

That night I found some newspaper articles which stated, on October 9, 1976, the Carr house had been lit on fire by a Molotov cocktail. I already knew their dog had been shot, now I'm seeing the same crimes that were done to the Netos, were being done to the Carrs.

The next morning I called Sylvia and asked if her family had ever spoken to the Carrs, she didn't think so. When I told her about the Carr house getting firebombed and their dog being shot just like theirs, she knew nothing about those incidents. How could the Carrs and the Netos not have talked with these identical crimes happening to both of them just yards away from each other? I know these incidents happened to the Netos, but how true were the incidents that happened to the Carrs? Were they staged?

During this conversation, Sylvia and I laughed about how protective her mother still is with her. She complained her mother didn't allow her to do anything when she was younger. Everytime she was outside her house playing, her mother would be screaming, "Sylvia, come inside." The harassment to their family made her mother Maria worry a great deal and she could not rest unless Sylvia was in her sights.

On December 31, 2021, I called Carl about the Borrelli letter and what I thought it meant. I always wanted to know Carl's point of view. His insight and opinion mattered to me most. I was desperately trying to seek out someone who would tell me I was wrong. I couldn't believe how much sense it all made. Carl thought it sounded right, and so did everyone I presented this theory to.

I wanted to be wrong. Did John Carr really sit in those woods and torture that family? Did he really miss stalking Sylvia because he was trucking around with Berkowitz and murdering people? Poor Joaquim Neto, I felt deeply broken-hearted for this man.

After speaking with Carl, I called the only person I knew who had hung out on the aqueduct in the Wicker area...Albie. I asked if he ever heard of anyone bothering the Netos. He replied, "Do you mean when they got stoned?" I never heard of the rock-throwing incident before interviewing the Netos. How did he know about this?

When I questioned Albie about this incident, he told me the cops interrogated him and his friends on the aqueduct the day after it happened. I asked if he knew who did it and he said, "I heard John Carr was bothering the Netos." "Why?" I responded. "I don't know why anyone bothered the Netos," was his answer.

January 2, 2022, I hadn't spoken to Larry about the Borrelli letter or the Netos yet. He was avoiding conversation since I found what I thought was the meaning of the letter. I needed to talk to people, and it wasn't happening.

As of recently, Sylvia and I would talk a lot about the case and her family incidents. She was so helpful with information and was such an important person in all this. I really bonded with her mother Maria and had a great relationship with the two of them. The Netos were a very nice family that reminded me of my own.

Larry finally called me later that night with an attitude. The past few days I had been talking to Sylvia and emailing Larry information from her. He started complaining about how he should be the one talking to Sylvia, and if he was not going to be the one getting the information firsthand, things were not going to be good. Was this kid serious? What was stopping him from calling Sylvia?

I let him raise his voice for about ten seconds before I stopped him. "Listen, first of all, I have become friends with the family. They are Yonkers, you are not. I am doing nothing different than what I have been doing this whole time. You should be grateful you even got to speak with them." He needed to be reminded he was an outsider.

Sylvia was comfortable talking to me, and so was her mother Maria. I prefer Larry form his own relationships with the people I brought forth. I could connect him to people, but I couldn't make the people like him.

Larry did not have good social skills to make people feel comfortable talking to him. He was all about just getting information. He made you feel that way too, and I could see that after the Neto interview. People don't like to feel used, it is not how you build a relationship. If Larry and I didn't have a bond by now, how well could he connect with strangers?

On January 6, 2022, I decided to look into the Wicker Street mailman, Andrew Dupay, who committed suicide shortly after Berkowitz's arrest. Maury felt Dupay might have known something about the cult in the neighborhood. Dupay's father also worked for the City of Yonkers and retired in 1974. Sam Carr retired in 1977, so there was a good possibility they knew each other.

I found two contacts still alive for the mailman Andrew Dupay, his daughter Noel and his sister, Suzanne B. Dupay. After a few hours, I had contact information for both of them.

On January 10, 2022, Carl went on Larry's show to talk about his recent visit with David Berkowitz in prison. He told the audience Berkowitz denied he shot him, said it was a woman, but he wouldn't tell him the woman's name. Carl was also told by Maury it was possibly Wheat Carr who shot him, so this made sense to him. Before Carl left the prison, Berkowitz gave him pamphlets to take with him about The Process Church. Carl did not discuss what was in the pamphlets with Larry's audience, he said he hadn't finished reading it.

I emailed Larry in the morning.

Paul: Ok, so, Berkowitz is trying once again to lead everyone into thinking a big group was involved. How didn't Carl read the entire pamphlet? Maybe he just doesn't want to share that information yet. Carl is a victim trapped in this game for years, he should get a free pass no matter what. If a couple of California kids came to Yonkers saying they were part of The Process Church…whatever. I'm staying on Wicker with the characters I am positive played a part in this. I'll go where all this takes me and if The Process pops up, God have it and so be it, but until that happens, I'm staying on Wicker.

After Larry's interview with Carl, he began telling his audience he didn't believe Carl went to visit David Berkowitz. Two days after Carl was on

Larry's show, Larry was already fighting with him and continuing his ways of use and abuse.

On January 17, 2022, Sylvia, Maria, and their family member Teresa Ramos, agreed to meet again at 18 Wicker Street for another interview. Teresa lived on the second floor with Maria's mother during those chaotic times in 1976 and was receiving phone calls to her apartment saying she was beautiful. Some of the calls were complaining about Rocket, the Netos' dog. She also saw the letter that was sent to the Neto home and told us Maria's mother tore it up and burned it. The letter had upside-down crosses, pentagrams, and talked about demons living in their attic having orgies in their basement. The basement is where Teresa said all their family parties took place.

During this interview, I did not like Maria Neto's body language. I could tell something was off. At one point, Maria interrupted Teresa to tell her the calls were coming in asking for Sylvia, and looked annoyed Teresa was saying the calls were coming in for her. Teresa was at the house the night Rocket was shot, and the story she told, was not told to me by Sylvia or Maria in any of our prior conversations.

On December 24, 1976, Teresa was with Sylvia playing the piano when she heard two gunshots. Teresa ran to the window and saw somebody running away. She and her uncles went outside to see what happened and noticed their dog had been shot. From the front porch of the house, Teresa saw a man in a white T-shirt who looked like Berkowitz, running with a rifle toward Warburton Avenue to an off-white colored car that someone was driving, waiting for him. As soon as she said this, I didn't like the feel of the interview. I had spoken to Maria and Sylvia plenty of times these past couple of weeks, and there was no mention of this incident. Who was driving the off-white getaway car Teresa saw?

On this visit to the Netos, I asked Maria if we could go up to the attic. "Of course," she replied. Larry went up the wooden ladder, took a peek, and came back down. He was not interested in seeing the attic. There was no way I was passing up the opportunity. I climbed the wooden ladder and pulled myself up. I couldn't wait to look around where Berkowitz said demons were, hoping to find some writing on the walls or clues. I walked around the entire attic trying to find anything that might have some meaning. There was nothing but empty bottles of wine wrapped in newspapers dated 1958. The bottles were made by a company called Gallo, and there didn't seem to be any significance with the fifty or so empty bottles. After a while, seeing it was okay to come up, Larry joined me. I still remained off camera, but my voice was heard.

When we came down from the attic, Larry immediately wanted to leave and was rudely rushing to go home. He did this the previous time also. I had no control over him, only myself. I wasn't leaving without an espresso and some of Maria's stories of her old country, Cuba. I stated they are a Portuguese family, but Maria was from Cuba. Her husband Joaquim was from Portugal.

I continued small talk with the family in the kitchen as Larry twice now said he had to head home while he stood in the hallway facing the door. As Larry was trying to rush out, I asked the Netos about the residents at 22 Wicker Street, the house next door. This is when Teresa started to complain about the residents at 22 Wicker having a German Shepherd that would not shut up, it was constantly barking. I asked her what the dog's name was and she replied, "Duke." As soon as she said the name "Duke," I looked at Larry, "Did you get that, get that on video?" The name Duke was mentioned in the Breslin letter, "*THE DUKE OF DEATH.*" Could this dog Duke who lived at 22 Wicker Street possibly be who the Breslin letter was referring to?

With the information I got from the Netos, the next day I found the lady who lived and owned 22 Wicker in 1976. The lady was married to a man who was a member of an Italian club which my family belonged to. Her husband was deceased now, but my father and uncle knew this lady's husband.

This lady did not want to be known, but I talked her into trusting me, and she agreed to do an off-camera interview. She confirmed she had a dog named Duke, and even showed me photos of him. Her family got along with the Netos very well, her father was close with Joaquim. She went on to tell me after Rocket was killed, her father gave the Netos a new German Shepherd for their protection. When I asked if she knew what the Netos named the dog, she replied, "King." Are you kidding me? "King?" 22 Wicker had a dog named Duke and 18 Wicker had a dog named King. "*THE DUKE OF DEATH*" and "*THE WICKED KING WICKER*" were clues left in the Breslin letter. It seems to me these two dogs were exactly what the Breslin letter was referring to.

In the Klausner book, Berkowitz talks a lot about demon dogs that were around him, torturing him. Duke and King, I'm sure were those demon dogs, as they were only a block away from his apartment at 35 Pine Street. "*THE TWENTY TWO DISCIPLES OF HELL,*" and "*JOHN WHEATIES,*" were grouped with these dogs' names in the Breslin letter as clues. According to Berkowitz, "*JOHN WHEATIES*" occupied 22 Wicker Street, which was a Holiday Inn Hotel for demons. Demons would travel through the earth on missions and stop at 22 Wicker Street to rest. These clues were directing you to the demon dogs "*DUKE*" and "*KING*" on Wicker Street, "*JOHN WHEATIES*" could also be found there. The clues were telling you where the demons were, where he was. "*THE TWENTY TWO DISCIPLES OF HELL*" were not people, they were the demons resting at 22 Wicker Street... demons are disciples of hell.

While this lady was living at 22 Wicker Street in 1976, she recalled a time when she was undressing in her bedroom and noticed a man looking through her window. She screamed and called the cops, but no one was caught. Another incident was when she lost her cat for a few days and then found it dead in a garbage can near the Carr house.

During our conversation, I brought up to this lady who Maury alleged was "*THE WICKED KING WICKER,*" Alfonso Carozza. According to Maury, Alfonso had a cousin who owned a yacht in New Rochelle and

Berkowitz claimed to Maury he was on it. This cousin of Alfonso was mysteriously killed on this yacht in the early '80s and the killer was never found. Maury thought Alfonso was a member of the twenty-two disciples of hell, and the cult was some how connected to Alfonso's cousin's death.

After hearing this information, she was extremely insulted and did not like one bit what I was telling her about Alfonso. She knew him very well, as he was her brother's best friend growing up. I explained to her it wasn't me accusing Alfonso of these things, and I apologized. She stressed Alfonso was Catholic and was a very good person, he would never be a part of any satanic cult. Alfonso was good friends with her family, and they rented an apartment to him and his wife at the house on Wicker Street when he first got married. She last saw him at her brother's funeral a few years ago.

I spoke to a lot of people about this lady who used to live at 22 Wicker Street and I heard nothing negative. She was soft-spoken and didn't have a bad bone in her body. One of my uncles loved her husband, as he had gone hunting with him. Her husband also ran for a council seat in the City of Yonkers and John Spencer had known him, he was a good man. She gave no signs of hiding anything, and I don't think she would have talked to me if she had anything to hide.

So some guy gets mysteriously killed on a yacht that Berkowitz claimed he was on, with the same last name as a resident at 22 Wicker Street, and Maury just assumed they were related...and Alfonso knew Berkowitz. Great...can't wait to get to the bottom of this one.

I then called Sylvia and asked if she got another dog after Rocket was killed. She repeated the same story about how 22 Wicker gave their family a German Shepherd after they lost Rocket. I asked her what the dog's name was, she confirmed, "King."

I'm realizing from research, and from speaking to residents, Berkowitz's center of activity was on Wicker Street. Untermyer Park was not the reason

David Berkowitz moved to Yonkers. Maury used "*THE GUTTERS OF NYC*" from the Breslin letter as his theory of where Berkowitz was, the aqueduct path that ran through Untermyer Park. Well, the same aqueduct path Maury was on in Untermyer, also ran right through Wicker Street, right between Berkowitz's apartment and the Carr house. From Berkowitz's 7th floor apartment window, he could watch everything that went on with the Carrs and families below at 18 and 22 Wicker Street…the activity was on Wicker Street.

January 20, 2022, all this Wicker Street information I was finding was amazing. I was lucky to be able to speak to these people, as Maury could not. Sylvia told me her father would not speak to Maury when he came by the house. Joaquim would not talk to anyone about any of this once he knew who it was and it was over. Who knows what else happened that Joaquim kept from telling his family so they wouldn't worry? Maury did manage in 1997 to speak with Teresa Ramos and Maria Neto's mother, but he failed to find out the dogs' names, obviously.

That night Larry got a response from an email he had sent to Craig Glassman's daughter.

Larry: Shayna Glassman, Craig Glassman's daughter, agreed to do an interview.

Paul: Excellent, should be interesting.

Craig Glassman was receiving crazy letters during the "Son of Sam" shootings while he lived beneath Berkowitz at 35 Pine Street. He died in a car accident in 1991. Maury suspected he had something to do with Berkowitz and the cult. Craig's daughter was a great find. Anything connected to this story was essential to color in.

The next day Larry emailed me.

Larry: My spidey sense is telling me this lady from 22 Wicker is lying for Alfonso.

Paul: Listen to me, please. The lady from 22 Wicker is a saint. The Netos also say her family was good. I have close friends who know both these families. These are not just contacts I talk to, they are family and friends, they are Yonkers.

Larry: Patrick O'Shaughnessey is a key player in all this, and he is still alive.

Patrick O'Shaughnessey was a Yonkers Police Officer who grew up in Berkowitz's Bronx neighborhood. According to John Comparetto, O'Shaughnessey should have known Berkowitz. Some of the Yonkers Police Comparetto knew suspected O'Shaughnessey of being the "Son of Sam." I talked to a Yonkers Police Officer, Joe Barca, who was O'Shaughnessey's partner, and he confirmed that suspicion. The brass of the department actually took O'Shaughnessey's work-issued .44 revolver and gave it to the NYPD for tests...it came back clean. Patrick O'Shaughnessey was in *The Ultimate Evil*, but Maury called him Peter Shane. According to Maury, O'Shaughnessey was asked by the Queens District Attorney if they could question him and he was never seen again. He retired from the police force to enlist in the Marines. Berkowitz did say a police officer was involved, and they were from the same neighborhood growing up.

Maria Neto called me that evening and asked if she could one day face David Berkowitz. She had so much heart, but just might be too tough for her own good. I had gotten close to Maria in the past couple weeks, and her heart was one of the purest I ever came across. She told me many stories of her life, from helping needy kids in the neighborhood, to bringing money to Cuba, so she could donate to the hospital her father died in. There was no bad in that lady, and I could feel her pain from miles away...she missed her husband so much.

January 22, 2022, always doing research and always getting contacts, I emailed Larry that morning.

Paul: I got some contacts for Alfonso, I'm going to soon put that to bed. I'm also going to knock on Steven Cassara's door. He lives ten minutes from my house...I found him.

Larry: I think Alfonso might be dirty and this lady you found is covering for his ass.

This kid did not want to listen. These families I was talking to were good families and had nothing to hide. I will prove all this.

Paul: Don't think that way unless she gives you reason to. I do not feel she is lying at all. If anything was going on with Alfonso, she did not know. They were good people like the Netos. If Alfonso was connected to all this, I feel she knew nothing. We just opened this door, let's see what's inside.

That afternoon, I got a call from one of Carl's researchers, Jess. We talked for hours about many suspects and this case. She, like Max, was extremely knowledgeable with the "Son of Sam" shootings, and there was much to gain from talking to her.

Jess was into a lot of cold-cases, her heart was in the right place. To her, it was all about helping Carl. She stressed she really liked Detective Geiss's work and asked if I could connect them. Geiss did me a favor and spoke to Jess over the phone, making her extremely happy. Putting people together was very important to me.

My conversation with Jess gave me the motivation to go knock on Steven Cassara's door. That's how this game was played. Sometimes the fuck-it feeling just came rolling in and you had to act on it, make that phone call, take that drive, knock on doors...enter Steven Cassara.

I hopped in my car and put Steven Cassara's address into my GPS. Ten minutes away is what it read, this should be easy. I tried to call Steven a few times and got no answer. I had no choice but to knock on his door.

I arrived ten minutes later, just like the GPS had said, then walked up to the front door and knocked. A bearded man in a red flannel shirt opened the door and I asked if I could speak with Steven Cassara. "Sure, that's me. Come on in," he replied. He invited me right in and didn't even know what I was there for. This was going to be a tough opening delivery.

I made sure I wore white to present myself in a surrendering way, every detail mattered. Steven's wife stepped into the room as I stood by the doorway. She was all smiles, a very nice lady. I politely told them I was working on a documentary about David Berkowitz and wanted to know if they could tell me anything about him. Steven, upon hearing Berkowitz's name, became a little agitated and said, "This again, I don't want to talk about this." I told him I was sorry and meant no disrespect, but if I could just ask him a few questions…I promised him, I meant no harm. He allowed me to speak, so I asked if his family had rented a room to Berkowitz in 1976. He answered, "Yes." I then wanted to know if Berkowitz was normal when they first met him, when he moved in, or did they notice he was a little off from the start. Steven recalled, "He was normal, had a job. I don't know what happened with that guy. He started bitching about our dogs and he got in my face one morning about it."

When I asked Steven if he knew the Carrs, he quickly responded, "I don't want to talk about this. It was so long ago." I told him I understood, but I had been looking into this case and think Berkowitz did not do everything they claimed he did. Steven looked at me puzzled and said, "The guy was nuts. He was shooting people." I agreed, but told him I thought there was more to the story than what was told to us, that there might be other people involved. Steven walked into another room and pleaded, "See, this is why I don't want to talk about this. Now you're telling me there were other people involved. I don't need to be bothered. Please, I don't want to talk about this."

His wife stood there smiling, telling Steven to relax. She mentioned she knew the Carrs and they were very nice people. I could tell I was aggravating Steven and didn't want to wear out my welcome so I thanked them both, apologized for bothering them, and let myself out. As I was walking out the door, I asked Steven, "Was Berkowitz really annoyed with your dogs?" He replied, "Yes, he hated my two dogs." I then squeezed in one more, "What kind of dogs were they?" Steven answered, "German Shepherds." I said, "Thank you Steven be good, thank you." I smiled at his wife and left. Hopefully, I would see them again.

I drove back home extremely disappointed, this was the first time I struck out. Steven did not want to talk to me. Even though I got some information, I know Steven knew more. I definitely thought he was not guilty of anything and had no involvement with Berkowitz's crimes, as they too seemed like just another family that was affected by Berkowitz's actions.

Steven was the son of Jack and Nann Cassara. He had a reason why he didn't want to talk. In June of 1977, Jack and Nann Cassara received a get-well card which was signed by Sam and Frances Carr. They soon found out the Carrs did not send them the card and Steven was the one who figured out Berkowitz sent it, causing his parents to alert the police. That is what was said in all the books and articles I read. He had reason to be scared. He was involved in a way like no other person I had spoken to. Steven got agitated during our conversation to a point where I felt bad. I hated I couldn't get an hour with him to decipher his memories. What he thought were just normal memories could be clues to what was really going on. It was killing me he was ten minutes away with answers.

On January 25, 2022, I researched a man named Richard Sperrazza, another suspect who Maury claimed was possibly a cult member. Jess helped me out a lot with information on Sperrazza and sent me a newspaper article which stated he worked with Berkowitz at the Texaco Building

Construction site in Harrison, N.Y. He began commuting to and from work with Berkowitz in October of 1976.

Sperrazza had Berkowitz over his house on several occasions during the time they worked together. Berkowitz even talked to his wife and kid a few times when he visited. He traveled in Berkowitz's cream-colored Ford Galaxie, but had no idea he was the "Son of Sam." Sperrazza added that Berkowitz did not like his German Shepherd and never came into his house unless the dog was put out back. One of the times Berkowitz went inside his home was on December 24, 1976. "*He had a few drinks and something to eat and then said he had somewhere to go,*" recalled Sperrazza. Remember, December 24, 1976 was when the Netos' dog Rocket was shot dead. Berkowitz left Sperrazza's house that night at 10 p.m., Rocket was shot at 11 p.m.

At the end of the article Sperrazza stated, "*I'm kicking myself in the head, I'm out thirty-six thousand (the reward money for the capture of the Son of Sam), but it's not the money that bugs me, it's the fact that I could have prevented some of the killings.*"

On January 26, 2022, I met Larry at Wicker Street to film a video…it was time I showed myself. Before we filmed, I walked with Larry on the aqueduct path, showing him all the room to roam, and how open peoples' homes were for stalkers while on *"THE GUTTERS OF N.Y.C."* Berkowitz was here, not Untermyer Park. The park was a good half-hour walk from here, there was no need to travel. If it was Untermyer Park that made Berkowitz move to Yonkers, he would have moved closer to that park. I was explaining and trying to stress to Larry that Wicker Street was the center of activity for Berkowitz, not Untermyer Park.

Larry and I filmed the video while walking the aqueduct, talking about all the Neto findings. This was the first time Larry's audience was seeing me, they only knew of me from my posts on Larry's website.

After filmimg, I took Larry to the Carr house. We met some construction workers who were by the back garage and were able to get a contact number for the current owner. We then went to the front door and began ringing some bells, to no avail.

When we left, Larry suggested we cross Warburton Avenue to check out Point Street, where the motorcycle club was that Berkowitz visited on August 6, 1977 looking for Mickey Carr. I told Larry it was not a good idea, as from the corner of my eye, I could see kids staring at us from the nearby deli. Larry was not street smart. He did not understand the law of the land around here. In Yonkers, be careful of the areas you travel in. Even I was an outsider in this area, and outsiders are smelled out in an instant. I entertained him a bit and crossed the street, but I could feel the tension from those kids at the deli...we needed to leave. Of course, he didn't understand, but playtime was over. We crossed back over to the other side of Warburton Avenue and headed back to Wicker Street.

I got what I needed from Wicker Street for the moment and began to think about how this all ended up this way. Where did David Berkowitz go wrong? His friends who grew up with him all agreed he was normal, a nice guy. John Comparetto insisted Berkowitz was not the same person when he returned home from his three years of service. This is when I started to research Berkowitz's Army years. I needed to find out what went on with Berkowitz during his three-year Army tour.

The next day Larry emailed me.

Larry: I booked Shayna Glassman for Monday's show and she is not responding to my emails now.

Later on that day...

Larry: Shayna backed out of the show. She didn't speak to her agent and it's too soon to talk before the release of her book. She somehow thinks she is a major celebrity and her book is going to be a bestseller.

Larry immediately began to trash Shayna Glassman all over his website and Twitter. I called Larry and asked him to calm down. If she couldn't make the show, he should relax and wait until she was ready. Losing her did nothing and we needed her, he should not insult her. Her agent was right, she had her book to protect. He should be grateful she was willing to even speak with him and to let her talk when she was ready. Of course, our discussion went to deaf ears as he continued to trash Shayna all over the internet. I guess there would be no information coming from Shayna in the future...great.

On January 29, 2022, Larry was editing the video we made, getting it ready to air. Me, I was visiting Caveman, making sure everything was alright with him. Caveman was a good guy, and I admired his attitude. Caveman didn't care about money or material things. He just lived and breathed.

That evening Larry released the video we did together, it was a hit, packed with information from the Neto incidents. This video should help get more people's attention and open more doors. It was new information that nobody heard before.

The next morning, I woke up and the video reached two thousand views overnight. That was fast for Larry's videos.

I was feeling good for about ten minutes until Larry emailed me.

Larry: The video was a hit, but somehow I am losing subscribers, oh well.

Losing subscribers? I can see he gained 20 subscribers since the video aired...why was he telling me the opposite?

Paul: I'll call you in a few, great video.

A few hours later, Larry emailed me again.

Larry: I weirdly lost quite a few subscribers today. I'm down to seven hundred and five from seven hundred and twenty-eight, oh well.

Again Larry was pointing out to me he lost subscribers, but what I saw by the end of that day was a rise from 708 to 741. Larry gained 33 new paying subscribers in one day after our video was released. I could see that, Penny could see that.

On February 2, 2022, Detective Geiss and John Rinciari came through once again. John Rinciari put together a squad of retired law enforcement who were friends with Berkowitz growing up for a meeting and wanted Larry and I to attend. The Yonkers Police had really stepped up and done things on their own without even being asked. They really were interested in this investigation, they gave their time and effort genuinely.

I emailed Larry, reminding him to be appreciative.

Paul: Make sure you thank Geiss. Yonkers Police have done the right thing with all this.

Larry and I discussed the upcoming meeting with the detectives and I told him I didn't need to be there. I asked him to do me a favor and attend the meeting with Carl instead of me. Larry did not want that, but I explained to him it was important Carl was included, and I would gladly take a back seat for him to attend. It was more important for a victim of this case, who was trying to find out who shot him, to be there. I also wanted Carl to connect with more law enforcement. "The two of you are just as good as if I'm there anyway," I said. It took a while to convince him to ask Carl, but he eventually did. Olive branches once again on the menu.

Larry: I emailed Rinciari asking him if it was okay to include Carl.

Paul: Thank you…you are making the right decision.

Larry: I also emailed Carl telling him we are on the verge of speaking to Alfonso Carozza and he is getting kinda weird about it. I think he is afraid we are going to dismantle yet another Maury myth. He said, "Why would he admit being a part of it?" That was it, that was his argument.

Paul: But when I do get in touch with Alfonso, all I can do is question him, there is nothing else I can do. I know Alfonso will know my family. I almost don't want to talk to him. I'm not trying to bother anyone, I'm just asking questions and bringing back answers.

I stopped by Maria Neto's house that night and she gave me all the newspaper clippings she had about the incidents which occurred at her home in 1976. Maria was a pioneer of the true American way, like my family before me. She came to this country to work, as did my family. These working people are what made America. The different cultures, from different countries, all working together is how this country was built. These people came together on this land to make a good life by working. Maria Neto was a true American pioneer.

On February 4, 2022, Larry sent me an email trying to convince me Patrick O'Shaughnessey was the cop Berkowitz claimed was involved with the shootings.

Larry: Zeman gave me the okay to use O'Shaughnessey's photo. I am going to confirm it's actually him by asking Rinciari and Comparetto before I post it. They both knew him. I want to make sure it's really him.

This is exactly why I wanted peace between all. People had information and everyone needed to share it to move this case forward.

The next morning Larry emailed me.

Larry: The photo of O'Shaughnessey is not him according to Rinciari and Comparetto who all knew him well. I sent Josh an email asking if he knew who this guy was and why Maury thought he was O'Shaughnessey.

Paul: We need everyone to come together as one and start over. We can't force anyone, but we can stay welcoming. I reached out to many people online to join, there are still a lot of people out there to reach. Don't be so hard on Carl and Josh, they are Maury's notes they are following which Berkowitz ok'd. Please, Carl and Josh are trying to help, don't bash them for Maury's mistakes. If I can maintain peace, so can you.

Here is an article I came across with a statement from Mike Novotny, a Yonkers Police Sergeant in 1977:

"At the time I didn't think anything, and then I began to realize that there may be more people involved in this." When asked by the reporter to give a ballpark number of people he thought might have been involved, Novotny replied, "Oh, I'd say half a dozen."

On February 7, 2022, I received a phone call from a retired New York City Detective who had spoken to Detective Joseph Borrelli. Detective Borrelli was sure David Berkowitz acted alone. Here are some of the points he made to back up his claim.

After the arrest, Berkowitz was interrogated for over eleven hours by numerous detectives and they all came away convinced he acted alone. Even Dr. Daniel Schwartz, the court-appointed psychiatrist who examined Berkowitz right after his arrest, agreed Berkowitz committed all these murders on his own.

Only Berkowitz's fingerprints were found on all the weapons that were confiscated and the Borrelli letter. Borrelli said the NYPD were in the YPD for several hours after the arrest and there was no discussion of any accomplices with the information they had on the case. Two Yonkers Police Officers, Peter Intervallo and Thomas Chamberlain, officers who dealt directly with the case, had no suspicions of any accomplices involved.

At five of the eight attacks, there were witnesses who only saw a single white male as the shooter.

The last point Borrelli made was the obvious, the attacks stopped after Berkowitz's arrest. The "Son of Sam" shootings did not continue once David Berkowitz was captured.

Detective Borrelli's statements were hard to swallow. The thought of Berkowitz acting alone after everything I had been hearing and reading did not seem possible to me. Still, I had to take what Detective Borrelli said with great weight as he dealt directly with this case.

I woke up the next morning and decided to look into an incident Maury reported happened at the Candlelight Inn restaurant located in Scarsdale, on the border of Yonkers. I have been there a million times as it was, and still is, very popular to all Yonkers residents for its chicken wings. After work, I took a ride up to the Candlelight Inn and had myself a Guinness at the bar.

This incident Maury reported came from a bartender who worked at the Candlelight in the '70s. The bartender told Maury that David Berkowitz, Robert "Tocco" Grady, and Michael Carr were in the establishment, got into an argument with someone, then exited. Shortly after they left, a lady was shot in her leg by someone outside the restaurant. Maury blamed this shooting on Berkowitz and company. On another occasion at the Candlelight Inn, Maury reported Wheat Carr shot out a clock above the bar. I already knew Tocco was not involved in this, but I still wanted to see if anyone had any information about what really happened.

As I drank my Guinness, I struck up a conversation with the bartender, "Hey, by any chance is the owner around?" He replied, "Yes, he is my father. What can I do for you?" I told the bartender I was working on a documentary about David Berkowitz and asked if I could speak with his father. The bartender was thirty-two and had no idea who David Berkowitz was. He called his father to let him know I was there, then told me his father would be down in a minute.

I continued small talk with the bartender, he was a retired Marine and was starting to learn the restaurant business. His grandfather ran the place before his father, and it was now his time to take it over. His family has owned the place since 1955. He recently finished six tours of duty in Iraq and was back home to run his family's business. Just then, his father came rumbling down the stairs and asked who needed to see him.

I greeted his father by shaking his hand and introduced myself as he took a seat next to me at the bar. I knew a few people from this neighborhood and mentioned some names to him so he would feel comfortable speaking with me. I told him I was doing a documentary on David Berkowitz and asked if he ever saw him in the restaurant or knew him. He shook his head and said, "No." I continued, "Was there ever an altercation in this place that involved David Berkowitz?" "Absolutely not," he answered. When I told him about Wheat Carr shooting the clock out above this bar, he laughed and said, "Didn't happen…a woman was shot in her leg while she was playing a video game here once, but no one was ever caught for it."

My next question was if he ever read *The Ultimate Evil.* He quickly responded, "Oh, that bullshit. I did read it, and none of that happened here." I asked when the lady got shot, was anyone blaming Berkowitz at the time? He said at the time, there were a lot of random shootings going on in the vicinity, but no one ever mentioned David Berkowitz as being responsible. I then asked, "So no one ever heard that story until Maury's book came out?" He replied, "Correct, I mean, no one was ever caught, so I'm not saying it wasn't Berkowitz, but that accusation was never heard until Maury's book came out. I can tell you for sure there was never a clock shot out in here, that I know. When the lady got shot, I was not here at the time, but my family has owned this place since 1955, and after the shooting happened, there was no suspicion of David Berkowitz at any time as being responsible."

I finished my Guinness then said, "Thank you sir, your restaurant has been a staple to the people of Yonkers for years. Your family should be proud of the memories it has been a part of. Thank you for your time." He told me to come back anytime and wished me luck on my documentary.

Just great...now what do I do? Larry was going to have a field day with this. I already knew Tocco being there was false. Now so was the altercation and Wheat shooting out the clock. The owner was right, no one ever caught the shooter, so who knows, but no one ever blamed Berkowitz until Maury's book came out.

I emailed Larry about my visit to the Candlelight Inn. He quickly emailed me back.

Larry: Do you think I should post about the Candlelight Inn?

Paul: Your show, you make the call...just do it right. Maury could be right, I didn't talk to the bartender that he did, but this is what the owner of the restaurant at the time said...the story Maury told never happened. Berkowitz was not there to his knowledge. The clock in his establishment was never shot out by Wheat Carr. An altercation with Berkowitz never happened at the bar. Remember to point out the owner never heard of these rumors until Maury's book came out, eleven years after the incident.

Larry posted on his website what I uncovered, and it caused all the Maury Terry people to go berserk. A few of them started to challenge my findings, claiming there was a newspaper article about this incident which included Michael Carr and Berkowitz's name. If this is true, then we would have proof that Berkowitz knew the Carrs.

I begged these people to produce the article, which they could not...but I could. A quick call to Penny, and in five minutes, I had the newspaper article. Nowhere in this article did it mention Michael Carr or David Berkowitz. It stated a lady was shot in the leg while playing a pinball machine in the front of the bar area, no one was ever caught. Maury had spoken to the bartender, not the owner. Maybe the bartender knew things the owner didn't know, but I think the owner for the past sixty-plus years would have heard the story Maury told before he read his book.

On February 11, 2022, Larry and I filmed a video while walking the aqueduct path. We discussed when Sam Carr's black Labrador Retriever Harvey was shot and the Neto incidents. I also brought to his attention Michael Lorenzo, a Yonkers Detective who was assigned to most of the incidents around Wicker Street during the shootings. I found an article, which after reading, looked like Detective Lorenzo was not taking Nann Cassara's complaints about David Berkowitz seriously. Why was Detective Lorenzo not paying attention to Nann's complaints and just brushing her off? I told Larry I had a few friends who knew Detective Lorenzo's son and were in contact with him recently. Detective Lorenzo's son, Mike, was also a retired Yonkers Detective.

The next morning I went into work and was stationed at a firehouse to repair the interior. Upon my arrival, I was greeted by my good friend, the fireman who had told me about Randy Hughes. He remembered from months earlier I was looking into the "Son of Sam" case and had a friend that got a hold of some files on David Berkowitz. These files were left to his friend's parents by a Yonkers Detective who passed away. I asked what the files were about and he had no idea. I have known this fireman for over thirty years and was grateful Justine's leads connected me to him again. If I hadn't reached out to him months ago, he would not have had these files for me. I couldn't wait to see what they were.

I started working on the repairs to the firehouse when my supervisor stopped by. We didn't have the right materials for the job, so I packed up my tools and took the rest of the day off. I drove to the Yonkers courthouse to sign out of work and I saw a man I knew very well in the parking lot...Frank Carozza.

I approached Frank with an extended arm and gave him a hug. Frank is from my father's neighborhood, our families have known each other a long time. Once I got the small talk out of the way, I asked if he knew Alfonso Carozza...Alfonso was his uncle. As I started to tell Frank the allegations against his uncle, he laughed and said, "I will call my uncle for you and ask him about this. Give me a day or two and I will get back to you." Before I left, Frank mentioned a friend of his, Sal DiMaggio, a retired YPD Captain, had information about the "Son of Sam" and would have him call me later.

I left Frank and walked into the courthouse to sign out when I ran into my manager, the stepson of retired Yonkers Detective Joe Surlak. Joe Surlak and his partner, Anthony Cerasi, were Yonkers Detectives assigned to the "Son of Sam" case. Anthony Cerasi was still alive, but Joe Surlak passed away a few years ago. My manager was walking with a man named Bob Cacace, the son of the judge who signed David Berkowitz's search warrants the night of the arrest. I asked Bob about that night, he said he would never forget it, and remembers that night like it was yesterday.

Three detectives came to Bob's house the night Berkowitz was arrested and needed his father's signature to issue the search warrants for David Berkowitz's car and apartment. His father did not like what he was signing because he wasn't sure if the detectives had the legal right to have already searched Berkowitz's car. When a judge is presented an application for a search warrant, he should have time to review the evidence thoroughly. These detectives needed his father's signature immediately, there was no time to waste, so his father signed it instantly. His father never did that before, but it needed to be done in order to stop the "Son of Sam."

Knowing this information meant if the search and seizure was illegal, all the evidence seized from Berkowitz's car would not have been admissible in court. I think the police may have known this was an illegal search and seizure, which is why they sealed all records. What gave the detectives the right to search Berkowitz's car before having a warrant?

When I got home that evening, Frank Carozza's friend Sal DiMaggio called me. Sal explained at the last shooting in Brooklyn, Berkowitz received a parking ticket on his 1970 Ford Galaxie, which was registered to Berkowitz's Yonkers address. On August 9, 1977, a day before Berkowitz's arrest, Sal was working with Wheat Carr at the Yonkers Police Dispatch when New York City Detective James Justus called asking about David Berkowitz's parking ticket. Sal answered the phone and spoke to Detective Justus briefly about the situation. After hearing Berkowitz's name, he realized Wheat would be better for Detective Justus to speak with and handed her the phone. Sal said Wheat had been accusing David Berkowitz of being the "Son of Sam" to him and his colleagues for weeks prior to this call...how did she know this?

I asked Sal, "How long was Wheat accusing Berkowitz of being the "Son of Sam?" "It was about a month before Berkowitz's arrest," he recalled. Remembering Larry's conversation, I asked Sal if he had ever heard of Berkowitz and Wheat dating. He laughed as he answered, "No, I have never heard that before." I then questioned him about Wheat's character. He described Wheat as being a tough girl who was a know-it-all. He only knew her for two years from work and didn't know her very well. He couldn't believe she was right, that Berkowitz was the "Son of Sam." What made Wheat think Berkowitz was the "Son of Sam?" Sal's response to that question was, he didn't know, he just recalled Wheat's house had been fire-bombed and their dog was shot. She was telling everyone at work, prior to the arrest, David Berkowitz was responsible. Sal confirmed those incidents really happened to the Carrs, but nobody knew who had done them at the time they occurred.

How did Wheat know Berkowitz was the "Son of Sam" prior to his arrest? I know she told Sal that Berkowitz was responsible for the harassment to her family, but what made her connect Berkowitz to the "Son of Sam" crimes? I was definitely missing something here.

Sal ended the conversation by telling me, throughout all these years of this story being told about the parking ticket call, his role of handing the phone to Wheat has never been mentioned. Well, here you go Sal, you are finally getting the credit you deserve.

What a day it was at ground zero, and the day was not over just yet. I did some research and came across a lady named Sarah Wallace. Sarah was an investigator who had followed the "Son of Sam" case. She felt Maury Terry gave Berkowitz an open door to make up false narratives.

Next, I researched an incident reported by Neysa Moskowitz. She was the mother of Stacy Moskowitz, the girl who was shot and killed by the "Son of Sam" on July 31, 1977 in Brooklyn. Neysa was broken-hearted from the loss of her daughter, it really affected her life. She believed Berkowitz killed her daughter at the time of his arrest, but as time went by, she started to believe what Maury Terry was reporting in his newspaper articles, that Berkowitz didn't act alone. Neysa was then left thinking the person who shot her daughter was still at large.

In 1981, Neysa reported to the police that two men broke into her apartment, tied her up, cut her arm, and made her suck her own blood. The two men left Neysa tied up and told her as they exited not to mess with David. Neysa had the scars on her arm to prove it.

What I found extremely odd about this incident is, Maury Terry did not mention this in his book. How could Maury not include this in *The Ultimate Evil*? It was good evidence showing other people were involved with Berkowitz. This incident was supporting Maury's claim of a satanic cults involvement, but it was never mentioned in his book...why not? This incident occurred well before Maury published *The Ultimate Evil* in 1987.

I feel Maury didn't include this incident in his book because it did not happen, and Maury knew that.

After the arrest, law enforcement closed the case and were not looking for any accomplices. I feel Neysa lied about this incident to get the police to look for other suspects as she was convinced her daughter's killer was still out there. She was desperate to find her daughter's murderer, and no one was looking. I would have done the same.

Why didn't Maury look for the two men who supposedly did this to Neysa? These men seemed to have been directly connected to Berkowitz as they went and threatened a victim's mother to leave David alone. I think Maury knew this was a lie and didn't want to include this in his book in case Neysa was ever to admit it. I feel Maury had his own things to defend and didn't want to risk his own credibility. Nothing was ever reported on this incident again, but I did see a newspaper photo of Neysa at one of Maury's book signings. Wouldn't she also be questioning why her incident was not in the book?

This day would never end, as I researched a few articles on Berkowitz's Army years, specifically when he was stationed at Fort Knox in Louisville, Kentucky. It was there under a pastor named Tom Wallace, Berkowitz learned about Jesus Christ and was baptized. I was amazed at the articles I was reading. How did Berkowitz go from following Jesus Christ, to taking people's lives?

CHAPTER XI

END OF THE YELLOW BRICK ROAD

On February 14, 2022, Larry had me come on his show so he could formally introduce me to his audience. During this show, he repeatedly disrespected Maury, which was something I did not want to be a part of. His public insults toward Maury were unacceptable. Stating the facts I was finding was all he needed to do. Yes, I too felt Maury was wrong, but I chose to keep my opinions about Maury away from the public.

On February 16, 2022, the nonsense continued with this email from Larry.

Larry: Carl just emailed me saying the truce is off. This is his email.

You got to be kidding me! I realize you need to entertain your paid subscribers, but you have gone way too far. I have received quite a few of your tweets and I choose to ignore your mean-spirited messages to your subscribers. For the most part, the Facebook people have adhered to the truce and have kept their comments to themselves. You on the other hand have not. I'm extremely disappointed in the fact that I trusted you and I paid a very high price asking the Facebook people to cease and desist. Now you mock our silence and think it's proof that you are right! That is rich! By the way, accusing Maury of leading Berkowitz in the 98 interview was fair. You seem to have learned from your master when you interviewed the Netos, not only leading but actually putting words in their mouths. I don't know why you have to insult people, your videos and your interviews stand on their own, why do you feel the need to bash pretty much anything that isn't your idea? People talking about incidents that happened 45 years ago, falling over their facts and you think you proved Maury wrong? I don't get it, this is the third or fourth time you got someone to say something different than Maury and now their story is more valid than Maury's? How does that work? I hope you continue to investigate the case and I hope you realize that bashing and mocking people is not going to solve the case.

Why was Larry continuing to cause problems? In my conversations with Carl, he was always behind the investigation…all he wanted was answers. I tried over and over to tell Larry to cut out his insults, have more respect for people. Before I started fact-checking Maury's work, no one, including him, knew anything but what Maury reported. Bashing people for standing behind the only research they had to go by all these years was wrong.

I emailed Larry to send me the information he had on Alfonso Carozza.

Larry: This is what Maury Terry had on Alfonso Carozza.

ALFONSO CAROZZA, YONKERS: Alfonso operated pizza joints on White Plains Road in the Bronx (relevant area) and later in New Rochelle. During SOS he lived at 22 Wicker Street in the Pine Street neighborhood. He was a cousin of Joseph Carozza, who was murdered on his yacht in a New Rochelle marina on New Year's Eve, '81. Unsolved case. DB, along with others, had been on Carozza's yacht. There is physical evidence of the relationship between Alfonso and Joe Carozza. At one point Joseph underwrote a loan to Alfonso for the purchase of an oven for the Bronx pizza place. Alfonso lived at 22 Wicker, as did cult associate Robin D'Acutis. It's possible they lived together in this two or three family house. (Alfonso not yet contacted).

Paul: Thanks, I want to show his nephew. I just got a call from Dave Butler, he is going to get Detective Mike Lorenzo Jr. to speak with us.

That night, I found an article on Andrea (Teresa) Ramos, the same Teresa I spoke to about the Neto incidents. As I mentioned earlier, Maury reported this article in 1997. He must have talked her into speaking with him while Joaquim Neto was not around. She recalled when someone opened fire on the Neto house on Christmas Eve in 1976, killing the family dog. Also the bizarre campaign of terror waged against the Neto family throughout that winter. Teresa was only present for the dog shooting, but remembered when a Molotov cocktail was flung onto the Netos' front stoop. There were also anonymous phone calls from a stranger complaining about their dog and an unsigned letter they received about demons in their attic having orgies in the basement.

How did she not tell Maury about the guy she saw after Rocket was shot, in a white T-shirt, running with a rifle down to an idling off-white car? This was a huge part to witness. Why didn't she report to Maury what she told me?

February 19, 2022, I sent Frank Carozza the allegations on Alfonso and asked him to call me after he showed his uncle. I knew his uncle was innocent, I just felt I had to prove it, not to prove Maury wrong, but to eliminate another falsely accused.

I emailed Larry after I spoke to Frank Carozza.

Paul: I talked to Alfonso's nephew, he said his uncle had words with Berkowitz on the street in front of 22 Wicker. Berkowitz said something to Alfonso's wife that he didn't like and Alfonso had an argument with him.

Larry: I'm nervous about Alfonso. I think he's a guilty party.

Paul: I think you need to think again, he did not hang out with Berkowitz. I know Alfonso's nephew for a long time and he thinks this is all bullshit. If Alfonso was guilty, his nephew would tell me to mind my business, and he wouldn't have gotten Sal DiMaggio to speak with me. His nephew would not entertain this if he thought for one second his uncle could be involved.

I spent that night looking into a criminologist named John Douglas. He was instrumental in developing and perfecting the science of criminal profiling. He interviewed and studied David Berkowitz. John Douglas described

Maury Terry as a person who was molded and influenced by his desire to make a case at any cost in order to sell his book.

February 21, 2022, I decided after I was done clearing Alfonso's name, I would no longer search for a satanic cult. I needed to let the real people who played a part in all this lead me. I still believed at this point, Berkowitz and John Carr were doing satanic rituals, asking to be filled with evil. I still felt John Carr was the true "Son of Sam."

Here are some excerpts from articles I found on Berkowitz:

Berkowitz would speak of demons taking his soul. When asked where he first experienced the demons, he said, "I began to hear them just after I moved to Yonkers."

Berkowitz said that demons and a barking dog of an elderly man, Sam Carr, ordered him to kill. Sam Carr's dog was really the spirit of a 6,000-year-old man. These demons would demand young blood. Berkowitz said he did it all and that he did it alone. Berkowitz said a lot of things, but in time not all of them would prove to be true.

After Berkowitz was captured and began serving his sentence, he told reporters that there was a cult active near his home in Yonkers but stopped short of saying he was a member of it. Berkowitz said that John Carr was a "devil worshiper," a statement that was later confirmed by John Carr's friends in North Dakota.

Berkowitz was asked by a prison guard while in jail if there were others involved in the killings. Berkowitz said, "Yes there are others." The guard asked who, and Berkowitz replied, "Sam's son...Sam Carr is the father and John Carr is his son. John has a brother named Michael. They will kill my family if I rat on them." Then Berkowitz tells the guard that he and the Carrs were in a devil worshiping cult and said the group was ruthless.

So you see, if anything, I needed to really look into John Carr and his family.

After months of research, I noticed something in all the books and articles about Berkowitz. There was no mention of Untermyer Park anywhere. Correct me if I'm wrong, Berkowitz referred to Wicker Street as being "*Satan's realm*" in Klausner's book. He never mentions the park in any of his interviews either, not until Maury's theories were released.

On February 25, 2022, I emailed Larry.

Paul: Alfonso's nephew is talking to his uncle and getting ready to meet me this week, put that down as done. I got some new contacts for Tommy Zaino.

Larry called me right away and wanted Tommy's contact numbers. How he never tried to reach a key witness to the last shooting was shocking to me. Sure, I would let him call Tommy, but I knew he was not good with people and could only hope he would handle it right. Letting Larry call was not the best way to succeed, but I sent him all the contacts anyway. I told him while he was at it, give the Dupays a call, and sent him their contacts as well.

Larry kept saying to me, "You're doing this all by yourself, what do you need me for?" I needed him for his videos, for the attention to the case. This was working, so I sent him the contacts to make him feel more involved. Larry reached out to Tommy Zaino and hit...Tommy would talk. Larry then reached out to Andrew Dupay's daughter and hit there also...good ol' Penny came through once again.

That night I did some research and came across this article:

It is difficult to square what Wheat told Detective Justus with Berkowitz later claiming that he didn't act alone. In fact, it's impossible. Wheat and

Berkowitz's descriptions of his interactions with the Carr family tells two entirely different stories.

Wheat's testimony is that Berkowitz was simply a deranged psychopath who acted alone. She does not say that her family was friends with Berkowitz or had any other association with him. According to her, Berkowitz was just some weird guy who lived nearby, became obsessed with her father and their dog, and began harassing them by leaving bizarre letters and trying to kill the dog on one occasion.

Berkowitz, on the other hand, told an elaborate tale in which he, John and Michael Carr were not only friends but were also active in a satanic cult together that practiced animal sacrifices and other dark rituals. Unless Wheat's brothers successfully managed to keep their dark dealings with Berkowitz a secret from her, there are only two possibilities...either Wheat is lying, or Berkowitz is lying.

If Berkowitz was really the fall guy for the Carrs' satanic cult, Wheat certainly created an excellent narrative to put the blame all on Berkowitz. Whatever the truth was of the matter, it was her conversation with Detective Justus that led to Berkowitz's arrest. As soon as Justus put the phone down with Wheat, he changed his mind about interviewing Berkowitz and instead ordered a stakeout at Berkowitz's apartment.

February 27, 2022 was the day of the detectives meeting held at John Rinciari's house. I hadn't heard from Carl in a few days and didn't know if he was going to be there. Larry was fighting with him and his group again, so I wasn't sure if Carl wanted to be around him.

I drove to this meeting with my detective friend Ryan. Attending were John Comparetto, John Rinciari, Detective Geiss, Larry, and a few other retired NYPD Officers who knew Berkowitz from his younger years.

I met John Rinciari and quickly realized we knew each other. I had only spoken to Rinciari over the phone, I hadn't met him in person yet. He was a

Yonkers Police Officer who was stationed at the 1st Precinct years ago when I was assigned to repair the building. I introduced myself to the rest of the men before I sat down, ready to soak in some names and numbers.

A retired NYPD Officer led the conversation with a billboard examining the shootings and their details. I needed this class, my investigation didn't get into the shootings yet. I was into the origin of Berkowitz's actions and planned to investigate the shootings once I was done with all the Yonkers incidents. I wanted to first find out why and when Berkowitz became this murdering lunatic. What caused him to commit these crimes?

According to John Comparetto, David Berkowitz was as normal as everybody else in the neighborhood. It was when Berkowitz returned home from his three years in the Army that Comparetto noticed he was not the same. Berkowitz worked at a fire auxiliary in Co-Op City with Comparetto and Rinciari for a few years in the late '60s before enlisting into the Army. They both said Berkowitz was very patriotic and eagerly joined to fight in the Vietnam War. All the detectives there who grew up with Berkowitz agreed he was not the same person after returning home from the Army and recalled his eyes were see-through, like glass. Berkowitz returned home after serving his country and his friends were no longer his friends, as they began to avoid him because all he did was preach the gospel. Berkowitz was preaching the gospel? What happened to Berkowitz in the Army?

The meeting carried on with everyone's personal connections and stories with David Berkowitz, it was very informative. The detectives before this meeting, on their own, did a thorough investigation on Patrick O'Shaughnessey. They remembered every time there was a shooting, he was mysteriously seen in the area by someone. O'Shaughnessey claimed he was a buff into the shootings and went to the crime scenes when he heard them over his scanner. They felt Berkowitz should have known O'Shaughnessey from Co-Op City because they all knew him from the neighborhood. The detectives confirmed O'Shaughnessey died in 2011. All of these detectives, except for Detective Geiss, thought O'Shaughnessey was involved.

Before I left the meeting, I asked Detective Geiss about what he thought going forward. He was in the middle of reading *Confessions of Son of Sam* by Dr. David Abrahamsen (published in 1985), and was now convinced David Berkowitz acted alone. This was the first person, besides Borrelli, to say this. Geiss was known to be one of the most respected detectives in all of New York State, extremely famous for never letting a case go unsolved no matter how many years went by. I have discussed this case with him many times, and this was the first time he was saying this. Sometimes you can come across evidence or read things that can change your way of thinking. I asked Geiss, "It's that book you're reading isn't it?" He answered, "Yes, I will give it to you in a few days when I'm done…you will see."

I handed two bottles of wine to John Rinciari for inviting me to his house, shook everyone's hand, and thanked them for their time. The meeting went well, but it kind of stalemated us all…where do we go from here? What could we actually do to get the right answers? One option they discussed was to have Wheat interrogated, but they said there was no way for that to happen. She would never agree to it, and couldn't be forced. That left only the idea to send John Comparetto into prison to see his old friend Berkowitz.

I left John Rinciari's house that day confident with the information I obtained. I felt I found the origin of the "Son of Sam," where Berkowitz started to become the ".44 Caliber Killer." It wasn't in Vietnam where he enlisted to fight for his country, as he was never stationed there. It was in Korea, where he was stationed on December 15, 1971.

I read a few articles about the U.S. troops who were stationed in Korea in 1972. It seems they were young kids wasting their time. There was nothing to do, no work after setting up camp, and too many troops with nothing but free time. There was no fighting going on in Korea, troops were stationed there as allies to the Korean Army. The United States needed countries close to Vietnam to help so the spread of communism would stop. The U.S. sent a ton of soldiers to Korea to make sure the alliance remained. It also served as a way to secure the U.S. evacuation from Vietnam, as it was a coastal country. With no war going on in Korea, soldiers began to fall into drug and alcohol addiction due to boredom. The troops also had sex with prostitutes during their lengthy spare time. With no women around for months, it was almost a sure thing among all the soldiers. In the long run, this was not a good recipe for the soul, especially if this was not what you signed up to do. Berkowitz enlisted in the Army to fight for his country, not sleep with prostitutes, do drugs, and drink alcohol.

I was a little upset Carl didn't come to the meeting, but I understood why, Larry was really disrespecting him lately. If I was Carl, I would never want to be in the same room as him either. I fought with Larry to include Carl. I even had Larry invite him so it looked like it was coming from him. I didn't want to ever give up on forming unity and putting people together, but I had to ignore the nonsense Larry was causing and stay focused on David Berkowitz. I posted on Larry's website how I felt.

I followed the yellow brick road and it led me the wrong way. I also have now exposed Oz from behind the curtains. All the people followed Oz without question. I don't fault the people for that, he was the only one to follow.

The next day, Carl and Max called to discuss how the meeting went. When I asked Carl why he didn't attend, he said Larry was sending him very nasty emails. He had it with his bullshit.

Carl already talked to John Rinciari about the meeting and was asking me if Detective Geiss was for real. "How could John Geiss think Berkowitz acted alone?" he asked. I told him Geiss was reading Dr. Abrahamsen's book, and you know from doing this case for so long how reading things can sometimes change your way of thinking. Both Carl and Max thought Detective Geiss was crazy. I didn't think Geiss was crazy, but I couldn't believe him myself with all the evidence Maury had pointing to accomplices. I still had to take what he thought with an open mind. I couldn't wait to read Dr. Abrahamsen's book.

On March 3, 2022, Larry asked me to join him on his show and share what I uncovered at the Candlelight Inn. I repeated what I was told by the owner, then displayed the newspaper article Penny found. I pointed out that nowhere in the article did it mention Michael or Wheat Carr…or David Berkowitz. The article stated the lady was playing a pinball machine when she got shot in the leg. The owner told me she was playing a video game. No one was arrested for the crime.

Before the show, Max allowed me to show Larry an article which stated the lady who was shot in the leg at the Candlelight Inn had visited Untermyer Park. All three of us found nothing of relevance with the article and I told Larry not to use it. He did, and used it to trash Max, taunting him by saying these were the stupid articles assuming things that meant nothing. He told his audience the "Terry Heads" follow this garbage and that's not what he does. After the show, Max sent me an angry text. I told Max I was not behind what Larry did, and was sorry I showed him the article.

The next day I called Frank Carozza and asked if he was finished speaking with his uncle. This was my conversation with Frank Carozza, and this was going to be the last time I entertain Maury's twenty-two disciples of hell cult.

Paul: Hey Frank, I'm sorry to bother you and your uncle with this.

Frank: No problem Paulie, how is your father doing?

Paul: Good, he came home the other day. Things are not the same here anymore. I'm trying to get out of New York myself.

Frank: Tell me about it. Everything is so expensive. Building materials these days are through the roof.

Paul: Is business good?

Frank: Yeah, I'm good. So what the hell is this guy telling you about my uncle?

Paul: Did you have a cousin Joe Carozza who owned a yacht in New Rochelle?

Frank: Absolutely not, there is a ton of Carozzas and we didn't have a relative named Joe.

Paul: Did your uncle know Berkowitz?

Frank: I told you, he had words with him one day in front of his house because he said something to his wife. After the arrest, he realized it was him.

Paul: Who did Alfonso live with at 22 Wicker?

Frank: He had just gotten married to my aunt Patty.

Paul: ...and your uncle knows nothing about a loan between him and Joe Carozza?

Frank: My uncle has no idea who you are talking about.

Paul: Crazy Frank, I can't believe I'm asking you if your uncle was part of a cult with David Berkowitz.

Frank: Paulie, our families have known each other all of our lives. You know we are very Catholic. Whoever told you this garbage is out of his mind. My uncle had absolutely nothing to do with David Berkowitz.

Paul: Did you ever hear of the twenty-two disciples of hell or the Wicked King Wicker.

Frank: What is that?

Paul: The twenty-two disciples of hell was the cult Berkowitz and your uncle belonged to and The Wicked King Wicker was what they called your uncle.

Frank: You asked me that last week. I have no idea what the hell you are talking about. My uncle has no idea what you are talking about either. Who is this guy saying all this?

Paul: Maury Terry, he wrote the book The Ultimate Evil. Did you ever read his book?

Frank: No, is he still alive?

Paul: No, he passed away in 2015. Listen, I'm sorry I bothered you and your uncle with this. I know your family is good. You have no idea how many inaccuracies I have come across looking into this case.

Frank: What the hell was this guy Maury doing? I laughed with my unlce about this. The guy goes to church religiously all his life and of all the people to accuse of doing devil bullshit, they got the wrong guy for that.

Alfonso Carozza was positively, without a doubt, not involved with David Berkowitz. Frank was clearly annoyed at all this, as was I. I regret bothering Alfonso and my mood paid for it when I was done talking to Frank. I was really ashamed of myself after this interview. I apologize to the Carozza family for my unwise decision. I am smarter than this, and should have known better. I didn't need to question this family, I already knew the truth. I was done with this satanic cult, this was the last straw. By this point, I doubted a satanic cult involving Berkowitz even existed.

On March 7, 2022, Larry did another one of his videos walking around Untermyer Park discussing the twenty-two disciples of hell. While he walked around that park for the hundredth time, I started to research what mattered...Berkowitz's Army years.

CHAPTER XII

THE ARMY YEARS

In the Army, while stationed in Korea, Berkowitz was sending letters home to his friends that suggested his conservative views were turning more liberal. One Army buddy, a friend of Berkowitz's from the Bronx, said the letters bragged about using stimulants, depressant pills, and on occasion LSD. Berkowitz was changing while in the Army, and I wanted to know why.

David Berkowitz converted from Judaism to Christianity while stationed at Fort Knox, Kentucky. He was baptized at the Beth Haven Baptist Church in southern Louisville. "*He made a profession of faith in Jesus Christ here*," said his pastor, Tom Wallace. "*I baptized the fellow. I noted he was a Jewish boy who had found Christ. He was lost in the world.*"

Records show Berkowitz was baptized on May 6, 1973, and was among 2,200 people who were baptized at Beth Haven Church that year. Those who remember Berkowitz from his church-going days in Louisville said he was an exemplary Christian. It was almost impossible for them to believe he was being accused of killing six people and terrifying New York City for over a year. Pastor Tom Wallace recalled Berkowitz experimented with hard drugs while stationed in Korea, just prior to coming to Fort Knox. He stated, "*My initial impression of him was that I never met anyone more sincere or none honest. Everybody was relaxed about him.*"

The man who invited Berkowitz to Beth Haven Church, fellow Fort Knox soldier Jim Almond, said Berkowitz accepted Christ on his first visit to the Louisville church. Almond stated, "*I just asked him to go to church with me one day. Berkowitz said to me, 'but I am a Jew.' I told him I didn't care what he was, did he want to go to church? We went and he really enjoyed it. He went forward at the invitation, and after the service, he came up to me grinning and laughing saying, 'man I'm saved.' Then Berkowitz came back that day for the evening service, and he went forward again at the invitation. He told me afterwards that he just wanted to make sure it took."*

Jim Almond, who called himself "*probably the last friend David had,*" said Berkowitz led an energetic Christian life at Fort Knox for about a year. He began "*back sliding*" shortly before his discharge from the Army in June of 1974. "*I think his parents got to him. They practically disowned him when they found out he had become a Christian. He started hanging around with guys who drank and smoked pot and had dirty pictures on their walls. Maybe he worried about going home and being lonely.*"

Beth Haven Church members who were friends with Berkowitz, portrayed him as a pleasant and effusive type, whose appetite for spiritual food could not be satisfied. He routinely attended Sunday worship services, Wednesday evening prayer meetings, and Thursday evening Soul winners classes at the church. He also would go out witnessing his faith door to door. "*He wasn't at all like they say he is,*" said Sue Winfrey, who was a member at Beth Haven who frequently sat with Berkowitz during worship service. "*David was a really nice guy, friendly to talk to, he talked a lot, sang songs and played the guitar. He seemed to be real strong in his faith.*"

Terri Luce, another Beth Haven member, served as a stewardess on one of the church's buses that transported soldiers from Fort Knox to Beth Haven Church. She said Berkowitz was always there when the bus came around. Terri stated, "*He was really a fantastic guy with a great personality. On the bus he would tell Bible stories to the kids. We talked all the time, mostly about church activities and spiritual things. He was in the Army, and my dad was in the Army. My parents really thought a lot of him.*" She recalled Berkowitz would study the Bible with vigor.

Rosalie Luce, Terri's mother, described Berkowitz as "*a great soul winner, I never heard him say an unkind word. He brought a lot of GIs in from base.*

It breaks my heart to see what has happened." She goes on to say "*I still don't believe it was him, but if it was, I'm just thankful he was saved. The Bible says, once saved, always saved.*"

Davi Zammit was stationed at Fort Knox and remembered Berkowitz as always having a clean-cut appearance, his uniform was always pressed, his shoes were always shined, everything around him was always in order. Zammit stated, "*He was telling the guys they shouldn't be drinking and swearing and running around with women. But as an individual, I didn't think he was bad. He was a little off sometimes, but so were a few other guys who seemed just as strange.*"

An Army buddy from Fort Knox, Paul Billow, said Berkowitz used to brag about using pills. Billow stated, "*When I met Berkowitz, he seemed to have been completely recovered from all he went through in Korea. He seemed to change drastically in other ways, from gregarious to reclusive, and toward a revolutionist form of the Baptist religion.*" Berkowitz was baptized, went to revival meetings, and according to Billow, tried to convert others. "*He told me that if I did not have Jesus Christ as my personal savior, I would be damned.*" Two months before leaving Fort Knox, Billow said Berkowitz started to swear. Billow suggested, "*Maybe he went back to drugs because somebody doesn't change like that overnight.*"

Terry Peterson, who was stationed in Korea with Berkowitz said he would be willing to testify as a defense witness if Berkowitz went to trial because, "*The Army may have screwed him up. When he came over to Korea, he wasn't a killer. Being over there, and his relationship with the military, may be what caused him to become a killer now.*"

When Berkowitz went into the Army in 1971, he began writing letters to his girlfriend back home, Iris Gerhardt. Iris was only fourteen years old when she started dating Berkowitz, and barely sixteen when they broke up. They continued to be close friends, and his letters to her helped shape a story of how a young soldier, corrupted by drug use and a rebellion against the war he was in, had changed. Iris said in the beginning, the letters seemed to be in good nature, but as time went on, she noticed something was not right.

Here is the first letter Berkowitz sent to Iris from his basic training at Fort Dix, New Jersey on July 8, 1971:

> *I have been at Fort Dix for over fifteen days. Basic training is sure hard. I have to run 5 miles everyday. Getting up at 4:30 in the morning isn't easy.*
>
> *I am not really unhappy at all that I enlisted. Even though this life is very hard, I felt I just had to go. I always wanted to be on my own. I wanted to take up some responsibilities. There was nothing for me to do back home anyhow. There is one thing I miss, that's my friends...You had better write soon.*

The next letter Berkowitz sent was received by Iris on August 5, 1971:

> *You can see that I put in many hours of hard labor. I guess it's the price of wanting to serve my country. I had nothing to lose coming here. I should be home next week on a pass. I hope to see you. I haven't changed much except I lost 25 pounds. Better not get me mad because I'm good with a gun! Don't make me use it on you. Love, Dave*

After Berkowitz completed his basic training at Fort Dix, he visited Iris back home and she noticed no change with his behavior at that point. When Berkowitz returned to the Army, he was stationed at Fort Polk, Louisiana, for his advanced training courses. When he completed his advanced training, he was then stationed in Korea. This is when Iris began to notice a change in Berkowitz's behavior.

Here is a letter from Berkowitz to Iris while he was stationed in Korea dated January 21, 1972:

Happy sweet sixteen...Did you know that I was in a down mood when I got your letter, then I read your letter and it totally paralyzed my mind. I think it's my fault that our going together never worked out. I never put any effort into our relationship. So don't apologize because you have nothing to worry about.

I'll tell you what when I come home in June. I'll promise to make love to you all weekend long, okay? Will do it for old times sake.

My mind has completely blew out. I have changed. You will probably be disappointed not to see the same old Dave anymore. I don't play anymore conservative patriot scenes. I woke up. The world is all fucked up (thanks Nixon). We've got to have some peace.

The only thing on my mind is Drugs, Music, Pollution, Poverty, Peace and Love. I really got into drugs ya know. It's different, kind of messed up. I guess I'm all fucked up but it's part of life. I despise religion, hate prejustice greed, etc. That's all the world is. A cold mass of hell. It sucks. We're all doomed to the grave. When you think of death do you lose your breath or do you keep your cool?

Listen love, think of God, it's the only way. I can't live in a world of atomic fear. I think there is some love left in the world. Oh man, Im all fucked up. Please straighten me out, please. I love you. Dave

The next letter Berkowitz sent to Iris was received on February 2, 1972. This is the first time we see Berkowitz rebelling against the Army, refusing to carry a gun:

I'm glad your happy about getting my picture. It's not a joke picture, that's the way I always am. Hey, you must be getting mad at me for writing all these unhappy letters. Well, I guess I shouldn't sound so down all the time, but I can't help it. The fact is, I am feeling down, all the time.

I suppose Ed is doing okay in the Coast Guard. But you have to realize that the Army and the Coast Guard are two different services.

Hey, guess what? They might transfer me to another unit. I'll either be a firefighter, medic, ecologist, or game warden. I have finally proven to them that I'm not going to play with there guns anymore. I made myself promise that I was not to carry any weapons while my unit was on the field. So that day while I was in the chow line, a major and a captain walked up to me and said, "Private, where is your gun?" And I said, I didn't bring it to the field and I refuse to bring it to the field. Well, all hell broke out after that. They just can't tell me when to carry a gun. I explained to them but they didn't do much good. I also explained it to the chaplain. And guess what? He's with me all the way. He never carried a gun in his life. He is trully a man of God, and so am I and he knows it. Of course, I'm for a court martial but I'll win. I'll have to prove that I'm a conscientious objector, which I am. It's going to be a ruff fight but I have one thing going for me. That is God. He's on my side.

There is one thing you must admit about me. That is, when have you ever known me to say things about love, Peace, God, etc. I mean, can you ever remember me talking about all this back in the world.

These feelings have been deep inside, now don't think I'm going insane or anything like that because I'm not, yes it's the real me, they come out with a little help from my friends. I must truly thank my friends for helping me. Because now I'm an individual again. Free from the war pigs and there evil ways. I wouldn't want you to meet my friends. There not very nice.

On February 21, 1972, Berkowitz wrote Iris back after she sent him a letter trying to help with the changes he was going through:

I like what you said in your letters. I guess I'll straighten out eventually.

The following are in my very own writings about today's society. I hope you will not be displeased with me for what I wrote. This is what's been on my mind. I've always had a guilty feeling about the stand I took when I was back home.

You will note that I have gone one extreme to another. That's because I am finally facing reality. I am writing you with the hope you will understand. I hope you will express your feelings truthfully. One thing I admire is a trully honest person. I hope you make out okay in school. Don't sweat it. I hated school too. Now I hate the Army more. I guess I'll have to suffer until I get out. I'm looking forward to seeing the world again. Take care, love Dave

On March 1, 1972, Berkowitz sent Iris this letter as he was dealing with his inability to cope with his Army life:

My court martial is coming up in a few weeks. I have a good chance of winning according to the facts and review. There's a good chance that I'll be fined $50.00. If I win I can tell them to get fucked and I'll be transferred to another job which does not involve handling guns and ammunition.

The reason I got court martialed was because I failed to obey a direct order from my company commander. The C.O. noticed that I didn't have any weapons. When he asked me where my weapons were I told him very politely I didn't bring them and I went into telling him how I felt about carrying and using weapons. I said, "Sir, I politely refuse to carry them because of my moral beliefs."

Well, he got kind of pissed off. He is a true lifer, who dedicated his mind and body to the Army. So it's obvious I cannot talk to him about the peace movement. The only thing I'm worried about is my jurors. There all lifers too. They only think Army and kill the enemy.

I'll beat these lifers, keep straight, I guess you get a chance to see all my friends so say hello. They probably won't remember me. If you see Ed call him a war pig and a rightist militant. If he hits you let me know. Then I'll take care of him myself.

I can't wait until tomorrow, it's pay day. I'll have to go and get some heavy acid and morphine so I can last out the month. Wish me Luck. Love, Dave

In this last letter, Berkowitz littered it with cartoon drawings and quotes: "*Ecology for Survival*," "*Love Shall Dominate*," "*Smog Kills Kids*," "*Hawks Vs Doves*," "*Love is?*," "*Death Is?*," "*Pleasure*," "*Peace means*."

Iris at this time was trying to write Berkowitz back as fast as she could to help him keep it together. Berkowitz to her, was now a different person than the one she knew. On March 14, 1972, Iris received this letter from Berkowitz:

I'm sorry you had to wait awhile for this letter but it was hard to start. I could ask you how things are back in the world but I know you are making it okay.

Do you know what the lifers made me do? They made me take a haircut. Man am I pissed off. Just because they love crew cuts, they gotta try to chop my head up. I'm still trying to find a way to go straight. It's not easy to find a way so I'm still searching.

Leave it up to the fucked up Army. They postponed my court martial a week. I can't wait to get it over with.

So far from reading this you would think I'm getting by okay. Well, I'm not. I've got some bad news for you. You know how the Army messes and changes things around the last minute. My original mid-term leave was for June. They had nothing better to do so they moved them back to late August or September.

I feel pretty bad now because I really wanted to get back to see you. I had my hopes up so much. I'll have to write you another letter real soon. I happen to be speechless right now. Love, Dave

Four days later, on March 18, 1972, Iris received this letter from Berkowitz:

Boy, love, you know I'm really down. I was just waiting and waiting to go home. Since I got here all I've been doing is fighting the establishment. It gets pretty hard to keep fighting all the time but I and a few others know where right. I'm just to anxious to see this great new world develop. But I get down sometimes when I see and think that I'll be dead before I can ever see this change take place. I don't feel like fighting. When I say fighting I don't mean with any violence. When do you think people will see the light.

It gets really bad when I get the impression that I have no support from anybody and I'm fighting a losing battle. I often feel this way so I get the urge to escape for awhile. In other words I just take my mind out of the rat race and get into deep meditation. When I do it gives me a chance to think and plan my next move. However lately I found I have been escaping quite often and I got in quite a mess. The weird thing is I sometimes like the mess I'm in.

Do you think you really know what love is? I was looking forward to heading back home. It would of given me a chance to rest my mind a bit before it bursts open. I just might turn out to be one of those unhappy citizens who gave up fighting a long time ago and just fell helplessly into the usual rat race. Sometimes I feel that the only time peace will come is when I'm dead. Or I might turn out to be a lifetime freak. I will write you soon because I love you. Love, Dave

Iris then sent Berkowitz two letters before receiving this one from him on April 8, 1972:

I really dig love and peace. Do you know what? I feel just like a useless expandable machine. That's right when I look in the mirror all I see is one green soldier looking back at me. I feel like a robot being told when and where I can do things. I wish I could get a bike and travel around the open plains of the land.

Say, how is Oscar the owl? I remember that old fat fellow. I'm getting jealous of him. I don't want him to stay in your bedroom. I'd rather be there myself.

How is America? Do you know that for the last few days, I've been so doped up that I feel I'm on a flying carpet. Wow, what a head. Well at least time floats by. I wish I could move the clock forward.

Guess what? I've come across an amazing discovery. I have finally made a conclusion. That is, God is real. Believe me, he's as you and me. I can't begin to tell you about it. Imagine if there were no countries to fight and die for. Imagine if man had no religion. I'm not the only dreamer. Love ya, Dave

On April 22, 1972, Iris received this letter from Berkowitz:

I know that I haven't wrote for awhile. My court martial was put off. I'm sure you know what's going on in Vietnam. Our officers would sure like us to go. We all think they are insane since we're on standby for 'Nam and figuring the war won't be over until the year 2001, you can assume I won't be home for awhile.

Let us drink a toast to the government for there very cool ingenuity in getting us back in 'Nam.

Oh by the way. Don't worry about me killing myself on drugs. I've got too much to do in life to sky out to soon. I'll be around for awhile.

Hey do you know that I miss you? I really do, so hang in there. Blessed are the Peacemakers. For they are the children of God. Love, Dave

Berkowitz was obviously going through a lot in Korea. He didn't like what he was a part of, so he turned to Jesus Christ for support. On May 5, 1972, Iris received this letter from Berkowitz:

Jesus Christ fought real hard and he never lived to see the changes. They haven't come so he's still waiting. I've committed my body to an evil organization. I think it's time to uncommit myself. I have much hope and faith in God and Peace. I have much love for people like you. I don't want to learn how to kill my fellow man. There ain't nobody gonna get rich over my dead body. Nobody is gonna send me to a war so they can make money by having me use their products like guns, bullets, bombs, etc.

When I get back you will see a new Dave. The Army doesn't like the changes that came over me so they try to break me. The Army reminds me of a baby. If a toy works, he throws it on the floor and drops it in the bottom of his toy chest. So until I get my head together, I'll be thinking of some solutions. Remember I love you! Dave

Berkowitz was clearly unhappy with his decision to enlist in the Army. He regretted wanting to fight for his country as he felt the war was all wrong. Iris received this letter from Berkowitz on June 7, 1972:

As far as the Army goes it's just one big bummer. We don't get along too well. I think it's because I see the Army as nothing more than a tool of the government to use against another nation. It's just a game of politics. I cannot see why man would wage war on another man. We're all supposed to love each other but we don't. I want to promote love and brotherhood. We don't have much love here on earth. War never did a person any good. I want to be free, I will be pretty soon. There is something I must do first. Give me about 50 days for planning. I sure would like mankind to be free. Hey love, tell me how to be free, tell me how to find peace. I haven't found any answers yet. Can you think of some? Love ya always, Dave

These letters are essential to read as I think this is where Berkowitz was changing into who he became. Iris received this next letter from Berkowitz on August 14, 1972:

They taught me how to fight. They taught me about many weapons, demolition, riot control and self defense. All of these courses will come in handy one day. I plan to use them and it's not going to be the way the lifers want me to use them. I will use these tactics to destroy them the way they destroyed millions of people through the wars they started. One day there will be a better world. After a few heads from the heads of state are removed. The poor man is not lazy like the rich man. I am displeased with it and I will try to change it. I will make it my resolution to find out what is in the heads of our fearless leaders. I will find out what is in their heads even if I have to crack them wide open. I hate rebels but I love revolutionaries. Love ya always, Dave

Iris only saw Berkowitz twice after his discharge from the Army. Once at Bronx Community College where they both attended the fall semester in 1975. Iris recalled, "*He seemed much more grown up and mature, but there was a change. Then I saw him again and I knew he needed help, but there was little I could do.*" When Iris was asked why she didn't help Berkowitz seek psychiatric help, she replied, "*I just thought he wasn't a violent person. He never got into fights. I only saw him angry once. He had an argument with his friend Ed, and he just said, 'I'm not talking to Ed for a while.' He never talked badly about anyone.*" Iris got married in 1975 and last heard from Berkowitz when he called her house. She wasn't home to receive his call, so he left a message with someone to have her call him back...she didn't...and a few months later the shootings began.

His friends said he was very patriotic and enlisted in the Army to join the fight for his country. Unfortunately, Berkowitz did not do any fighting against the enemy, only his country did he fight with. He was stationed in Korea where he spent his time doing drugs and other horrible things that came with boredom. Berkowitz was eager to fight for his country, but his country wasted his time and polluted his mind with evil.

On January 4, 1973, Berkowitz ended his hell tour in Korea and was then stationed at Fort Knox, Kentucky, where, as you have read prior, he tried to change his life and accepted Jesus Christ.

David Berkowitz was discharged from the Army on June 24, 1974. He left the Army with a horrible taste in his mouth, regretting he enlisted, resenting his government for the war he felt was wrong. The Army had accepted his courageousness to only waste his time, which made him a confused person who just wanted to go home.

When Berkowitz returned home to his adopted father and stepmother Julia, he quickly moved out on his own that November of '74. In February of 1975, Berkowitz's father moved to Florida with his wife Julia, away from his Jewish son who became a Christian, abandoning him in New York City. Berkowitz was then alone, with no friends or family, with no direction in a world he didn't understand.

I began to search for all the people in these Army articles so I could contact them. Good ol' Penny would come through once again with the most important of them all...Pastor Tom Wallace, a ninety-one-year-old wonder of the world. A man with more saves than the great New York Yankee,

Mariano Rivera. He was alive, living in Tennessee, and was still very active in spreading God's truth.

I emailed Larry later that day.

Paul: What is going on with Zaino and Dupay?

Larry: I'll try to call Zaino again. Dupay seems to have ghosted me. I called Mike Lorenzo Jr. at the record shop you told me he owned. He is ok to meet up. I'm going to wait until you can go see him with me.

Paul: I'm sure I know him when I see him. Sounds good, I told you he was coming.

CHAPTER XIII

PASTOR TOM WALLACE

March 9, 2022, I started to contact all the people I found in the Army articles. I got a slight hit with Paul Billow, I spoke to his wife. She confirmed Paul was with Berkowitz in the Army and would tell him I called, but I never got to speak directly to Paul, he never called me back. I tried Jim Almond but couldn't get passed his answering machine. Finally, I did connect with someone...God's gift to the world...enter Pastor Tom Wallace.

Paul: Hi, may I speak to Tom Wallace please?

Tom: This is him, who is calling?

Paul: How are you doing Mr. Wallace, my name is Paul Agostino. I am doing a documentary on David Berkowitz and I came across your name as his pastor in 1974. Are you okay with me speaking to you?

Tom: Yes, sure.

Paul: I'm from Yonkers and I have been going around my city asking questions about what happened with David Berkowitz. When I came across your articles, I saw that David was like how the guys who grew up with him said, a good guy, a good person. This doesn't add up to how Berkowitz has been portrayed to the public. I was wondering if you could help me out a bit. I don't think the story that is out there is the truth.

Tom: Well, let me give you my view of it and exactly what took place. David was in the military during the Vietnam War. He was a typical young fellow pulled out of his life and sent to all that tragedy over there. He got on drugs and the alcohol and sex and everything that goes with it. They then shipped him to Fort Knox, where I was pastoring at the time. We ran buses out to Fort Knox and picked up soldiers who wanted to come on a voluntary basis. We had two or three busloads of course, our church was a pretty good size. Some of the guys got David to come and he got into some of our youth activities. Now typically when a guy's on alcohol and on drugs striving for women and all that kind of stuff, he is unhappy and misled and can't find what they are looking for. David got into our young people here, who were delightful and happy. They were clean-cut kids, Christian families. We had a tremendous youth group teaching our children to get people converted to Christ and get the Lord in them to help them. Also, to teach a biblical plan for their life so they could have some eternal purpose. David saw these kids all happy, singing happy songs and all these activities. We alerted them to the evils of drugs and alcohol and sex. David saw the happiness in these people, and he wanted that, so he responded to our invitations, and he went through the motions. He responded to our invitations to accept Christ, and then he took a stand and was willing to be baptized to testify what had happened to him, but he didn't get it, and when he left and got back to New York, he was empty, and had all these temptations. Then he just went crazy. I think he just got tricked into a bunch of demonologies, and then he says he heard a dog talking to him. Then he went crazy and started shooting people. They gave him three life sentences I think for that. Now after this, I've been in contact with him in prison. I've been in contact with him several times. I subscribed for him a Christian magazine for him in prison. I was up there one time, and I called his lawyer to ask him if they would let me see him, and the lawyer said, you don't want to go in there. Normally it would be great, but you don't want to go today. It's like every time his mother goes to see him, he is like a tiger, an animal, and he goes wild, you don't want to go around him, so I didn't do it. When I got back, I corresponded with him, and somehow, some of the people came in there and had religious services in the jail. David had had a little taste of it here but didn't get it. When he heard in prison, these services, he responded and really got a hold of it. I send him literature and I've corresponded with him by email and by letter and he just got transformed. Now he is a very happy man, and he is involved in helping the elderly prisoners. Of course, he's going to be there three lifetimes and there's no possibility of parole, so he's not interested in that, he just wants to help. David has a beautiful spirit. I correspond with him now. I got a letter from him about a month ago and the guy has really, really become a Christian. Now before he tried to be, but he didn't know what to do and it didn't take, but he really got a hold of it, and he has Christ in his heart and he's helping. He's been appointed assistant chaplain, so he has some purpose there from keeping him from going crazy.

Paul: So you think it's real? David is born again?

Tom: Yup, what he has got now is real. When I baptized him, he wanted it, but he didn't have it. He had no understanding of any of it and he was just in Satan's control. He was just living off the energy of drugs and his appetite for alcohol and sex, and all that crazy stuff that people who have no direction, or purpose, as far as God is concerned. Anyway, I think he met Christ. I think the Lord came into his heart and he became a Christian.

Paul: But why won't he tell the truth? I know a victim that is still alive, and he won't tell him who shot him.

Tom: Ah, listen, we have two philosophies here. One is the secular philosophy and what we call the left, and the right is of biblical philosophy. The Bible talks about the difference between when a person has a spiritual insight or they have the Lord in their heart, or they have a Bible to guide them on what's good and what's bad, and without the Bible, people follow philosophies who don't think they need God in their lives, and they don't believe there is a heaven or hell. Folks who go that secular route, they are the newspaper people, and they report from their viewpoint. From a biblical viewpoint, I see an entirely different David Berkowitz. He talks my language now. I'm ninety-one years old and I have been at this for seventy years. I'm convinced that David has a relationship with the Lord. He is sincere and honest and clean-cut now. He knows that drugs would ruin everything for him. He knows that alcohol will kill him before his time comes, and so he is learning these things from biblical principles. If a person absorbs biblical principles, they can absorb these principles and allow Christ into their hearts. The Lord is real. God came into the body of Jesus and lived among us, and then went to the cross and made a total payment for the sins of the world. According to the Bible, our Lord offers the free gift of eternal life. This whole thing, in the secular world, they cover a lot of philosophies to try and justify what they want. The result of that philosophy is crime, and we have drugs and alcohol and immorality, and the teaching of sexuality, freedom for all these people. Some of these philosophies just don't want Jesus in the picture. David is a genuine, sincere Christian now, and may not be perfect. He may have all kinds of problems, but I do believe the guy is genuine. I have had a lot of contact with him. There is an account in the Bible. Jesus gave a story of a man who had a demon in him, and the man heard the gospel and he wanted it, so he chased the demon out of his life, but he didn't get Christ in him. He just cleaned up his act and quit doing bad things. When this guy chased the demon out, the Bible says that the demon went out and couldn't find a place, so he gathered up more demons, and a whole bunch of demons came back into the man, and the man was ten times worse than before. When the newspaper people from New York came with their lawyers to interview me, I told them David cleaned up his act here when he saw our young people happy. He tried on his own, but he didn't get Christ in the picture and as a result, he had an empty house. The Bible says that a man in the New Testament swept and garnished his house, cleaned everything up, but when the demons came back, and they found his house empty, they moved right back in. If the demons had knocked on the door and Jesus answered, they would have gone away. What happened is, he cleaned up his act, because he wanted it, but he did not get Christ in his heart, and as a result, when he got back to New York, he got possessed with devils. One of the lawyers wanted me to testify in court and he told me what he wanted me to say, and I said well, you don't want me up there because I'm going to say the opposite of what you're trying to get me to say. They said heck, if you're going to say that, then we don't want you up there. They have to be sensational in order to sell their stuff. They add their flavor to it, it's not truth. Some of the TV personalities have interviewed David over the years and David made them look like fools. They weren't prepared for what he was going to say. I would just be clapping my hands when David would go off.

Paul: When you met him, what was he like? Was he messed up? What did Korea do to him?

Tom: One of the fellows who brought him came from a good church foundation. He had Christ in his heart, and he wanted to help him, so he encouraged David to come. Now that guy had been in the same setting in Vietnam as David was. That fellow had no problems there because he had Jesus in his heart. When David was over there, his heart was empty. He didn't have anything to help him from getting pulled into it. The guy who brought him here helped David try and find the Lord. As a result, we didn't get the job done but we planted a seed. When he heard all this in prison later on, he was open. He knew he saw sincerity, honesty, integrity, character in our young people. He remembered that, so he didn't reject it when he heard it. A lot of people just keep on rejecting it because they never saw it, heard it, or felt it.

Paul: I grew up here in Yonkers and I am pretty sure David did not do all this himself. The Son of Sam is not him, why does he accept that? I think there were other people involved with him.

Tom: Now I don't know about all of that. David liked to play with the TV people.

Paul: How was he when he left to go home?

Tom: He was just about as bad when he left here as when he came here, even though we had exposed him. He was trying hard, and he just didn't see it. He didn't understand it. He really has absorbed it now. He has become a new creature. He wasn't a new creature here. He went through the motions of the public procession of being baptized and so forth, you know. These people came here and wanted to see his baptism card. They were doing that so they could laugh at us. I wrote a story about all this with *The Sword of The*

Lord papers. They asked to print it. I told them under one condition...you don't change a period or a comma, anything. You put it exactly like I said, don't edit it.

Paul: The first time you saw David in prison, was he accepting to you? Was he remorseful?

Tom: He has written to me many times about how sorry he is. He was not in control of himself.

I got off the phone with the pastor and was again hearing about a completely different David Berkowitz. What really happened to him when he returned from the Army? His friends said he was preaching Gospel when he first returned home, yet the pastor said before his discharge, he went back to his rotten ways.

I told Larry about the pastor, but he wasn't interested. Larry didn't like the pastor was telling me Berkowitz acted alone, it went against the narrative for his show. The lone-shooter theory was not an option to discuss for him.

Pastor Wallace sent me the article he wrote for *The Sword of The Lord* newspaper which was published in 1977. He expressed in this article what he thought happened to Berkowitz. I think this is where the media got the idea that Berkowitz called himself the "Son of Sam" because he was a product of "Uncle Sam"...a product of our country.

Here is what Pastor Tom Wallace emailed me:

David Berkowitz told his doctor that a 6,000-year-old voice from a neighbor's dog told him to do it. He was going to rid the world of sinners. "That boys a victim of the crime infested streets of New York," said one man. "It's the result of watching all that killing on TV and in the movies," testified another. Some blamed it on a broken home, others spoke of drugs, public school exposure, rock and roll influence, and still others associated it with a tour of duty in Korea.

Mark Life, a journalist with The New York News, blamed The Beth Haven Baptist Church of Louisville, Kentucky for the whole thing. In a syndicated news story, a New York Daily newspaper wrote that Berkowitz had picked up the inspiration to rid the world of sinners while attending services at our church.

Charles Daley, editor of The Western Recorder, Kentucky's voice of Southern Baptists, blamed the aggressive outreach evangelism program.

May I share with you my thoughts on the matter, under the headings, "Son of Sam? Son of God? or Son of Satan?" My thoughts are related to the words of the apostle Paul in the book of Romans "and even as they did not like to retain God in their knowledge, God gave them over to a reprobate mind to do those things which are not convenient." (1:28)

Son of Sam? David Berkowitz gave himself the name "Son of Sam." I took this to mean "Uncle Sam" and surely the ".44 caliber killer" was indeed a "Son of Sam," a product of "Uncle Sam."

David Berkowitz was a product of "Uncle Sam's" crime infested city streets. New York City's crime increased 300 percent in the prior ten years, while Tokyo showed a 2 percent decrease in crime. Tokyo's secret...family closeness, a two-hour moral and educational teaching time, strict law enforcement, and a requirement that all policemen must visit and become acquainted with all those families in the district. Dr. Bertrand Brown, Director of The National Institute of Mental Health wrote, "Repeated exposure to violent programming can produce sensitivity to cruelty and violence and builds the feeling that violent behavior is appropriate under some conditions." In a society where there is murder every 26 minutes, a violent crime each 31 seconds, and 21 serious crimes every minute, we are not surprised any more when some fellow goes berserk and on a killing spree. Resentment, anger and disappointment had been brewing inside David for years and it finally boiled over. Reasons cited were family, relationships, drugs, TV and his frustrations over the war.

David Berkowitz was a product of "Uncle Sam's" public school system. David did not have the advantage of a Christian school education. At this time a lot of new philosophies were telling all who would listen that "God is dead." The "Son of Sam" was taught naturalistic, secularist reasoning built upon few facts, much theory, and assumption. David was surely a product of "Uncle Sam's" secular schools.

David Berkowitz was a product of "Uncle Sam's" rock music culture. Elvis and The Beatles were in full swing. Hard, acid rock music had its message. It was specifying sex, drugs, and suicide. When listening to this music, it becomes a direct line of communication with the philosophy of individuals whose lives are often controlled by Satan. Hard rock is Satan's tool, brainwashing those to accept this concept of life. With heroes like Brian Jones, who drowned after an overdose, Johnny Winters, who ended up in a mental institution. Jimi Hendrix, who collected $100,000 for a one-night performance and suffocated in a pool of his own vomit that same night. Janis Joplin, the lesbian with V.D., who tried suicide 6 times and finally succeeded. All these heroes, plus a crowd of others, how was David to end up any different?

David Berkowitz was a product of "Uncle Sam's" Hollywood films and TV. The projector and a screen have proven to be the best teaching tools invented to date. Hollywood propagates the world views on sex, drugs, alcohol and divorce, for hours a day sins are glamorized. Morals and principles of ethics are of no concern to producers of Hollywood films. David Berkowitz was indeed a "Son of Sam."

David Berkowitz was also a product of "Uncle Sam's" drug culture. Smoking marijuana, sniffing cocaine, shooting heroin and morphine, and popping pills have become a way of life. Teens are suffering from the aftereffects of drug use. Suicide, the eventual end of heavy drug use, is accelerating at an unbelievable rate.

David Berkowitz was a product of "Uncle Sam's" broken homes. One Psychologist told of David's desire to locate his real mother. Broken homes have always had their effects on the children. Could this tragedy in New York have been prevented by a family altar?

David Berkowitz was a product of "Uncle Sam's" liberal, modern view of religion. America was falling away from God with all the sins that distracted American's young minds. The young people of America have long ago lost confidence in the diluted, middle-of-the-road, liberal national council of churches approach. We have seen this country pass through the cycle from red-hot evangelism to an evangelistic position, then to an orthodox stand, on to dead orthodoxy. From there it has gone to liberalism, on to modernism and from that, to radicalism, and finally to revolution and anarchy. A wave of burning buildings, riots and sit-ins brought us to a stark realization that revival was our only hope. With the excitement of drugs, sex, pornographic literature and rock music, the "Son of Sam" looked upon the sick, anemic, formal religious systems that he knew as a joke. When he saw the reality of the young people with changed lives, high standards, good habits and clean language, he was willing to take a second look. The sincere message of the gospel was different, and he listened to it carefully.

Son of God? David Berkowitz was sincere when he came to Beth Haven. He saw reality and liked it. The seed went forth. He received it gladly, it was such a welcome contrast to religion. Forgiveness, peace, happiness were appealing words to him. He heard and responded, but obviously, we think, did not repent and exercise faith. Jim Almond testified that as long as he kept on David and worked with him, it was great, but as soon as he eased up to give him opportunity to show his faith, he turned immediately back to the "Girly" pictures, the drinking buddies and the foul language. It is possible, of course, for a person to really be born again and then get away from it, like the prodigal son. Paul the apostle taught "therefore if any man be in Christ, he is a new creature, old things are passed away, behold, all things become new," (11 cor. 5:17). David had an interest in getting away from the Army base, circulating among the girls in the college and career class at Beth Haven, and even enjoyed the music and message of the church services, but he did not become a new creature. I do not believe he was a son of God. He may have been, but this is my belief.

Son of Satan? One doctor who spent hours on this case remarked, "I have never heard anything so strange in my life." He referred to the stories of the experiences of David Berkowitz. Did this boy actually hear a voice talking to him from a dog? Was it Satan or maybe a demon? Nobody really knows! However, in this day when we "Wrestle not against flesh and blood, but against principalities, against powers, against the rulers of the darkness of this world, against spiritual wickedness in high places" (Eph. 6:12), It would be good for us to "Put on the whole armour of God." In our text, Paul speaks of those who "Did not like to retain God in their knowledge as being turned over to a reprobate mind." (Rom 1:28)

Jesus told of the case of a man who had a demon. The demon became restless and departed from the man. it went wandering in dry places and could find no rest. When it returned, the house was empty, swept and garnished. The demon entered back in and brought with it seven more wicked spirits, worse than itself. (Matt. 12:44,45) I personally believe that this poor, unfortunate boy came seeking for peace and help. In the favorable atmosphere of our church, he reformed and threw out some of the wicked things in his life, but because he did not get Christ in to fill the empty place, it all returned and with more wickedness than before! David was obviously overcome by a demon of insanity. There is really no way to be sure whether the killings by "Son of Sam" were demon inspired or not, but we can form opinions as we read the bible and look to the Lord for spiritual insight.

Now years have gone by since that time and there have been some interesting developments in David's case. He is serving out three life sentences in Attica State Prison in New York. He sent me an email sharing his testimony. Some folks came to the prison, and he stated that he put his faith in Christ. He began to assist the chaplain in the ministry at the prison. David works with inmates, counseling and assisting in the ministry of the chaplain. I believe we planted the seed, others watered, and God gave the increase.

On October 8, 1997, I received the following letter from David Berkowitz, #78-A1976 in Attica Prison, New York, it reads as follows:

Dear Pastor Tom Wallace,

I was so blessed, encouraged and touched in my heart to receive your letter. I miss you and the folks at Beth Haven very much. It was more than two decades ago but everything is fresh in my mind. Those days were good times for me, the very good days of my life before many bad things happened. I appreciate all the prayers you've said for me, the times you were thinking about visiting, and even the subscription to The Sword of the Lord. I love this newspaper. It is probably by far one of the best Christian publications that's around these days. If you would send me a subscription again I would be most grateful. I would also share it with the brothers here in the prison chapel. Pastor Wallace, so much has happened over the years. I am deeply sorry for all the hurt and pain I had caused to many lives. Through it all I have discovered- and I cannot even find the words to describe it all- but I have experienced the greatest level of God's love and mercy. Perhaps this is something of what the apostle Paul felt the moment he stopped being Saul of Tarsus. I love Jesus with all my heart and I thank him continually for his abundant mercy and grace. Yes, I am with Christ now and it is wonderful. Today the Lord has me working as the chaplains clerk at this prison. He has also made many ways for me to share my testimony to glorify the Lord. I am enclosing some messages the Lord has allowed me to write. Hope they will encourage you. My heart has been touched by your letter. God bless you, Pastor Wallace, in Christ's love, David Berkowitz

Pastor Wallace believed Berkowitz acted alone. He blames this country for producing the "Son of Sam," the son of "Uncle Sam." Pastor Wallace felt our country was once a strong country, when it had God as its foundation. He believes our nation fell out of sync with Christ in those days of war, and the people, including Berkowitz, suffered. Pastor Wallace painted a picture of a boy who was lost and couldn't find his way home. Berkowitz was abandoned by his country, abandoned by his friends, abandoned by his family, and eventually...he would feel abandoned by God.

Pastor Wallace blames the culture Berkowitz was a part of, the music his generation listened to. He thought the music in those days influenced people's minds in a bad way. During his Army years, Berkowitz was clearly influenced by a rock band called *Black Sabbath*. Proof is in his letters to Iris as he recites songs from their album titled, *Master Of Reality*. *Black Sabbath* produced music preaching anti-war and pro-God, what Berkowitz came to be.

Hollywood movies were also influencing Berkowitz's generation according to Pastor Wallace. In 1976, before Berkowitz began his attacks with his .44 revolver, he saw the movie *Taxi Driver* and I can assure you it triggered the green light for Berkowitz to start his revenge. The main character in the movie, Travis Bickle, was a vietnam veteran who returned home and did not fit in with society...identical to Berkowitz's life. Seeing this movie definitely influenced Berkowitz to act the way he did.

I emailed Pastor Wallace the next day to thank him for his time and insight. I'm very thankful and grateful to have been able to talk to a man like Pastor Tom Wallace who is responsible for saving so many lives. He is a true soldier of Christ, a ninety-one-year-old blessing to the world from God.

Paul: Thank you so much Pastor Wallace, I'm trying my best. I don't know why I'm trying to figure this all out. In my heart I think God is doing something to me. I knew nothing of David Berkowitz a year ago, just a crazy man who talked to a dog that was from my city. When I started to run into lies, I kept walking around asking more questions to get the right answers. Everything has been coming at me, victims, witnesses, inmates, locals, you... it hasn't stopped for a year. Extremely strange coincidences have been going on the entire time and it will not stop. I have not made one dollar and every person that has come to me and helped me find the truth, I have taken in as family. I don't know what I'm doing, but something keeps me going. I can only ask that you help me from the evil that comes with this investigation. I feel great, my heart is always with Jesus, but you never know when evil will fight back, pray for me. I have gotten very ill reports on people who have looked into this case before...I'm just an Italian street kid from New York who shouldn't be looking into any of this. Thank you always for saving so many people. I can only beg God to make me half the man you are.

Here is a letter Berkowitz sent to his father Nathan while he was stationed in Korea:

Dad,

Although I'm your only son, you must admit we have never been close. Actually, it's all my fault. I mean before I was just too stubborn and immature, Dad. I know I often hurt you but I didn't know better. I didn't mean to do all the things I did because I've always loved you and mommy. I just didn't know how to say it. I know I was adopted, but I'm grateful for you because you gave me all you could. The love you and Mom gave me was more than I ever deserved.

When you married Julia, I was very happy although I never expressed it. I was cruel to her. I don't know why. I'm really very very grateful to her because she has given you a new life. After Mom died you became a vegetable, Dad. I felt sorry for you because you didn't deserve it.

I'm glad that you enjoy life. You should, because you deserve it. You have really been a good father. You've worked hard and done your share.

I just can't explain my ideas and philosophies to you. You wouldn't understand. It's all too deep. I feel like a saint sometimes. I guess I'm kind of one. Dad, believing in God is wonderful.

Well, I'll make out okay, I got this thing called faith.

To be honest with you, I have never really told you anything about myself. I really can't now. But just trust me, please. Everything's fine. I hope to see you soon. Just be happy and please try to forget about me, Dad. Make believe you don't have a son please. It's better this way because we may not see each other for a long time.

I hope things are ok in the store. I'm sorry that I can't live up to your expectations. I'm sorry that I'm nothing in society, that is I feel sorry for you because you don't see my point. I'm happy with the way I see things, it's wonderful.

You know Dad, with you and Julia together you may as well be honest with yourself. You know you can be just as happy with yourselves, without me around. I've been a burden to you all your life. Well, I won't be anymore.

I've been too much trouble to you all along and I'll be even more trouble with you now. So please try to forget me Dad, please it will be easier on you. I'm very content with my thoughts. Peace to you. Love to you. Love all of you. Sincerely, Dave

I think David Berkowitz began to change in the Army, Korea to be specific. This, to me, is where Berkowitz started to become the ".44 Caliber Killer." This, to me, is where he started to realize he was alone, and would be alone. His struggles in the Army had him looking for support. When he found the support he needed by becoming a Christain, he would lose his support from his friends and family.

CHAPTER XIV

COPS AND CONVICTS

I was definitely feeling like this investigation was progressing. Giving Larry all this information to use as content for his show was working. I just needed to stay focused on Berkowitz...that's all I had to do.

Larry told me that morning the Dupays stopped responding to him, he lost them. I gave him Zaino and the Dupays weeks ago to contact, I hadn't heard anything back on either of them. I should have contacted them myself.

At this time, I was reading Dr. Abrahamsen's book, *Confessions of Son of Sam*, and can assure you this is also essential to read. Dr. Abrahamsen was the closest doctor to Berkowitz after the arrest and told him right from the beginning of their relationship, he didn't want to hear about Sam and the demons, he wanted to hear about David Berkowitz.

I ended that night finding this article:

Saying he was possessed "by howling demons." Berkowitz told Dr. Daniel Schwartz, "I'm the Son of Sam. It's not me. I was their tool. I want to be David Berkowitz only. He tortured me, never let me sleep, rest, or have peace of mind." Berkowitz said, "They encircled me. They wrecked my life. I know in my heart I'm a good person. My conscience doesn't bother me. I didn't hate these people. Sam did it through me for blood." Then in a grim warning, Berkowitz told Schwartz, "He still wants me, he is still around, he's inside of me."

The next day I emailed Larry, impatient for information.

Paul: Do you want me to call Tommy Zaino? I can talk to him if you think that will work better.

Larry: Yeah, give it a try, I can't seem to connect with him.

On March 11, 2022, Larry made plans with Mike Lorenzo Jr. to meet us at his record shop in Hastings, N.Y. He wanted me to go with him because he wasn't comfortable meeting Mike alone. I told him not to sweat it, when I see Mike, I will know him. Sure enough, as we were walking to Mike's shop, Mike was standing outside, and of course I knew him. He broke up a few keg parties I was at in Untermyer Park.

I shook Mike's hand and told him I remembered him from hanging out on Lake Avenue. Mike did not remember me, and he shouldn't have, he was much older than I was. I was a street kid when he was a cop on our block. He most likely chased me through a few yards back in the day. I probably ripped a few shirts hopping fences from him.

Mike was familiar with just about every person I knew from the Lake Avenue neighborhood and we started to play the famous Yonkers game, "Do you know this guy?" Mike's attitude was exactly like mine, identical. I started to think to myself as I was listening to him talk, I was the way I was because of his generation that came before me, we were raised on the same streets. Mike told Larry everything about Yonkers that I had told him prior. He confirmed there was no twenty-two disciples of hell cult that existed in Yonkers because no one would have tolerated it. The Yonkers locals never took well to outsiders.

Mike was a retired Yonkers Detective who ran into a lot of bad stuff in our city during his years patrolling the Yonkers streets. He entertained Larry and I for over an hour, talking about many of the strange people he came across during his years of service.

After speaking to us about all the evils of Yonkers he came across as a cop, he walked us downstairs to the basement of his record shop. Larry brought his film equipment with him, and Mike agreed to do an interview as he had some original police reports his father left him from the case. The reports were on the Carrs' harassment incidents and his father's phone call with Nann Cassara. The reports showed the Carrs' house had been firebombed and their dog Harvey was shot, but no suspects were ever caught. He told us his father was not ignoring Nann Cassara's complaints when she spoke to his father on the phone about David Berkowitz, but rather, his father was not letting out information to a civilian about the case.

In one of Mike's father's reports, I noticed a cop named Hoyt Rodgers was the police officer who responded to the Carrs' house the day their dog was shot. He also was the officer who spoke to Sam Carr and a witness at the scene who saw a man with blond hair and a rifle, running south on the aqueduct after the incident. I asked Mike if Hoyt was still alive and he said I could find him at Gianna's restaurant in Yonkers. Done deal, I would be seeing Hoyt soon.

I left Mike's record shop that day with some exceptional information, and Mike was on board for future discussions. I got home and talked to three of my friends who were locked up by Mike when they were young. They should have been better at hopping fences.

The following day, I called a good friend of mine who knew the owner of Gianna's restaurant and asked him to tell the owner when he saw Hoyt Rodgers, have him call me. Within one hour I was speaking to the responding officer who had taken Sam Carr's report when his dog was shot at the Carr house. I told Hoyt who I was, what I was doing, and asked if he was comfortable meeting to discuss the reports he took that day. He was busy at the moment but agreed to meet with me on a later date.

That night while I was doing research, I came across an article titled, *Larry Dunn: A Bronx Native and Son of Sam*. Larry was interviewed by a reporter a few weeks prior, and this is what I read:

With his investigative team consisting of former Police Officer John Comparetto, along with his local informant, Justine, Larry may be destined for justice.

Now isn't this something. Larry only knew Comparetto because of me, so I know this article was done when I was involved. Justine had been gone for a long time now, how was she his local informant? He didn't even mention to me he gave this interview.

On March 14, 2022, I went to visit my friend who had worked with Sam Carr…just another day at ground zero. He had a next-door neighbor called Fingers who was fresh out of prison, and guess who he knew? Fingers spent his entire life in and out of prison since he was sixteen. He was used his whole life as a body for hire.

Fingers was sitting on his front porch, so I asked my friend if I could speak with him. It couldn't hurt to ask about David Berkowitz. My friend called him over and introduced us to each other. I knew who he was, but he didn't know me. About ten years ago, Fingers roughed up a guy who owed a friend of mine money. Money on the street must always be settled or messages need to be sent so that others don't make the same mistake.

This was my conversation with Fingers.

Paul: Hey, what's up man?

Fingers: How you doing?

Paul: My friend here says that you knew Berkowitz.

Fingers: Well, I had a problem with him, uh. He was in PC's, a high form of protection. He was fucking a homo. A lot of guys don't know about it. He was fucking this guy named, uh, I can't think of it.

Paul: He was definitely gay?

Fingers: Absolutely, he was fucking a guy that had tits and everything, looked like his girlfriend, you know what I mean. He was telling everybody, no not me, this guy's just my friend. You don't get lost with a guy in a cell for two hours and then tell me your his friend. He would come out smiling, you know.

Paul: What year did you run into him?

Fingers: I did thirty years. He was in PC and there was a guy in there I couldn't stand. I told Berkowitz to do me a favor and get that guy over there. He says what, so you can start yelling? I said what do you give a fuck what I want to do. Go get the guy before I fuck you up when I see you. So, he goes to me, oh you wouldn't talk that way about me if I was... I said you're not a tough guy. You were shooting girls from a distance.

Paul: You had an argument with him?

Fingers: Yeah, because of him I couldn't get close to home. This is how fucked up the government is. They put him in Sullivans County and I'm trying to get there in the worst way. I had about twenty-something years in already. I was ready to go home. I said put me close to the city. They said we can't because David Berkowitz ratted on you and said you had a beef with him. So I said well why can't I go there. They said because he is there and he put a separation order on you. Because what happened was, when I was yelling at him, I couldn't get him. He was behind a gate in APPU, a higher form of protection. Half the population wanted to kill him. Only now he is in a soft jail. They don't do nothing over there. Now he turned his life over to God, he's another bullshit artist. Anyway, I went to go walk away and I said, you fucking rat bastard, and everybody started calling him a rat. Then Berkowitz says, how the fuck am I a rat? How are you a rat? You said the dog made you do it and when you gave up the dog, they put the dog to sleep, you fucking rat. I made a joke out of it and all my friends started laughing at him and started throwing shit at him, real feces.

Paul: Real shit?

Fingers: Real shit. They were throwing it at him through the gates and then he got transferred to Sullivan.

Paul: Did you hear of Berkowitz getting stabbed in prison?

Fingers: That guy was my friend, Hauser. I was with the guy that cut him.

Paul: Oh shit, that is the guy.

Fingers: Yeah, the guy cut him on his neck. Berkowitz was giving Hauser water... Listen, the guy Hauser was a friend of mine. Berkowitz was giving out water and Hauser goes, watch, I'm going to get this cocksucker. I said what are you waiting for?

Paul: Why did he do it?

Fingers: He said that the mafia was going to give him money. That the mafia promised to give guys money.

Paul: Now the mafia was upset with Berkowitz running around the neighborhoods right?

Fingers: The mafia is upset with everybody that makes their neighborhood hot, but their not going to pay you to hit David Berkowitz. They don't pay me for hitting guys that do belong to them.

Paul: So what was his reason for slashing him?

Fingers: Number one, he wanted to get popular, that's the real reason. He said that the mafia was going to pay him, there was a million-dollar contract on him, which…David Berkowitz ain't worth two Snickers bars.

As far as the mafia being involved with the "Son of Sam" crimes, that is completely false. If you look at the history of organized crime, during WWII, you will see law enforcement legally cooperating with the mafia. The mafia played a crucial role in WWII, using its power and control over New York City ports to keep an eye out for boats, or any other suspicious characters entering New York. They even used their leverage to get the U.S. Navy inside an off limits foreign consulate believed to have crucial information on the Nazis. The "Son of Sam" case is the only other time in history you will see law enforcement, without coercion, working together with the mafia as they both were desperately trying to catch the "Son of Sam." New York City in the '70s was completely controlled by organized crime. All of the streets in New York at that time were protected by the mafia, and the "Son of Sam" was insulting them.

The story I get from all the old-timers whenever I bring up the "Son of Sam" to them is always the same…they were waiting for him to come to their neighborhood. Not only was the "Son of Sam" disrespecting their neighborhoods which they were personally in charge of protecting, he had the cops out all over the New York City streets messing with their lifestyle and money. Law enforcement was out heavily and they hated it. They desperately wanted to get the "Son of Sam" off the streets of New York themselves. The old-timers I talked to said they were waiting for the "Son of Sam," loaded and cocked.

I called Hoyt Rodgers that night to see when he was available and we agreed to meet at 3:30 p.m. the next day. I tried to get in touch with Larry to see if this would be a problem for him, but it was 7:30 p.m., and he would never answer his phone after 7:00 p.m.

The next day I emailed Larry.

Paul: I called you last night to see if you were free, but you didn't answer. Hoyt can meet us today at 3:30 p.m. at Gianna's. Bring the reports, he wants to read them.

Larry: Cool, see if you can reschedule for tomorrow. I have a busy day.

I immediately called Larry to tell him this was when Hoyt was available, and I already said we were going to be there. If he picked up his phone the night before, I could have arranged it better. I took what I could get. Hoyt told me 3:30 p.m. today, so I was going with or without him. I didn't need Hoyt to have time to change his mind. Larry sucked it up and agreed to make time for Hoyt's interview.

We met Hoyt that day with Mike Lorenzo Jr. at Gianna's restaurant. I introduced myself to Hoyt and ordered a round of drinks for the table as Hoyt looked over the reports. Hoyt remembered he was sent to the Carrs' house the day their dog Harvey was shot and a bullet, or casing, was taken back to the precinct as evidence, but when he checked a few weeks later, the evidence was missing. Hoyt did not see the dog that day as it was taken for medical help before he arrived.

First question I asked Hoyt was, "Did the Carrs tell you it was Berkowitz who shot their dog?" He said the Carrs did not know who shot their dog at the time. When he interviewed Sam Carr that morning, Sam said he heard gun shots and ran outside to help his dog which he saw had been shot. Sam then saw a man wearing a jean jacket and dungarees carrying a rifle, running north on the aqueduct, but didn't recognize the man, and never mentioned the name Berkowitz to him at all.

I questioned Hoyt, "Do you think the Carrs were involved with Berkowitz?" He firmly answered, "No chance." Hoyt knew Wheat personally and said the Carrs were definitely not involved with Berkowitz. When I asked Hoyt about the witness he had taken a report from that day, who saw a man with blond hair running south on the aqueduct with a rifle, he didn't remember taking that report.

What I took from Hoyt's interview was Harvey, the Carrs' dog, was definitely shot, and this incident was not staged. Hoyt knew Wheat personally and said she did not know it was Berkowitz who shot their dog when the incident occurred. Sam did not know of Berkowitz at this time either, or he would have told Hoyt it was him. If Sam or Wheat knew Berkowitz, why wouldn't they have told the police that morning it was him who shot their dog? Sal DiMaggio told me Wheat knew Berkowitz was harassing her family, and he was the "Son of Sam" before the arrest. What happened from April 27, 1977, to August 9, 1977, that would make Sam and Wheat accuse David Berkowitz of being the "Son of Sam," the man responsible for harassing them.

After our meeting with Hoyt, Larry asked if I would come on his show that night after he interviewed Andrew Dupay's daughter. I agreed so I could thank her for giving us her time.

Before the show started, I set up my laptop and put my earbuds in so I was ready once Larry was finished with the interview. He started his show by telling his audience how he woke up the other day and all the Dupay contacts were in an email thanks to his amazing team of researchers. Team? What team? Who were his amazing team of researchers? He was manipulating the situation like he had done so many times before. His ego wouldn't have it any other way. Now it was an imaginary team he was giving the credit to.

A month earlier, Larry did an interview with another podcaster to discuss the Wicker Street and Neto findings. He discussed all my thoughts and theories as if they were his. It was clear what Larry was doing. I ripped off my earbuds, turned off my computer, and continued to read Dr. Abrahamsen's book.

The next day I reached out to Tommy Zaino. He was a street guy like me, we had a lot in common. After we got a little acquainted, Tommy began to open up and started to tell me what happened at the Moskowitz/Violante shooting.

On July 31, 1977, around 2:10 a.m., Tommy and a girl he was with parked his car in a spot under a streetlight on Shore Parkway, near the Bath Beach Park in Brooklyn. After a few minutes, because of the light, he moved his car forward to another spot. A few minutes later, Stacy Moskowitz and Robert Violante parked in the same spot he had just moved out of. Tommy said he knew Stacy and Robert before this incident, they were friends. When the shooting happened, he saw a man through his rearview mirror come out of the park, shoot into Stacy and Robert's car, then ran back into the park where he came out from.

Right after the attack, Tommy held a bloody Stacy Moskowitz in his arms as he was trying to help her. He then went to the closest precinct to report the incident. I asked Tommy if he thought the shooter was Berkowitz and his response was, "No, the shooter's hair looked completely different from Berkowitz's."

Tommy remembered seeing a yellow Volkswagen bug parked a couple cars in front of him with a female in the drivers seat, and noticed a white van parked down the road behind him during the shooting. He saw no one with the shooter, but didn't think who he saw was Berkowitz. I asked if he had seen anyone near the white van because supposedly there were people filming this shooting. Tommy didn't recall seeing anyone around the white van.

Tommy visited David Berkowitz in prison a few years after this attack, and Berkowitz told him, "You're lucky you pulled your car up a few spots or it would have been you who got shot." Berkowitz denied to Tommy it was him who shot Stacy and Robert.

In the end, Tommy did not think Berkowitz was the shooter in Brooklyn that night, and Berkowitz during his visit, confirmed that. My last question for Tommy was if he liked Maury Terry. He and Maury had gotten along well and were very good friends.

This was all very confusing. I had two legendary ace detectives and a pastor telling me Berkowitz acted alone. I had Maury's researchers and Tommy Zaino telling me there were others involved. At this point, I was already convinced there was not a cult of twenty-two people that Berkowitz belonged to, but I still questioned if he acted alone.

On March 18, 2022, Dave Butler called me after he spoke with Jim Faulkner, Wheat Carr's close friend and former business partner. The guy who bought the Carr house for a suspiciously low price and excavated the backyard right away. Dave told Jim the police were looking into things again and he immediately asked Dave, "What are the cops looking for? Berkowitz was crazy and the Carrs were as innocent as the victims he shot." He mentioned to Dave it was Berkowitz who shot Harvey and rushed off the phone saying, "I have a new life now, away from Yonkers, I got to go." Jim Faulkner insisted the Carrs were good people, that they were victims like the others in Berkowitz's path.

That very same day, John McCabe, Wheat's ex-husband, was contacted by a friend of mine. McCabe said Maury Terry was full of shit and the Carrs were not involved with Berkowitz. He rarely saw John Carr, as John wasn't around Yonkers much. He felt bad for Michael Carr because Michael was gay and misunderstood, Michael was very confused. Jim Faulkner and now John McCabe, who were close to the Carr family, were both saying the Carrs were not involved with Berkowitz. Hoyt Rodgers also recently told me the same.

Larry emailed me later that day.

Larry: I talked to Tommy Zaino. He feels good now about what we are doing.

Yeah, Tommy felt good…me and him hit it off well like two kids who had grown up together, I really liked the guy. Of course he was now comfortable to talk. I did not email Larry back.

Larry: You should email Wheat and give her the old Agostino charm.

Paul: It's too late for that.

This kid had been insulting the Carr family, calling John Carr "Jelly Head John," referring to John's death picture for months on his shows. Wheat stopped emailing him, he had no manners or respect. He was now asking me to email her because he obviously does not know how to talk to people.

I begged Larry this entire time to drop the attitude, lose the ego. Try to be thankful to everyone for giving us their time and trust. That all proved to be way too hard for him to do.

On March 21, 2022, I stopped by Chief Monaco's office to see if he could put me in touch with Peter Intervallo's brother Frank. Frank was a retired Yonkers Police Captain I met a few years back while refurbishing his precinct. Frank's brother Peter, along with Thomas Chamberlain, were police officers assigned to the "Son of Sam" case in Yonkers during the shootings. They were on Detective Michael Lorenzo's reports and dealt with the crimes at the Carr house. Frank was stopping by tomorrow and Chief Monaco said he would give him my number. He also told me Peter's two sons were now working on the force and he would put me in touch with them shortly.

Chief Monaco then handed me reports that were given to him recently from one of his detectives. It was Yonkers Detectives Anthony Cerasi's and Joe Surlack's reports on the "Son of Sam." I quickly skimmed through them as I went to see Detective Geiss. I knew he saw these already and I wanted to know his opinion. I left Geiss's office that day with reports that changed everything.

CHAPTER XV

THE TURNING POINT

After reading these reports, nothing was ever the same again. These were the first Yonkers Police Department reports the public had ever seen since Berkowitz's arrest. They were not official police documents, but were an in-depth summary of David Berkowitz from his birth to his arrest, and all the Yonkers Police work pertaining to the case. Some incidents were missing, so I added everything that was necessary, and corrected all minor mistakes. Here it goes, the turning point in this investigation...the untold truth.

David Richard Berkowitz

Alias

"Son of Sam"

On June 1, 1953, Richard David Falco was born to Joseph Klineman and Elizabeth "Betty" Broder Falco out of wedlock. He was given up for adoption to a Jewish couple four days later. Falco was the last name of Elizabeth's ex-husband Anthony who had left her for another woman more than a decade earlier.

On December 20, 1954, eighteen and a half months after being born, Richard David Falco was officially adopted by Nathan and Pearl Berkowitz of 1105 Stratford Avenue, Bronx, New York. An amended birth certificate was filed in the name of David Richard Berkowitz.

In September of 1957, Berkowitz attended public school #77.

In September of 1964, Berkowitz attended Junior High School #123.

In 1967, Nathan Berkowitz owned a hardware store on Melrose Avenue in the Bronx.

On October 5, 1967, Pearl Berkowitz passed away from breast cancer.

In September of 1968, Berkowitz attended Columbus High School.

In May of 1969, Nathan and David Berkowitz moved to Co-Op City, 170 Dreiser Loop, apartment 17B.

In 1971, Nathan Berkowitz re-married a woman named Julia.

In June of 1971, Berkowitz graduated from Columbus High School.

On June 23, 1971, Berkowitz enlisted into the United States Army and took his basic training at Fort Dix, New Jersey.

On December 15, 1971, Berkowitz was stationed in Korea.

On January 4, 1973, Berkowitz was stationed in Fort Knox, Kentucky.

On June 24, 1974, Berkowitz was honorably discharged from the Army at the rank of Specialist, Fourth Grade.

In November of 1974, Berkowitz moved into studio apartment 5E at 2161 Barnes Avenue in the Bronx. During that time, an eighty-three-year-old woman, who lived under Berkowitz, received threatening letters regarding her noisy television set. Also the superintendent of Berkowitz's building who lived across the street at 2150 Holland Avenue had his dog shot dead.

In 1975, Berkowitz worked for I.B.I. Security Company on 161st Street, Jamaica, Queens. Berkowitz was assigned to guard the Universal Car Loading Company at 351 10th Avenue in Manhattan.

In February of 1975, Berkowitz's father Nathan retired and moved with his wife Julia to Boynton Beach, Florida.

On January 26, 1976, Berkowitz purchased a .45 caliber Commando, Mark III, semi-automatic carbine for $152.50 from Barbara Rutuelo of the Empire Gun and Coin Store on 8th Avenue and 56th Street in the Bay Ridge section of Brooklyn. At that time, Berkowitz produced a validated New York firearms permit.

On February 18, 1976, Berkowitz moved into a second-floor apartment in a private house at 174 Coligni Avenue, New Rochelle, which was owned by Jack and Nann Cassara.

On February 28, 1976, Berkowitz purchased a .22 caliber Glenfield model 60 long rifle.

On April 15, 1976, Berkowitz moved into apartment 7E on 35 Pine Street, Yonkers, New York. Berkowitz at this time drove a yellow, with black top, four door sedan, 1970 Ford Galaxie, registered with the license plate #561-XLB.

On May 13, 1976, at 3:30am, there was a small fire to the exterior of a three-story framed house at 18 Wicker Street, owned by Joaquim Neto. The fire was caused by someone throwing a Molotov cocktail at the second-floor window. Firemen responded and extinguished the fire. Police Officers Jesse Taylor and Kelsey Hogue as well as Detectives Michael Lorenzo and Edward Oakley responded to the scene and investigated the arson.

On May 15, 1976, there was a report of shots fired at 35 Pine Street. Police Officers Dennis Shayne and Guido Fiorelli investigated this complaint which was made by an anonymous telephone call.

On June 10, 1976, at 11:27pm, there was a report of shots fired in the Wicker Street aqueduct area which was investigated and unfounded by Police Officers Fitzgerald and Joseph Kostik. The complaint was made by an anonymous telephone call.

On June 12, 1976, Berkowitz purchased a .44 caliber Charter Arm Bulldog revolver, serial #212927 from the Spring Branch Jewelry and Loan Company in Northwest Houston, Texas. The gun was purchased by a friend of Berkowitz, Billy Dan Parker, who is a twenty-four-year-old construction worker. Berkowitz told Parker it was a long ride home and he needed the gun for protection.

On June 29, 1976, Berkowitz quit his job as a security guard.

In July of 1976, Berkowitz began working for the Co-Op City Taxi Company.

On July 29, 1976, at 1:00am, Donna Lauria, eighteen years of age of 2860 Buhre Avenue in the Pelham Bay section of the Bronx, was shot in the back and killed instantly as she sat in a parked car outside of her home with her friend Jody Valenti, nineteen years of age of 1918 Hutchinson River Parkway. Jody had just driven Donna home. Donna worked as an Emergency Medical Technician for two years at the Empire State Ambulance Service with headquarters at New York Hospital. Donna and Jody were discussing summer vacation plans when the killer walked up to their car, looked directly at them, drew a pistol, and opened fire without saying a word. Jody, a nurse, was wounded in the left thigh as she sat in her double-parked car with Donna in front of Donna's six story apartment building. Jody described the killer as a white male in his late thirties wearing a blue striped shirt.

In August of 1976, a complaint was made that Joaquim, the owner of 18 Wicker Street, was killing everyone in the house. Officers responded and searched the house for dead bodies to no avail. The owner of 18 Wicker Street, Joaquim Neto, knew nothing of what the police were talking about nor who called them. The complaint was made by an anonymous telephone call.

In September of 1976, Berkowitz began working for the Wolf and Murnier Sheet Metal Company in Elmsford, New York.

On October 9, 1976, a Molotov cocktail was thrown through the window of Sam Carr's house at 316 Warburton Avenue in Yonkers at 4:15am. The Molotov cocktail landed in a small office of his telephone answering service which Sam Carr extinguished with a fire extinguisher. Firemen responded and the damage was minimal. Police Officers Berletic and Mazzella as well as Detectives Thomas Dugan and Andy Cavallo investigated the arson.

On October 23, 1976, Carl Denaro, twenty years of age was shot in the back of the head at about 2:00am as he sat in a parked car with his girlfriend, Rosemary Keenan, on 159th Street and 33rd Avenue in Flushing, Queens. Rosemary was also injured during the attack. Carl had shoulder length brown hair and in the dark he might have been mistaken for a female. Carl was hospitalized for three weeks at the Flushing Medical Center where steel was placed in his skull. The injury disqualified him for service in the United States Air Force which he had been about to enter.

On November 27, 1976, Joanne Lomino, eighteen years of age of 83-31 262nd Street, Bellrose, Queens, was shot in the back while sitting with her friend, Donna DeMasi, on the front porch of her home at 12:40am. Joanne and Donna had just returned by subway and bus from a movie in Manhattan. They were alone on the porch when the killer walked up to them and asked for directions. The killer then drew a gun from under his coat and fired several shots at them. One bullet lodged in Joanne's spine and she is paralyzed from the waist down. Joanne is a graduate from Martin Van Buren High School. Donna, seventeen years of age of 8629 267th Street, Floral Park, Queens, is a senior at Martin Van Buren High School. Donna, who was shot through her neck, described the assailant as a white male, between twenty-five and thirty years old, wearing a brown and green three-quarter length coat.

On December 24, 1976, at 11:01pm, Joaquim Neto of 18 Wicker Street reported his German Shepherd had been shot and killed. Two bullet holes were in the aluminum siding in front of his house where the dog was shot. The bullets could not be retrieved as they bounced in an unknown direction. Police Officers Thomas Chamberlain and Peter Intervallo as well as Detectives Walter Moray and William Mcbride conducted the investigation where it appeared that an apparent .22 caliber weapon was used.

On January 30, 1977, Christine Freund, twenty six years of age of 58-18 Linden Street, Ridgewood, Queens, was shot to death at 12:30am as she sat in a parked car in front of 1 Station Square, opposite the Forest Hills Inn at the Long Island Railroad Station in Forest Hills, Queens. Christine was employed as a secretary by Reynolds Security located at 22 Broadway, Queens. John Diel, thirty years of age, a bartender at the Ridgewood III on Grand Ridgewood Avenue in Ridgewood, was unharmed and was with Christine when she was killed. John lives at 6158 Gates Avenue, Ridgewood. John was Christine's steady boyfriend for seven years and was to become her fiance in two weeks on Valentine's Day. The couple had seen the movie "Rocky" at the Continental Theater and ate at the Wine Gallery, both of these places were on Austin Street. When John and Christine finished eating, they walked to John's car, a 1976 red Pontiac Firebird and sat in the car for two minutes while the engine warmed up. The killer approached the car from the rear, firing three shots through the car window that struck Christine in the head and right shoulder.

On March 8, 1977, Virginia Voskerichian, nineteen years of age of 5911 Exeter Street, Forest Hills, was a junior at Columbia University majoring in Russian language studies. Virginia was shot to death between 7:30pm and 7:45pm as she walked in front of 4 Dartmouth Street, not far from her home in Forest Hills. Virginia was slain only a half block from the spot where Christine Freund had been killed five weeks earlier. Virginia was shot in the mouth from close range and was found lying down in shrubbery near the sidewalk. Her purse and some books were lying nearby. Virginia was on her way home from school and had left the I.N.D. subway station at Continental Avenue.

On March 12, 1977, Berkowitz began working at the Bronx General Post Office on Grand Concourse and 149th Street as a mail letter sorter.

On March 15, 1977, Craig Glassman moved into apartment 6E on 35 Pine Street, Yonkers, New York, right beneath Berkowitz.

On April 11, 1977, Sam Carr received an anonymous letter complaining about his dog being a nuisance in the neighborhood.

On April 17, 1977, Valentina Suriani, eighteen years of age of 1950 Hutchinson River Parkway, the Baychester section of the Bronx, was an acting major at Herbert H. Lehman College Bronx, N.Y. She was shot and killed at 3:00am as she sat in a parked car with Alexander Esau in front of 1878 Hutchinson River Parkway near her home. Alexander, twenty years of age, who lives with his father at 352 West 46th Street, was employed as a tow truck operator helper. He was also shot and killed. They had attended a movie prior to being in this location. Both were sitting in the driver's seat when the killer approached on the driver's side and fired through the closed window. Donna Lauria and Jody Valenti were shot just a few blocks away. At the scene the killer left a letter addressed to NYC Detective Joseph Borrelli. The letter was described by police as rambling, incoherent, and ghoulish in tone. The car Alexander and Valentina were sitting in belonged to Alexander's brother.

On April 20, 1977, Sam Carr received a second anonymous letter complaining about his dog being a nuisance in the neighborhood. This time the author of the letter was threatening Sam Carr.

On April 21, 1977, Sam Carr of 316 Warburton Avenue reported to the Yonkers Police that he had been receiving threatening letters. One which came on April 11 stating legal papers would be filed relative to his dog barking. He received another letter on April 20, complaining again about his dogs barking. This time the writer claimed his life was being destroyed and he had nothing to lose, no peace in his life, or his family's life, until Sam Carr's life was ended. The first letter was anonymous while the second was signed "a citizen." Wheat Carr, who is Sam Carr's daughter, was also present during this interview. Police Officers Peter Intervallo and Thomas Chamberlain as well as Detectives Reynold Baker, William Kennedy, Michael Lorenzo and Edward Oakley made the investigation.

On April 27, 1977, at 9:31am, Sam Carr of 316 Warburton Avenue reported his dog Harvey, a black Labrador Retriever was shot. Mr. Carr stated he heard three shots, went behind his house where he found his dog shot, then observed a white male wearing a dungaree jacket and pants, carrying a rifle, heading North on the aqueduct. Police Officers Wargoki and Hoyt Rodgers investigated the shooting and spoke to a witness who refused to give his name. The witness reported he had observed a white male with blonde hair, six feet tall, about eighteen years old, carrying a rifle, running south on the aqueduct.

On June 6, 1977, Jack and Nann Cassara received a get-well card with a picture of a dog on the front. The get-well card stated the sender was sorry to hear Jack Cassara had fallen off the roof and for him to be careful and let the writer know if Nann needed anything. The card was signed Sam and Frances, and the return address on the envelope was Mr. and Mrs. Sam Carr of 316 Warburton Avenue. Nann Cassara, upon receiving the card, called the Carr residence and realized the Carrs did not send the card, nor did the two families know each other. They both arranged to meet at the Carr house on June 9.

On June 7, 1977, Craig Glassman received a threatening letter which referred to him as "Satan's child." The letter also called him "Master Glassman," claiming if he didn't "obey thes commands, the commands of your father then you will be punished." The return address on the envelope of this letter read: Mother, The Cemetary, 174 Coligni Avenue, New Rochelle, New York 10801.

On June 9, 1977, Jack and Nann Cassara met with Sam and Frances Carr at their house with the get-well card. Sam Carr, upon seeing the writing of the get-well card noted that it appeared to be in the same handwriting as the threatening letters he was receiving.

On June 10, 1977, Nann Cassara discusses with her son Steven Cassara her meeting with the Carrs, and how the get-well card handwriting matched the Carr's threatening letters. Nann's son Steven points out that the front of the get-well card had a dog on it and the Carr letters were complaining about a dog. Steven then reminds his mother about the tenant, David Berkowitz, who they were renting the apartment to a year ago, left their house in a rage complaining about their dogs. Steven's father, Jack Cassara, then looked up David Berkowitz's name in the phone book and realized Berkowitz was living right behind the Carr house at 35 Pine Street in Yonkers. Nann Cassara then calls Sam Carr to tell him she thinks it is David Berkowitz, an old tenant of hers, who was sending those letters and Berkowitz was living right behind them at 35 Pine Street.

Also on this day, Sam Carr reports to Yonkers Police Officers Peter Intervallo and Thomas Chamberlain that David Berkowitz, who was living at 35 Pine Street, was responsible for sending those threatening letters to his house. Sam Carr also informed them about the get-well card the Cassaras received. Sam Carr now thinks Berkowitz was responsible for shooting his dog. Officers Intervallo and Chamberlain indicated that the Detective Division should be notified as they felt Berkowitz was responsible for the dog being shot and sending the threatening letters. Sam Carr then goes to the Yonkers Detective Division to report to them the same.

On June 23, 1977, Yonkers Detectives Michael Lorenzo and Edward Oakley sent samples of David Berkowitz's signature from his 35 Pine Street lease, along with copies of the threatening letters sent to Sam Carr and the get-well card sent to the Cassaras to the F.B.I. laboratory in Washington, D.C.

On June 26, 1977, Judy Placido, seventeen years of age of 2208 Wickham Avenue, of the Pelham Bay section in the Bronx, was shot in the right temple, right shoulder, and back of neck as she sat in a parked car at 3:20am with Salvatore Lupo, a friend, outside of 45-39 211th Street, just south of 45th Road and Bayside, Queens. The couple walked to their car from the Elephas Discotheque on 211th Street and Northern Boulevard. Judy and Salvatore were sitting in a car belonging to a friend of Sal's for about ten minutes when the assailant approached from behind and fired four shots wounding them both. Like many of the other victims, she had long brown hair. Salvatore Lupo, twenty years of age, a Maspeth, Queens resident whose address was withheld by Police, was shot in the right forearm as he sat in the parked car with Judy.

On July 12, 1977, Sam Carr contacted Jimmy Breslin of the Daily News to tell him he saw a composite drawing of the "Son of Sam" in an issue of Time magazine and thought it resembled David Berkowitz. Sam Carr also told Jimmy Breslin about the incidents concerning the threatening letters and of his dog being shot. Jimmy Breslin advised Sam Carr to call Inspector Timothy Dowd of the 109th Precinct in Queens. Sam Carr called the 109th precinct, but Inspector Dowd was not there. He gave his information to an unknown Detective.

On July 13, 1977, Craig Glassman received a second threatening letter telling him "Mister Carr" is his "commander," and not to "stop issuing Captain Carr's wrath upon the world." The return address on the envelope of this letter read: Bro Demesmutz, Command Post 316, Gibor Merritt Aves, Bronx 10475.

On July 31, 1977, at 2:05am, Police Officer Michael Cataneo Jr., of the New York City Police Department, issued a summons to a 1970 Ford Galaxie, New York registration #561-XLB for illegally parking next to a fire hydrant at 290 Bay 17th Street in Brooklyn, summons #906953-2. At this time a witness, Cacilia Davis of Bay 17th Street, Brooklyn, observed a man fitting the description of the ".44 Caliber Killer" carrying a package as she was walking her dog before the shooting occured. She notified Brooklyn detectives after learning about the shooting of Stacy Moskowitz and Robert Violante.

Also on this day, at 2:35am, Stacy Moskowitz, twenty years of age of 1740 East 5th Street Flatbush, Brooklyn, was shot in the head and killed as she was sitting in a car at a lovers' lane near the Bath Beach park in Brooklyn. Stacy was with Robert Violante, twenty years of age of 1972 Bay Ridge Parkway Bensonhurst, Brooklyn, who was shot in the head, wounded, and was blinded.

On August 4, 1977, Yonkers Detectives received the writing samples they sent to the F.B.I laboratory in Washington, D.C. and the tests came back inconclusive.

On August 5, 1977, Police Officers Peter Intervallo and Thomas Chamberlain report to Sergeant Michael Novotny their suspicions on Berkowitz being the "Son of Sam." The officers also went to the Yonkers Police Department Intelligence Division and spoke to Detective Richard Salverson of the New York City Police Department Intelligence Division and Detective William Grogan of the Yonkers Police Department Intelligence Division to give them Berkowitz's description, car model, color, and license plate.

On August 6, 1977, at 7:30am, Craig Glassman, who is a member of the Westchester County Auxiliary Sheriff's Department, and has a police officers status, reported an arson at his apartment 6E, 35 Pine Street Yonkers, New York. The fire was started at the front door of Craig Glassman's apartment. Garbage and .22 caliber bullets were placed at the base of his door and the fire was lit causing the bullets to explode, awakening Glassman and his neighbors. The fire was extinguished by neighbors and the Yonkers Fire Department who responded. The damage was contained mainly to the door and door frame. Craig Glassman gave a report to Lieutenant Starkey of the Yonkers Fire Department at 7:34am. The report stated Craig Glassman told Lieutenant Starkey he had complaints from a neighbor who lives directly above him about his television set being too loud. Lieutenant Starkey went to Berkowitz's apartment 7E and knocked on his door to speak with him about the fire, but there was no one home.

Also on this day, at 7:35am, Yonkers Police Officers Wisner and Thomas Chamberlain, along with Detectives Murdo Urquhart and Solomon Spivey interrogate Craig Glassman upon arrival about the fire set to his door. Craig Glassman then shows the officers a threatening letter he received regarding harm being done to him which was signed, "Deso Demesmutz." Craig Glassman states he received other letters which were part of an investigation which was being conducted by the Westchester County Sheriff's Department. Craig Glassman also states he was working with Investigator David Feliciano and refused to discuss it any further. Officer Chamberlain notices Sam Carr's name in Craig Glassman's letters and tells Glassman, Berkowitz is a possible "Son of Sam" suspect. Officer Chamberlain and Craig Glassman tried to contact Berkowitz by knocking on his door, but there was no one home. They also went up the fire escape to look into Berkowitz's apartment, but there were blankets covering the window.

Also on this day, Detective Urquhart, after viewing one of the letters Craig Glassman had in his possession, observed the name Carr and immediately realized there was a prior investigation being conducted by Detectives Lorenzo and Oakley, who he then summoned to the scene. After viewing the letters, Detectives Lorenzo and Oakley stated Berkowitz was a possible suspect, and along with Detectives Urquhart and Spivey, proceeded to Berkowitz's apartment and found no one home. They then searched the area for Berkowitz's car, but were unable to locate it. The detectives made three more visits that day to Berkowitz's apartment, to no avail. Upon leaving the building, after the fire, Craig Glassman found another letter in his mailbox from Berkowitz.

Also on this day, Sam Carr went to the 109th Precinct in Queens at 11:30am and informed an unknown detective and captain of his belief that Berkowitz was the ".44 Caliber Killer." Sam Carr also showed them copies of the threatening letters he received. Sam Carr then informed Detective Lorenzo by phone late that afternoon he had been to the 109th Precinct and gave them information on Berkowitz.

On August 8, 1977, Yonkers Detectives Lorenzo and Oakley notified Detective Richard Salverson of the New York Police Department of all the new information on David Berkowitz. The Yonkers detectives also met with Investigator David Feliciano and exchanged information.

On August 9, 1977, at 8:20pm, Detective James Justus of the New York City Police Department, Tenth Homicide Zone, Brooklyn, called the Yonkers Police Department and spoke to Wheat Carr, a civilian employee of the Communication Division for the Yonkers Police Department. Detective Justus explained he was working on the ".44 Caliber Killer" case and was trying to contact David Berkowitz relative to him receiving a parking ticket in the area of a shooting, as he might be a possible witness. Wheat Carr then informed Detective Justus she thought Berkowitz was responsible for her father's dog being shot and the threatening letters that were sent to her father Sam Carr. Wheat Carr also told Detective Justus about the Molotov cocktail that was thrown at her house and Craig Glassman's fire to his apartment. Wheat Carr then notifies Detective Justus that she had been working with Police Officers Peter Intervallo and Thomas Chamberlain on the matter.

Also on this day, Wheat Carr notifies Detective Lorenzo and Oakley that she had received a telephone call from Detective Justus regarding this investigation, where the detectives then spoke to Detective Justus and gave him the information and facts that they had on David Berkowitz, also that they had spoken to Detective Richard Salverson.

On August 10, 1977, NYPD Detectives Edward Zigo and John Longo of the 10th Homicide Division of Brooklyn, appeared at the Yonkers Detective Division and stated they were pursuing the ".44 Caliber Killer." They were notified of the telephone conversation between Detective Justus and Wheat Carr. They were also aware of the parking ticket issued to David Berkowitz's car on July 31, 1977, in the vicinity of the last homicide. Detective Zigo was given copies of the threatening letters received by Sam Carr and Craig Glassman and stated that he was going to speak with David Berkowitz. Detective Zigo requested to speak with Wheat Carr and arrangements were made with Captain Owen McClain for the interview to take place at 3:00pm.

After speaking with Wheat Carr, Detective Zigo and Longo proceeded to 35 Pine Street and observed Berkowitz's car, a 1970 Ford Galaxie, four door sedan, yellow with a black vinyl top, New York registration #561-XLB parked in front. Detective Zigo looked through the back window of the vehicle and saw what appeared to be an illegal weapon. Upon opening the back door, which was closed but unlocked, they found a .45 caliber machine gun, and a letter addressed to "Attention Suffolk County-N.Y.P.D. and Press." At this point the handwriting on the envelope appeared to be the same as the two previous letters sent to the press, which took credit for the .44 caliber killings.

Detective Zigo and Longo then notified their superiors in New York City, who then responded to 35 Pine Street. Detective Zigo, along with Detective Michael

Shilensky of the Legal Department of the New York City Police Department went to the Yonkers Detective Division and appraised them of the facts wherein a search warrant was drawn up for David Berkowitz's car and apartment.

During this time the search warrants were being drawn up, David Berkowitz's car and apartment were kept under surveillance by the New York Police Department. Craig Glassman exited from 35 Pine Street, approached David Berkowitz's car, and was stopped by the New York City Police Department. Craig Glassman stated his identification and told detectives he knew what David Berkowitz looked like and offered to assist in the identification of Berkowitz if, and when, he came out of the building.

At 9:15pm, David Berkowitz exited 35 Pine Street carrying a paper bag and entered his car, wherein he was apprehended, arrested, and conveyed to the Yonkers Detective Division where he was advised of his rights by Sergeant Frank Fernandes and Detective Michael Shilensky. At this point David Berkowitz admits he is the "Son of Sam." Berkowitz's vehicle and apartment were kept under surveillance as the search warrants were being signed by City Court Judge Robert Cacace at his home on Mohawk Road.

Detective Zigo then searched Berkowitz's car in the presence of other members of the New York City Police Department and Detectives Joseph Surlak, Anthony Cerasi and Sergeant Frank Fernandes of the Yonkers Police Department. On the front seat, wrapped in plastic and in a paper bag, a .44 caliber Charter Arm Bulldog revolver, serial #212927 was fully loaded and found. On the back seat, a .45 caliber Commando Mark III carbine, serial #23954 was found inside a cloth bag. There was also ten .45 caliber thirty round clips and one hundred and seventy-three rounds of forty-five caliber live ammunition. The aforementioned letter addressed to Suffolk County New York Police Department and Press was also seized.

Searching the apartment, the New York City detectives seized: A Ithaca deerslayer 12 gauge pump action shotgun, serial #371494956. A Charter Arms AR-7 Explorer, .22 caliber rim fire semi-automatic rifle box, serial

#TN3-13-155. A .22 caliber Glenfield model 60 long rifle, serial #2-5444401. A Glenfield 4x15 powered, Opti-centered scope. Also seized were a large amount of live ammunition, maps of New York and the surrounding areas, clothing, personal writings written by David Berkowitz, a Lafayette portascam receiver and a personal telephone book, along with other personal items. David Berkowitz was transported to the New York City Police Department, along with his car.

On August 11, 1977, New York City Police Department Forensic Unit, with Lieutenant Luisi in command, processed and photographed Berkowitz's car and apartment. They also made a diagram of the apartment. The apartment was secured by Detectives Thomas and Andy Cavallo. Detective McClain of the Yonkers Police Department Criminal Identification Unit responded to the apartment and took photographs. Other valuable property such as Berkowitz's television set, stereo unit, a fan, a vacuum cleaner, an alarm clock, were all transported to the property room of the Yonkers Police Department for safekeeping and the door was secure.

Also on this day, at 3:01pm, the following named persons were apprehended in David Berkowitz's apartment by Yonkers Police Officers John McCabe and Jesse Taylor after they broke into Berkowitz's apartment by going through a window from the fire escape: David C. Berliner, white male, thirty-four years of age of 175-20 Wexford Terrace Jamaica, Queens, who is a reporter for the Washington Post. Leonard Detrick, white male, sixty years of age of 28 Columbus Avenue, Closter, New Jersey, who is a photographer for the Daily News. Theodore Cowell, white male, thirty-four years of age of 585 West End Avenue, Manhattan, who is a photographer for TIME magazine. Robert Kalfus, white male, twenty-five years of age of 137-16 Booth Avenue, Flushing, Long Island, who is a photographer for the New York Post. All their used film was confiscated along with one cassette tape. They were charged with criminal trespassing and were booked at Central Booking.

On August 12, 1977, all those who trespassed into Berkowitz's apartment were arraigned in Special Sessions Court before Judge Robert W. Cacace who also issued an Order of Seizure for all types of film or photographs regarding the arrest of the photographers.

On August 13, 1977, photos of the inside of Berkowitz's apartment appeared in the centerfold of the New York Post. It is obvious that Robert Kalfus somehow managed to hide a roll of film from the Police.

On August 17, 1977, at a prearranged meeting with the Detective Division of the New York City Police Department, Inspector Timothy Dowd, Chief of the Queens Homicide Task Force, read out loud the personal writings of David Berkowitz which were seized from his apartment, pursuant to a search warrant which was executed on August 10, 1977.

The general theme of these writings was that a "Blood Monster" was contained within the house of Sam Carr. That Sam Carr, together with John Carr, and The Wicker Street Gang, which were living in satanic headquarters at 18 and 22 Wicker Street in Yonkers, were commanding Berkowitz to kill. A person named Joaquin from The Wicker Street Gang, Craig Glassman, Nann and Jack Cassara of New Rochelle, were the leaders and driving force of the satanic cult which commanded Berkowitz to go out and kill. It should be noted that all of the persons Berkowitz refers to...Sam Carr, Joaquin Goncalo, Jack and Nann Cassara were owners of noisy dogs, with the exception of Craig Glassman, who Berkowitz, in his writings, states that he played his television set exceptionally loud.

On September 1, 1977, Yonkers Police Department advised their Corporation Counsel that no material is to be released to any agency because of the pending lawsuits against the city.

And there you have it...the first Yonkers Police Department reports to ever be shared with the public dealing with this case.

Chief Monaco has done Yonkers proud, and I give him back my utmost gratitude. He is a brother of mine in this deep Yonkers family. Chief Monaco also gave this investigation Detective Geiss. These two men are responsible for releasing the truth, which had been held back from the public for over forty years. I am beyond grateful for knowing these two men.

Now, let's take a look at these reports. Remember, Maury did not see this during his investigation. The YPD closed this case after Berkowitz's arrest because of lawsuits from some of the victims' families. I originally thought they closed the case because of an illegal search and seizure done to Berkowitz's car...I was wrong. The YPD closed this case a few weeks after Berkowitz's arrest and the entire department was told not to discuss the case with anyone to protect the city from lawsuits.

On June 1, 1953, Richard David Falco was born to a single mother named Elizabeth Broder Falco. Elizabeth was divorced at this time for over ten years from a man named Anthony Falco who had left her for another woman. In 1952, Elizabeth became pregnant while having an affair with a married man named Joseph Kleinman. Joseph threatened Elizabeth not to keep the baby or she would never see him again. Elizabeth then made arrangements to give her child up for adoption to a Jewish couple named the Berkowitz' just four days after Richard's birth. On December 20, 1954, Nathan and Pearl Berkowitz officially adopted Richard David Falco and changed his name to David Richard Berkowitz. At a young age, David was told by his adopted parents his biological mother died giving birth to him and his biological father could not care for him alone, so he was given up for adoption.

In 1967, Berkowitz's adopted mother Pearl passed away from breast cancer. He was only fourteen at the time and it was the first real loss he experienced in his life. He loved his mother Pearl and from the research I have done, this loss greatly affected him. Less than four years later in 1971, Berkowitz's father Nathan re-married a woman named Julia, and I think this may have factored into Berkowitz enlisting into the Army. After just a few months of living with his father and Julia, Berkowitz graduated high school and headed straight into the Army for what would be the worst decision of his life. When he returned home from the Army in June of 1974 to live with his father and Julia, he moved out on his own only five months later. I think Berkowitz's relationship with his stepmother might have been a factor in some of the life choices he made, and those choices impacted his life not the way he wanted.

In November of 1974, Berkowitz moved to 2161 Barnes Avenue, Apt. 5E in the Bronx. While living at Barnes Avenue, an eighty-three-year-old woman, who lived beneath Berkowitz, received a threatening letter regarding her noisy television set. Also, the superintendent of Berkowitz's building had his dog shot and killed, which Berkowitz admitted to shooting in the Klausner book. This is the first report of Berkowitz being bothered by noise, sending threatening letters, and a dog being shot within the vicinity of where he was living.

In February of 1976, Berkowitz moved to 174 Coligni Avenue in New Rochelle, the Cassara house. I spoke with Steven Cassara, who told me Berkowitz was fine until one morning when Berkowitz got upset his two German Shepherds were barking and began pacing in his driveway yelling. Steven went nose to nose with Berkowitz that morning as they argued about his dogs. We see here again, Berkowitz is clearly bothered by noise from barking dogs.

In April of 1976, Berkowitz moved to 35 Pine Street in Yonkers, overlooking the beautiful Hudson River, but what Berkowitz didn't realize was, he moved into the worst possible place on earth when it came to barking dogs. His apartment window was above three residents he would come to hate. The Carrs had a dog, 22 Wicker had one, and 18 Wicker had one also. I talked to some people who lived in that area at the time, they said their dog never shut up. The Wicker area was notorious for public dog walking. There were dogs everywhere around Wicker Street. Berkowitz moved three times trying to get away from his uncomfortable surroundings, trying to help his situation, and here he was, in the absolute worst possible place.

The barking dogs around Berkowitz were a definite factor which drove him over the edge. A factor that for sure made him give up with no hope. Berkowitz tried to place himself away from what was bothering him, but it got worse every time he moved.

On April 27, 1977, Sam Carr's dog was shot at his home, 316 Warburton Avenue. Yonkers Police responded to the scene. I had the opportunity to talk in person with one of the responding officers, Hoyt Rodgers. Hoyt told me the Carrs did not know who shot their dog at the time. He knew Wheat on a personal level, he dated one of Wheat's good friends. He confidently told me there was no way the Carrs were involved with Berkowitz, and the Carrs definitely did not know him. The "Son of Sam" shootings started nine months prior to this incident and the Carrs knew nothing at this point of David Berkowitz's existence. Sam and Wheat did not know Berkowitz, but could it be possible they were unaware of John's relationship with him? After all, who was stalking Sylvia? Who started harassing the Netos before Berkowitz moved into town?

On June 6, 1977, Jack and Nann Cassara received a get-well card with a picture of a dog on the front cover from Sam and Frances Carr. When they called the Carrs to ask about the card, they were informed the Carrs did not send it. Both families then met on June 9th, and the Carrs showed the Cassaras anonymous threatening letters they were also receiving. The handwriting in the get-well card and the Carrs anonymous letters seemed to have been written by the same person, but they had no idea who it was.

This was the get-well card sent to the Cassaras:

Dear Jack,

I'm sorry to hear about that fall you took from the roof of your house.

Just want to say "I'm sorry" But I'm sure it won't be long Until you feel much better. Healthy. well and strong!

Please be careful next time. Since your going to be confined for a long time, let us know if Nann needs anything...Sincerely: Sam and Frances

The return address on the envelope was Mr. and Mrs. Sam Carr, 316 Warburton Avenue, Yonkers, NY 10701.

On June 10, 1977, Nann Cassara realized, with the help of her son Steven, Berkowitz was the person who sent them the get-well card. Nann immediately called Sam Carr to inform him of what they figured out. Sam then went to the Yonkers Police and brought Berkowitz to their attention as the person who was harassing him with threatening letters. Now Sam also thought Berkowitz shot their dog, as it was him who was writing the letters. Sam at this point did not say to the police Berkowitz was the "Son of Sam," but why didn't the police just go to 35 Pine Street and question Berkowitz about the letters sent to the Carrs? Regardless if the police thought they were crank letters and it was just a dog that had been shot, firearms were used, and this wasn't the only dog shot in the area.

A Molotov cocktail used on the Netos...no suspect. A Molotov cocktail used on the Carrs...no suspect. The Netos' dog was shot...no suspect. The Carrs' dog was shot...no suspect. A SWAT call to the Netos...no suspect. Shots fired at 35 Pine Street...no suspect. Shots fired in the Wicker aqueduct area...no suspect. Now they had a suspect, why did they not question Berkowitz?

On July 12, 1977, Sam Carr saw a sketch of the "Son of Sam" in *Time* magazine and contacted Jimmy Breslin at the *Daily News* to tell him the sketch looked like David Berkowitz. Breslin instructed Sam to call Inspector Timothy Dowd at the 109th Precinct in Queens, and give his tip to him. Sam did that, but Inspector Dowd wasn't there. He still gave his tip to a law enforcement officer. This is the first time Sam is suspecting David Berkowitz of being the "Son of Sam," the person harassing him.

How did Sam Carr know what Berkowitz looked like if he didn't know him? I will tell you how. A month earlier, with the help of the Cassaras, Sam and Wheat were told it was Berkowitz who was sending them threatening letters. Wheat Carr, who worked with the Yonkers

Police, had a few of her law enforcement connections look up David Berkowitz. What her connections came back to her with was a driver's license with Berkowitz's photo on it. You might say though, in the '70s, there were no photos on our driver's licenses in New York, and you are correct. Remember though, in 1976, Berkowitz was working for the Co-Op City Taxi Company, and in order to drive a taxi in New York State, you needed to have a photo on your taxi license. This was the license her connections produced for her. How did I know this information? You will find out later on.

Why did Jimmy Breslin not act on Sam Carr's tip? Breslin was probably receiving hundreds of phone calls a week from people who thought they knew who the "Son of Sam" was. Perhaps Breslin, in the beginning, did entertain a few tips, obviously with no success. After a while of unsuccessful leads, he started to direct all the information that came to him to Inspector Dowd who was in charge of the New York City Omega Task Force, which was designed to handle all of the "Son of Sam" tips. Breslin did not blow off Sam, in fact, he did what he was supposed to do, lead the tips to the professionals who were handling the case.

Why did the 109th Precinct not act on Sam Carr's tip? Again, you have to understand, the New York City Omega Task Force was receiving hundreds of phone calls a week on "Son of Sam" suspects. What should they prioritize, and how do they know what tips to pay attention to immediately? I'm sure they were going to look into Sam's tip, but they had an overwhelming job to do, and Sam's tip may have had to wait until other leads were done being looked into. This might have been perceived as neglect, and the families of the victims could have used this in their lawsuits, but in reality, the New York City law enforcement was undermanned and were 100 percent trying their best to get their job done.

On July 31, 1977, the morning of the Moskowitz/Violante shooting, Cacilia Davis, a key witness, had been out with a friend. When she returned to her home on Bay 17th Street in Brooklyn around 2:00 a.m., there were no parking spots for her friend to park. They double parked as she exited her friend's car, said goodnight, and walked to her building. This was when Cacilia noticed a policeman putting parking tickets on some illegally parked cars. She then went inside her apartment and got her dog to take him for a walk. While walking back to her building, a man came from behind a tree and walked toward her. The man gave her and her dog a long, sharp look, then turned and walked into one of the courtyards between the buildings. These sequence of events are the most important key moments in this entire case.

When Cacilia Davis decided to contact Brooklyn Detective Joe Strano a day after the shooting to tell him she saw a strange man in the area before the attack, she reminded him there was a policeman ticketing cars in front of her building that morning when she returned home. With this information, Detective Strano found four parking tickets issued that day in the area. One of them was issued to license plate #561-XLB, David Berkowitz.

On August 5, 1977, Yonkers Police Officers Peter Intervallo and Thomas Chamberlain are the first law enforcement on record to inform the New York City Police Department (Detective Richard Salverson) about David Berkowitz, as they suspected he was the "Son of Sam." This was five days before the arrest, and if Officers Intervallo and Chamberlain were paid attention to, we would have had a completely different scenario on how Berkowitz was captured. These officers did a lot of work behind the scenes to be the first to suspect Berkowitz of being the "Son of Sam." This is what Detective William Powers was trying to say in his letter to *New York Post* editor Steve Dunleavy. The Yonkers Police Department reported Berkowitz to the NYPD and was ignored.

August 6, 1977 was a crazy day for David Berkowitz. He lit a fire outside Craig Glassman's door and was seen walking around Warburton Avenue, wearing a wig, strapped with a gun, asking for Mickey Carr. Why was he looking for "Mickey," Wheat Carr? I think because Berkowitz knew his time as the "Son of Sam" was coming to an end and he wanted to kill Wheat before his capture. I think he knew Sam and Wheat were on to him. This was the day the Yonkers Police thought for sure David Berkowitz was the "Son of Sam" as Craig Glassman's fire alerted them to 35 Pine Street and they saw Glassman's letters.

The Yonkers Police and Fire Department tried to contact Berkowitz on this day, but were unsuccessful in doing so. After the fire to Craig Glassman's door, Sam Carr drove down to the 109th Precinct to speak with Inspector Dowd at 11:30 a.m. He didn't get to talk to him, but he did get to speak with a detective and captain at the precinct. Sam was clearly going out of his way to get law enforcement, and even Jimmy Breslin to pay attention to him, but they just wouldn't listen.

Before Berkowitz attacked Stacy Moskowitz and Robert Violente, he saw a police officer place a ticket on his car. Berkowitz's uncontrollable desire to continue his chaos and shoot Stacy Moskowitz and Robert Violante after he was issued this parking ticket shows you he was willing to take the risk of being caught to play his role as the "Son of Sam." To me, the couples in a parked car scenario at the park in Brooklyn that night for the taking was too much for Berkowitz to pass up. No parking ticket was going to get in his way of giving the media what they wanted. Targets had become scarce with everyone staying inside fearing him. He needed to take advantage of the perfect ".44 Caliber Killer" scenario...he needed his attention. This decision by Berkowitz to ignore the parking ticket would finally get the NYPD to contact the YPD on August 9, 1977, and find out that Sam Carr was right. This is where we can thank Wheat Carr. If Wheat hadn't been working at the Yonkers Police Dispatch to receive Detective Justus's call and give him vital information about Berkowitz, the Yonkers Police would have been dealing with the situation on their own. The New York City Police would have never quickly acted and been in Yonkers the next day without speaking to Wheat.

Sam and Wheat Carr, who for many years have been badly branded as a part of these crimes by Maury Terry, deserve the right recognition. Before these reports surfaced, we were made to believe Sam and Wheat were railroading Berkowitz to cover up what really happened and who was really involved. We were made to believe Sam and Wheat Carr were avoiding law enforcement by hiring a lawyer to protect them from being interrogated. I now see the Carrs were probably interrogated by law enforcement more than anyone in this case. The facts are in these reports, Sam and Wheat were actually working with law enforcement.

If Sam and Wheat Carr had anything at all to do with Berkowitz, why would they both go out of their way to chance bringing attention to themselves? We all need to stop thinking law enforcement was gullible enough to be fooled by Sam and Wheat. That was not the case one bit. Again, was it possible John Carr was involved with Berkowitz and Sam and Wheat did not know?

On August 17, 1977, Inspector Timothy Dowd read letters written by David Berkowitz that were confiscated from Berkowitz's apartment the night of his arrest. These letters claimed Sam Carr, together with John Carr, Joaquin Goncalo, Craig Glassman, Nann and Jack Cassara, were all a part of a satanic cult who commanded Berkowitz to kill. I have never seen the name Joaquin Goncalo before. Could he be "*Joaquin the Joker*," the person Berkowitz said lived at 18 Wicker Street?

These reports were extremely important to see. They are written evidence as to what really occurred from the people involved. This is the first time Yonkers law enforcement released anything they had on this case, and I am beyond grateful to be able to present this to you.

I met Larry the next day and gave him a copy of these reports. This was breakthrough material I was giving him, first of its kind. When I mentioned I was going to give a copy of these reports to Carl and Josh, he got extremely pissed off, then angrily said, "No, you can't do that, fuck them."

Carl has been under the impression for years that Wheat may be the person who shot him and these reports showed Wheat was innocent. It was important to me for Carl to see these reports right away, I knew he had not seen them before. Larry continued on with his tantrum saying, "If you give these to him, he will be handing it out to everyone before I can do my shows."

This kid was making me sick. I sat there listening to him complain about how Carl and Josh did nothing for him. Larry didn't understand how lucky I was law enforcement gave me these reports. I told him he had three days to put the reports out and then Carl was getting them. I gave him three days just to act like I was budging a little so he would shut up. How could I hold this information from Carl when it had Wheat all over it? I needed to show Carl Wheat was innocent.

Josh was also going to get these reports, he was why I was doing all this. These people have been at this for years and never saw the Yonkers law enforcement side of things before. These reports were the truth, and these people needed to see them. This wasn't about me or Larry, this was about the Netos, Carl, Wheat. This was about Yonkers and the people who had been wrongfully accused.

Later that day Sylvia Neto called after remembering there was a lady named Barbara Ivey who lived at 22 Wicker Street during the shootings. Barbara was a bartender at Dickies Lounge which used to be on the corner of Warburton Avenue and Wicker Street, right across from the Carr house.

Need I say this was a job for Penny? In one hour I had what I needed to contact Barbara. I got in touch with Barbara's daughter-in-law and asked if she could have her husband, Barbara's son Kevin, give me a call. She was happy to do that and began to tell me how interested Kevin was in the "Son of Sam."

As we talked, I mentioned some people I knew from her area. Turned out, Kevin's best friend was Paul Hudson. I grew up with Paul, he was on my basketball and football teams when we played for the North Yonkers Boys Club. Also friends with Kevin was Jason Phillips, aka Jason Glover, aka Jadakiss from The L.O.X., who also played on my football team growing up. Paul's father coached us in peewee football. He was one of the best coaches

I ever had in my life. Picture Lawrence Taylor as a peewee football coach, he put the fire in me. When I was twelve, he trained me like a warrior, I owed this guy. At the least with this contact, I could maybe get to speak with Mr. Hudson who I hadn't heard from in thirty-three years. I would love to thank him for what he instilled in me, the heart of a lion.

Kevin called a few hours later, his mother was sick in the hospital and couldn't speak. I was sorry to hear that and wished his mom well. I told Kevin I grew up with Paul Hudson and we talked for a while about Yonkers. Kevin was Yonkers, born and raised. I brought up David Berkowitz to him and he was very much into the case. He was only five in 1976 and didn't remember seeing Berkowitz in his neighborhood. I asked if his mother knew Berkowitz and he answered, "No, but we knew the Carrs, my mother was friendly with the family. I used to play with Wheat's stepdaughter all the time growing up." I cut to the chase and went right for the million-dollar question, "Have you ever heard the Carrs were involved with Berkowitz?" He replied, "No way, they were good people." Just like me a year earlier, he never heard of any of that, a true Yonkers resident answer. I told Kevin I would keep in touch and thanked him for his time.

That night, Larry wanted to do a show with the Surlak/Cerasi reports. Normally, I would just let him go on air and do it himself, but I needed to be seen so he couldn't tell the audience his imaginary team of researchers found them.

Going on Larry's show also gave me the opportunity to tell the audience Wheat Carr was innocent. Larry did not agree with me even after reading these reports. I was going by what I believed was the truth, it was Maury versus these police reports now. I had proven Maury wrong already by searching Yonkers for his satanic cult members and came up with nothing. Now I see what really happened with the people involved.

Since Larry showed his audience these law enforcement reports, the next day I sent Carl everything. He thanked me again for what I had done because no one in the history of this case had ever gotten Yonkers law enforcement to cooperate with information. Carl was extremely grateful and insisted I come see him so he could buy me dinner.

I spoke with Carl about these reports and Wheat's real involvement in all this. He was made to believe Wheat possibly shot him, and it was important for me to fix that. I know Wheat didn't shoot him. Wheat would not have been an instrumental part in catching Berkowitz if that were true. When I finished going over these reports with him, I felt I changed his mind about Wheat. Wheat didn't shoot him, but it was hard for him to let go of what he was told for over thirty-five years. I understood that, and I wasn't going to give up on him. Berkowitz told Carl to his face when he recently visited him in prison he was not the person who shot him, it was a woman. What was Carl supposed to think now? It wasn't Wheat, and I hoped he could see that after reading these reports. I got you Carl, no one has got more skin in this game than you, and I will not give up until God is done.

That evening Detective Geiss called me. Berkowitz recently received a letter he sent to him and replied. Geiss had communicated with Berkowitz before by letter, asking him about a crime that was committed at Untermyer Park in 1977. This time, he wrote to Berkowitz asking him to make things right with Carl, and tell him the truth. Detective Geiss did this on his own weeks ago. He thought Berkowitz acted alone and felt the need to help Carl.

Rumors were going around that Berkowitz did not like Larry and was not happy Carl did an interview with him after he visited...that rumor was incorrect.

Here is Berkowitz's letter to Detective Geiss dated March 19, 2022:

Detective Geiss,

I hope this letter finds you. I received your letters dated February 20th and 24th. I wanted to make a copy of your letters and send them to my attorney to let him know you wrote. Thank you for your patience. I am sorry to have kept you waiting.

I did have a visit with Carl Denaro recently. He and I had been communicating and we finally set a date for a visit. It was ok but it did not go as I had hoped. I wanted the opportunity to feel comfortable around him first, but we did speak. Right now things are on hold, but it may work out that he and I will meet again. Either way I wish Carl the very best.

As for the woman who was sadly abused and assaulted inside Untermyer Park, I do not know of this incident. Back in the 1960's and early 70's the park was in a state of despair and I'm sure all kinds of mischief went on. I do not, however, have any knowledge of this event. I am sorry I cannot provide you with more information as I have none. I can not begin to imagine the pain this woman has endured and the horrific memories she must be experiencing. I pray she will heal physically and emotionally. I don't know what else to say. If I think of anything that will be helpful I will contact you. Sincerely, David Berkowitz

This is why I got along with Detective Geiss, his heart was in the right place. A true detective does not wait for direction. They act and do at any time what they think might work to get answers. I didn't ask Geiss to do this, he acted on his own.

Larry was disrespecting Carl on his shows after their interview, accusing him of lying and never going to see Berkowitz. We can put that to bed now. To me, after reading this letter, it didn't sound like Berkowitz was upset with Carl for talking to Larry. It sounded like Berkowitz didn't get off his chest what he wanted to, and hoped in the future to see Carl again to do that.

Also, look at how Berkowitz talks about Untermyer Park. He knew the park was in despair, but it sounds like he wasn't in the park a lot as he says, "*I'm sure all kinds of mischief went on.*" Berkowitz is not saying he knew or witnessed any mischief. He is saying he is sure, like that's what was probably going on, but he didn't know. For someone who was portrayed as the devil king of Untermyer Park, that to me, was not a solid answer matching that characteristic.

I called Carl back to tell him this news and again he was beyond grateful. If I can add some comfort to Carl's life at any time, I will. He only did the interview with Larry because I asked him to, to show unity. If Berkowitz was upset with him because of that, I felt responsible. We now know he wasn't, and Carl felt much better about things.

Carl then told me a lady contacted him earlier that day and said she could get him files on the case from a detective she knew for five thousand dollars. I told him I would pay for the files and would even meet the lady to get them. Carl said, "NEO, you are a magician."

On March 26, 2022, I received an early morning email from Larry.

Larry: If a lady named Sharon tries to reach out to you, be careful. She is working for Carl as a mole.

I did not respond to Larry. I was completely tired of all his nonsense. I didn't have a clue who Sharon was. Her being a mole made no sense as I was telling Carl everything I did, and Larry knew this.

Later that day, Larry emailed me again.

Larry: I got some names for you. Artie Gardella from Warburton, Billy "Wags" Weider, Thompson brothers from 495 Odell Avenue and Jerry Emmett who hung himself at Untermyer Park. See what you can find on these guys.

I did not answer Larry, but I loved to hunt. I tracked down every name he gave me with contact numbers. Larry was wrong about Jerry Emmett. My brother knew Jerry and said he committed suicide at his home on Odell Avenue, not at the park. I thought we were done with Untermyer Park, what was this all about?

When I called Larry and started to give him all the contact numbers to these people he asked for, he stopped me saying, "I don't need those numbers. They were just kids who hung out in the park." I asked, "Then why did I just spend hours breaking these names down if you didn't need them?" His reply was, "Ah, now you know the people in your neighborhood better."

Really? I went silent as I wanted to reach through the phone and strangle this kid. He sent me names to look up for no reason. I said to him, "Are you serious? I just wasted my time doing this and you don't even want the contacts?" This kid just gave me bullshit names to look up, a Maury Terry move I read he did to the people investigating with him back in the day.

Larry was gaining quite a fan base with all the information I was giving him. I could tell he never had gotten the attention he was now receiving. The threat of losing that attention became a fear for him.

Some might say I was being used. I say only by God and what He has planned. I didn't want to do this. I never asked to do this. God just kept putting my life in the right places. God was using me. I believe in God, and this is how He works, through people. This is not me. I'm not an investigator, but I believe this all has a purpose, I accept that.

I'm not special, I'm not sinless, I'm not even worthy, I'm a street guy from Yonkers who is lucky to be alive. I'm extremely grateful for my life, and thank God for my survival. I'm grateful I think that way, I'm grateful for today.

During this past week, I talked Larry into working with another podcaster he of course didn't get along with, again trying to rid this community of division. Larry took my advice and the podcaster guy agreed to end their quarrels. For me, it was just one less person Larry was fighting with.

The next day I finished reading Dr. Abrahamsen's book and I could see a lot, not a little, but a lot of reasons why Berkowitz did what he did...alone.

Again, Dr. Abrahamsen wanted Berkowitz to forget about his demon stories, to forget about what drove him over the edge. He wanted to hear about David Berkowitz. This was smart because it wasn't just the demon dogs that made him kill. The dogs drove him over the edge by making his life hell, but he also killed because of what his life had become because of rejection and abandonment. Dr. Abrahamsen took a deep dive into Berkowitz's life, having him focus more on himself, not the demon stories he was telling everyone else.

After reading Dr. Abrahamsen's book, I could see why Berkowitz killed, and in no way was an accomplice even entertained. It was all about David Berkowitz and the underlying reasons in his life that made him feel alone in the world.

Dr. Abrahamsen's book is a must-read in order to understand Berkowitz's life and what he went through. The Klausner book is also a must-read as it is important to understand Berkowitz's crazy world of blaming people, dogs and demons for driving him over the edge. Personally, I stand in between both of these books.

To me, what drove Berkowitz over the edge was his never ending, uncontrollable surroundings. Klausner's book helps you see that factor. Abrahamsen's book helps you see why Berkowitz targeted women and hated who he was. Both books play a role in understanding what was really going on in Berkowitz's life.

I think Berkowitz had a lot of resentment towards God, he blamed God for everything. It came from not being able to truly understand Christ. Like Pastor Wallace said, "*he cleaned up his act, because he wanted it, but he did not get Christ in his heart*," he just didn't get it. His failure at being a Christian would be his last attempt at being a good person. To Berkowitz, he gave his life to God and nothing had changed, it was just more rejection, including from the people he loved. To Berkowitz, it wasn't the dogs barking, it was God allowing his life to be bothered by those dogs. I believe Berkowitz's main motive in all this was to get back at God for the life he hated.

My theory, at this point, was Berkowitz may have met John Carr, practiced satanic rituals with him, and then took things too far on his own. I think this could have started with Berkowitz hanging around John, but when he started to kill, John got away from him, and once again, Berkowitz was rejected and abandoned. Is this why Berkowitz fire-bombed the Carr house? Was he mad at John for what he introduced him to and then left him? The Molotov cocktail incident to the Carr house did happen after the first shooting. I now think the Borrelli letter was written by Berkowitz as he tried to frame John Carr. The Borrelli letter starts out, "*I AM A LITTLE BRAT*," as if he was mocking John. Any way you look at it, whether John knew Berkowitz or not, the shootings were done only by Berkowitz. To prove myself right, I felt I still needed more closure on John Carr.

I walked around Yonkers, knocking on doors, asking everyone I ran into about this case, and I was finding out Maury Terry had reported things wrong. Now I needed to talk to the people out in Minot, North Dakota about John Carr. I wanted to see if the reports Maury got from there were like the reports I fact-checked in Yonkers.

I was willing to go to Minot, North Dakota and asked Larry if he was interested. He quickly declined saying, "Hell no, that place is not somewhere I want to take a vacation. It is freezing out there." Unreal, I could care less about the weather out there. This was not a vacation I was offering to take. I wanted information and whatever it took to get it. I looked into some of the people Maury had spoken to from Minot and some of them were still alive. There were still some people out there to speak with who knew John Carr. Larry declined and told me good luck.

On March 28, 2022, I came across two newspaper articles I had never seen before:

"CARR'S QUICK TO DEFEND TALK OF LOCAL POLICE"

Among the first to rise to the defense of Yonkers Police following the filing of a second lawsuit against the department in the Son of Sam case were Sam and Wheat Carr, both of whom figure prominently in events surrounding the arrest of David Berkowitz, the suspected .44 Caliber Killer.

"As far as I'm concerned, the Yonkers Police Department acted in a professional and competent manner," said Sam Carr, a retired City of Yonkers public works employee who runs an answering service from his home behind the apartment house in which Berkowitz lived. Carr, whose home was firebombed and who received threatening letters about his dog barking, was said by Berkowitz to be the "Sam" of "Son of Sam," a six thousand year old "voice" that gave him instructions to kill through Carr's dog, Harvey.

Wheat Carr, his daughter, is a Yonkers Police Dispatcher credited with providing a vital link leading to Berkowitz's arrest by turning a telephone inquiry from New York City about a parking ticket Berkowitz received near the last Son of Sam shooting scene over to Yonkers Police who were working on several Yonkers incidents in which Berkowitz was suspect, including the letters to her father.

A notice of claim in a ten million dollar negligence suit against Yonkers Police was filed Monday by Robert Violante, who was shot and blinded in one eye July 31 in Brooklyn. A similar case was instituted against the department last month by the family of Stacy Moskowitz, Violante's companion, who was shot and later died. Both suits contend Yonkers Police had enough information on Berkowitz to have apprehended him before the shooting.

I am mixed about these lawsuits. I know Yonkers Police did not intend to do anything wrong, but the incidents on Wicker Street should have been paid more attention to. There possibly could have been no "Son of Sam" if the YPD stopped what was going on at the Neto and Carr homes. I don't hold the YPD at fault at all. I look at intent and I know for a fact the YPD did not intend to let Berkowitz go. I think I know the reason why these crimes were not investigated like they should have been, I'll explain later.

The article continues...

Sam Carr cited work on the case by Yonkers Detectives Michael Lorenzo and Edmund Oakley and Police Officers Peter Intervallo and Thomas Chamberlain all of whom were honored by New York City after Berkowitz's arrest.

"It is almost unbelievable, the work done by Lorenzo and Oakley, Chamberlain and Intervallo," said Carr. "I know the amount of work these two detectives and two patrolmen put into it. They did their job in a most professional way to my knowledge."

This is the second newspaper article I came across that day:

"BEAME TO HONOR 2 LOCAL POLICEMEN"

Two Yonkers Policemen and a part time Westchester Deputy Sheriff who were involved in the capture of David Berkowitz of Yonkers, the alleged Son of Sam, will receive certificates of appreciation friday from Mayor Abraham Beame in New York City. A Yonkers Police dispatcher will also be honored.

The presentation will be made while twenty-five New York Police officers, including Deputy Inspector Timothy Dowd, are promoted for their work on the capture of the suspect. Dowd is commander of the Special Homicide Task Force established to capture the .44 Caliber Killer.

I would like to point out, it was all Yonkers work, besides the parking ticket, that led to the arrest of David Berkowitz. Thank the people involved with the capture such as Cacilia Davis, Sam and Wheat Carr, the Cassaras, Craig Glassman, and Yonkers Police Officers Peter Intervallo and Thomas Chamberlain. Without these people, Berkowitz would not have been caught when he was. Officers Intervallo and Chamberlain were on to Berkowitz days before the parking ticket was discussed with Wheat. They were also in contact with New York City Police during the days before the arrest, following protocol to let the New York City Omega Task Force do their job handling this dangerous person correctly.

The article continues...

Yonkers patrolmen Peter Intervallo and Thomas Chamberlain will receive the certificates for their part in the investigation, as well as Craig Glassman, the volunteer Deputy who lived in Berkowitz's building and called authorities attention to Berkowitz's strange behavior.

Wheat Carr, the daughter of Sam Carr, will receive a citation from the mayor. She is the police dispatcher who played a part in alerting Brooklyn detectives to Berkowitz who had run-ins with her father, a neighbor of Berkowitz.

Among these being promoted will be New York police officer Michael Cataneo Jr. who processed the ticket on the car of Berkowitz when it was parked near the place where Stacy Moskowitz was killed in Brooklyn. The ticket helped place Berkowitz's car in the area.

In a related development, Police have said there is no evidence that Berkowitz, in the company of an unidentified companion, visited Mamaroneck Animal Shelter the day before he was arrested. The report had prompted speculation that Berkowitz may have had an accomplice.

Hmm...I wonder who gave that report of Berkowitz visiting the animal shelter a day before the arrest. This newspaper editor is calling that report a statement with no evidence to support it.

Where was all this before? How could anyone think the Carr family was fooling all these professional law enforcement agencies? The Carrs were the reason Berkowitz was caught, and to think they did all this to cover up their involvement is absurd. Do you see how many law enforcement agencies, as well as Jimmy Breslin, the Carrs were trying to alert? They even cooperated with the FBI. Do you really think Sam or Wheat would have been able to fool all these people they were contacting? I just don't see it. The mayor of New York honored Wheat and her father for their roles in Berkowitz's capture, this was not an act. The NYPD and the YPD had nothing crooked about them in this case, and neither did Sam or Wheat.

There was no way Berkowitz would not have told the authorities John Carr was an accomplice when he was arrested. I feel he was trying to kill Wheat days before the arrest, he hated that family. Why would he cover for John? Berkowitz claimed he couldn't say who was involved because these people involved would hurt his family if he told on them...but he does tell on them, he blames Sam as soon as he is arrested. If Berkowitz was trying to cover for John, blaming his father would not be the wisest decision. He had no family in his life to protect, which is why he felt alone in the world in the first place.

April 2, 2022, since I now believe Berkowitz was the author of the first letter to Borrelli, I had to eliminate my theory of the letter's meaning with "*I MISS MY PRETTY PRINCESS*." I thought John Carr had written this letter and I was wrong. Penny and I then came up with a different meaning for that passage.

Regarding "*I MISS MY PRETTY PRINCESS MOST OF ALL*." In a passage from the Klausner book, Berkowitz calls Donna Lauria his "*little princess*." Berkowitz was referring to Donna Lauria in the Borrelli letter.

With the words "*SHE'S RESTING IN OUR LADIES HOUSE*," Berkowitz was referring to Donna Lauria's obituary:

LAURIA-Donna A. Suddenly. Beloved daughter of Michael and Rose (nee Staltari). Devoted sister of Michael Jr. and Louis. Dear granddaughter of Louis and Catherine Barletti. Reposing RALPH GIORDANO FUNERAL HOME, 1727 Crosby Ave. Until Mon. Mass of Resurrection Our Lady of the Assumption Church, 10A.M.

Berkowitz was referring to the church Donna Lauria was laid to rest at, "*Our Lady*" of the Assumption Church.

"*BUT I'LL SHE HER SOON*." The letter was not misspelled as I had originally assumed. The word "*SHE*" was intentional. Berkowitz meant to say she, as in marriage. Penny and I found another passage in the Klausner book where Berkowitz explains this:

Right after Berkowitz killed her, Sam had promised her to him. He was supposed to marry her, he says. Sam told him that, Berkowitz says Sam promised Donna to him as a bride. Sam had led David to believe that Donna would someday rise from the dead to join him.

This all sounds right to me, but was this all planned by Berkowitz to make himself look insane? Or did he actually believe these scenarios in his mind for real?

I posted this theory on Larry's website, but he was still convinced John Carr wrote the Borrelli letter, so he didn't like I posted it going against his show's narrative. He also didn't like I posted without showing him first. I wasn't putting the post up to take a shot at his show's narrative, his narrative was once mine. I put the post up because I truly thought Berkowitz had written the Borrelli letter and what Penny and I came up with made sense.

Larry emailed me later that day.

Larry: I think the post you put up causes a lot of unnecessary doubt. It's interesting, but now people are going to use your post to go against the show's narrative.

I didn't see it that way. I was looking at this case differently now. I wasn't abandoning the work. This investigation was ongoing, and new evidence that was not seen before was now in front of me. I have been wrong many times, nothing wrong with that, as long as I get it right in the end.

April 3, 2022 was the day Larry held a Zoom meeting about the Surlak/ Cerasi reports. Attending were Bob Maitre, a retired Yonkers cop who Mike Lorenzo Jr. brought into this, John Rinciari, the podcaster guy, and Scarlett Diaz, a lady who frequently posted on Larry's website. I had to convince Larry to invite her to the meeting so she could take notes. We talked mostly about the Yonkers Police reports we just saw for the first time. It was some game-changing information and we all had our opinions. During this meeting, every time someone tried to speak, Larry would interrupt and tell the person they were going off track. The point of discussion was to open up our minds and try to see what others see. If you don't let anyone talk, you gain nothing. Sometimes the smallest thing said can turn the biggest wheel. Even the wildest assumptions can lead you to the truth. Before I left the meeting, I asked if anyone knew Anthony Cerasi, the detective on this case who was responsible for these reports to be made. Bob Maitre said he did and would give him a call. At least I got something out of this meeting.

The next day I discussed with Carl and Max about going out to North Dakota. To me, John Carr was the only one I needed to look into a little more. There has already been a lot of holes in what Maury reported with this case, John's life in North Dakota is what I wanted to know more about. Max then sent me documents someone sent him a day earlier about John Carr.

The documents Max gave me were interviews with friends of John Carr from North Dakota. There was nothing in these documents that connected John to Berkowitz so I didn't feel they were important in any way. Max asked me to keep these reports to myself, as they didn't belong to him.

I told Larry I got these reports, but they had nothing to do with Berkowitz so they were not important. Larry wasn't happy I wouldn't send him Max's reports, but this was the atmosphere he created. This kid put me in a bad position and I didn't like it.

So the Carrs didn't realize who was bothering them until June 10, 1977, and they were only on to Berkowitz at that time as the author of their harassing letters, not the "Son of Sam" yet. It was not until July 11, 1977, when Sam saw a sketch in *Time* magazine did he realize that the "Son of Sam" was possibly David Berkowitz, the man harassing him and his family. June 10, 1977 is when Berkowitz should have been spoken to by the Yonkers Police, and July 12, 1977 is when the New York City Police should have been looking into him. Again, the NYPD was getting a ton of phone calls from people with wild stories claiming they knew who the "Son of Sam" was from the police sketches, and that is what Sam had. What do they prioritize among hundreds of tips?

On April 5, 2022, Kevin Ivey called and asked if I wanted to speak with Mr. Hudson. I anxiously said yes and then heard Kevin yell, "Mr. Hudson," to put him on the phone. Once I heard Mr. Hudson's voice say hello, I started to form tears in my eyes. He sounded exactly the same from when I was twelve. I could not cry though, you never cry in front of Mr. Hudson. He built tough men, he built me. I told him how grateful I was to have had him in my life. How lucky I was to be molded by him. I told him he was the one who put the fire in my heart, taught me the fourth quarter must always be mine. To always get stronger as I go and always finish what I came to do. I told him without his seasoning, I would not be the man I was today. He thanked me for what I was saying, and if I could hear correctly, he was choking up a bit. I told him if there was anything I could ever do for him to call me, he had my number now. He was still coaching football and said he would take me up on that offer if he needed any help getting the kids some uniforms.

I thank God for these moments, for giving me the opportunity to thank this man. These are the things I receive in return for doing this. To get the chance to tell this man his life made a difference in mine was priceless.

April 7, 2022 was the most important day of this investigation. It started out like all the rest, but when you are at ground zero, anything can happen. I drove into work, had coffee with Detective Geiss, and reported to the fire-house I was working at for the past few weeks. While I was working, my good friend, the Yonkers fireman who told me a couple of weeks ago he had files for me, asked me over the loudspeaker to come down to his locker. I approached my friend and he handed me seventy-one pages of information on this case. They were the lost "Son of Sam" files from the Yonkers Police Department. Nothing was in Yonkers Records Department on this case, they disappeared years ago. Only the law enforcement who were on this case before all files were sealed had seen them.

CHAPTER XVI

THE LOST YONKERS FILES

I had in my hands what no one has seen in over forty years. Even John Geiss, in his forty-year career, has never seen these files. They contained photos of the inside of David Berkowitz's apartment that the Yonkers Police took the night of the arrest. Wheat Carr's entire phone conversation with New York City Detective James Justus on August 9, 1977. David Berkowitz's arrest records, what exactly was seized from his car and apartment, a treasure trove of evidence. The best of all...it contained seventeen handwritten letters by David Berkowitz. Some of these letters have never been seen before by the public and they prove to carry with them a lot of answers.

I thanked my fireman friend tremendously for this. He actually had no idea what he was handing me as I hugged him. I never in a million years thought he was going to be giving me the lost Yonkers "Son of Sam" files.

First thing I did was find a nice spot in the firehouse where I wouldn't be bothered and looked through it all...it was so overwhelming. After I skimmed through the files, I called Detective Geiss to tell him what I had. I owed the Yonkers Police that, they were behind me this entire time. Once I told Geiss I had something, he called me every half hour asking me when I was bringing them in. I love this guy, but I needed a minute alone with these files to look at what no one else has seen in over forty years with my own eyes.

I brought these files to Detective Geiss a little after noon, and when he laid eyes on them, he looked at me and asked, "Where did you find these? These are the Yonkers files that went missing." I laughed and said, "A friend gave them to me, end the interrogation there." He smiled and went to make copies. I asked if it was okay to present these to the public, as I didn't want to bother anyone. He had no problem with that, he just suggested I take it slow and I agreed.

These files were weeks worth of content for Larry's show, so I didn't want to give them to him all at once. He would just blow through it all right away. I gave no one these files but Detective Geiss.

The first report I would like to show you from these files is the phone conversation that occurred on August 9, 1977, at 8:20 p.m., between Yonkers Police Dispatcher Wheat Carr, and New York City Detective James Justus. Detective Justus contacted the YPD to ask about David Berkowitz and a parking ticket he received in the area of the last shooting in Brooklyn. Sal DiMaggio, who worked at the Yonkers Police Dispatch, answered the phone and spoke with Detective Justus briefly. After hearing Detective Justus ask questions about David Berkowitz, Sal immediately handed the phone to Wheat because he knew she had information about Berkowitz.

Here is the entire phone conversation between Detective James Justus and Wheat Carr:

Justus: *Yes, this is Detective Justus from the Brooklyn Robbery Squad, New York Police Department.*

Wheat: *Yes...*

Justus: *I'm working in the 10th Homicide Zone, now, on the .44 Caliber Killer...*

Wheat: *Yeah...*

Justus: *...and I'm trying to contact a party that lives up in Yonkers...who is possibly a witness to the crime down here. That's a Mr. David Berkowitz...*

Wheat: *Oh no...Oh no...*

Justus: *Do you know him?*

Wheat: *Could I...I was very involved...This is the guy I think is responsible...*

Justus: *David Berkowitz?*

Wheat: *...is responsible...my father was down there, yest...Saturday.*

Justus: *Yeah...*

Wheat: *...and you also got information regar...is he at 35 Pine Street?*

Justus: *Yes, dear...*

Wheat: *David Berkowitz, I don't know how you, or what, but my father went down to the 109th and you also...someone received information through uh... our police officers and that's because of some incidents involving a shooting where we have reason to believe that this person is responsible. He also has written similar type threatening letters to the Sheriff's Investigator who recently moved into his apartment. So, I don't...*

Justus: *Do you know David Berkowitz yourself?*

Wheat: *I don't know him, I, really, because of a shooting incident at my home and a fire bombing and threatening letters...*

Justus: *At your home...*

Wheat: *...and through investigation found out that this is probably the person...*

Justus: *Did you notify the police department on it?*

Wheat: *Oh yeah, there are numerous reports on it, and information regarding this guy was given to your department on Saturday.*

Justus: *Yeah, well I am doing it another way, he got a summons down here, that night, right in the vicinity...*

Wheat: *Oh my God...he...he...you know, because we have seen him and he fits the description, this is why my father went down there with his whole file...of copies of the letters we have received from him...and I believe that the Westchester County Sheriff's Department is now investigating him because he threatened a Sheriff's investigator, my dog was shot with a .44 caliber bullet...*

Justus: *Oh really?*

Wheat: *At least what was supposed to have been. The people who have seen it claim it was a .44...*

Justus: *ah...*

Wheat: *he...he...just scared me to death...now you are telling me he's a witness...*

Justus: *Well, we don't know, a possible witness, and from what you are telling me, a possible perpetrator...*

Wheat: *um...and he owns a yellow car...*

Justus: *He has a yellow...yeah, I'd say a yellow Ford, I believe it is...*

Wheat: *Yeah, yeah, yeah...uhuh...do you ...the 109th, is that Brooklyn?*

Justus: *No, Queens, we're working out of the 10th Homicide Zone in Brooklyn.*

Wheat: *Okay...well he went...my father went to the 109th on Saturday, okay... last week someone was up here at our Intelligence Unit and at that time spoke with Police Officers Chamberlain and Intervallo and they gave him information...just a long shot, now, because he does resemble the picture...I don't know him personally...*

Justus: *Alright, so you know of Berkowitz...*

Wheat: *Right...*

Justus: *...through...*

Wheat: *...incidents that have occurred that I have reason to believe that you could prove in court that he's responsible for a shooting incident at my home...*

Justus: *...Yonkers had at home and believes Berkowitz responsible...*

Wheat: *...he happens to be...he either was or is now employed as a rent a cop like a security guard...*

Justus: *rent a cop...you use the same terms we use down here? huh?*

Wheat: *Yeah*

Justus: *Your dog was shot...*

Wheat: *...with a large caliber bullet...it's never been confirmed because you know how it happens, right? Seventeen people have seventeen different jobs and nobody gets together and it's only in the last week that these two cops and I got together and put all the reports together and got the D.D. reports where he is doing everything...*

Justus: *Let me ask you something, honey? With his name, do you have a pistol license bureau up there that would a...*

Wheat: *...okay, supposedly he has a permit either to shoot by New York City or has an application now being processed in relation to this...*

Justus: *...in New York City...*

Wheat: *...he holds no permit in the City of Yonkers at this time...*

Justus: *...but possibly here in New York City...*

Wheat: *...possibly because he was employed as a security guard. Well, you know who you should get in touch with, and if you will hold on a minute, I will find out when he is working...alright...it is either Police Officers Chamberlain and Intervallo who for their own reasons put this all together, just because it happens to be their sector where I live...*

Justus: *Chamberlain or Intervallo?*

Wheat: *Yes.*

Justus: *Would you be able to do me the honors, please?*

Wheat: *Well, I'll find out where they are, they are not working right now, I know that, okay, can you hold on a minute?*

Justus: *Alright.*

As Wheat is getting information for Detective Justus, Justus talks to someone in the background.

Justus: *I have something beautiful here. I wanted to talk to this guy about a summons...lives up in Yonkers...I was talking to Yonkers to get a notification made and she says...oh no not him, he shot my dog with a .44 about a month ago, he's crazy, he's sending threatening letters to the Deputy Sheriff's Office...*

Wheat: *Could I get your name and I'll have one of them call you back?*

Justus: *Alright, my name is Justus...J U S T U S...uh I'm thinking what the hell number should I give you, I'll give you this one 946-3336, and that's a 212 exchange...*

Wheat: *212-946-3336 and you are Detective Justus*

Justus: *Right*

Wheat: *Okay, I have...*

Justus: *Can I ask you a favor, honey?...can I get your name please?*

Wheat: *Sure...my name is Carr C A R R*

Justus: *First name, honey?*

Wheat: *Wheat...W H E A T...now, my father...my father is Samuel Carr he went down there with all the information the other day.*

Justus: *Where do you live Miss Carr?*

Wheat: *316 Warburton Avenue...W A R B U R T O N Avenue, and that is immediately behind...the back of his house and the back of mine, the back of his apartment and the back of my home face each other...there is also a Westchester County Sheriff's Department investigation because he wrote letters to this Sheriff's investigator who has the apartment underneath him saying that my father planted him there and he is going to get us instead. But, I'll have Pete or Tommy call you back...I'll call them at home...*

Justus: *Do you know how to spell the last guy's name, not Chamberlain, the...the...*

Wheat: *I N T E R V A L L O, just like it sounds...right*

Justus: *Okay doke, honey...*

Wheat: *Thank you a lot...*

Justus: *Thank you very much, dear.*

Wheat: *Bye, bye...*

Wheat Carr then informed the Yonkers Police Department that she had spoken to Detective Justsus from New York City and had them contact him to exchange information...causing all of Yonkers Police, New York City Police, and the Westchester County Sheriff's Department to converse and work together.

I want to focus a moment on Yonkers Police Officers Peter Intervallo and Thomas Chamberlain. Look at, "*Okay...last week someone was up here at our Intelligence Unit and at that time spoke with Police Officers Chamberlain and Intervallo and they gave him information.*" This phone call was on August 9th and Wheat states that someone from the NYPD (Richard Salverson on August 5, 1977) was in Yonkers already speaking with Officers Chamberlain and Intervallo, showing you days before the arrest, these two officers were after Berkowitz as the "Son of Sam."

Also look at, "*it's only in the last week that these two cops and I got together and put all the reports together and got the D.D. reports where he is doing everything...*" Officers Peter Intervallo and Thomas Chamberlain, with the help of Wheat Carr, had Berkowitz as a "Son of Sam" suspect a week before this conversation, a week before his arrest. The real investigative work that solved this case was done by these three people, the Cassaras, and of course good ol' Sam. I really would like to see how this would have played out if the New York City Police Department had acted on Intervallo and Chamberlain's information.

So what would've happened if Wheat Carr was not at work that night to speak with Detective Justus? What if Steven Cassara never figured out the get-well card sent to their house was from David Berkowitz? What if Sam Carr never realized the letters sent to him and the Cassaras' get-well card were both written by the same person? The Yonkers Police were on to David Berkowitz because these people figured things out. The fire at Craig Glassman's apartment was the point where the YPD were sure Berkowitz was the "Son of Sam" because of the letters Glassman showed them. The parking ticket Berkowitz received only threw the New York City Police in the mix. So was it the parking ticket that got Berkowitz caught, or was it the people he was messing with?

The following is a Detective Report by assigned Yonkers Detectives Joe Surlak and Anthony Cerasi:

August 10, 1977

The assigned spoke with New York City Detectives Edward Zigo and John Longo, who related that they were pursuing the .44 caliber homicide investigation in New York City and are here to interview one David Berkowitz, male white, 24 years, of 35 Pine Street, Apt. 7-E, relative to him receiving a traffic summons on his vehicle, a 1974 Ford, New York Reg. 561-XLB, yellow with a black vinyl top, which was issued to him shortly before and in the same area of the last .44 caliber killing in Brooklyn, New York.

Detectives Zigo and Longo were then informed that this Department was conducting two investigations: No. 1-Investigation of threatening letters received by one Samuel Carr of 316 Warburton Avenue; the first being issued on April 21, 1977, and the second investigation being a suspected arson, the complaint being one Craig Glassman of 35 Pine Street, which occurred on August 6, 1977.

Said Detectives proceeded to 35 Pine Street and thereat observed David Berkowitz' car parked near the main entrance and upon looking into same, they observed what appeared to be the butt end of a machine gun which was in a sack in the back seat. Detective Longo kept surveillance on the vehicle while Detective Zigo returned to this Division and notified his superiors, and Detective Michael Shilensky of the Legal Counsel of the New York City Police Department who responded to this office and made application for search warrants of David Berkowitz' car and apartment.

Inspector Dowd and Chief of Detectives Keenan also responded to 35 Pine Street and were in charge of Detectives at that scene. As they were drawing up the search warrant, David Berkowitz came out of his apartment at approximately 2115 hours and entered his vehicle and was immediately apprehended and placed under arrest. Berkowitz was conveyed to this office where he was advised of his constitutional rights by Detective Sergeant Frank Fernandes.

The assigned along with Detectives Zigo and Shilensky, proceeded to the home of City Court Judge Robert W. Cacace where after reading the application of the two search warrants, he endorsed same.

The assigned along with said Detectives returned to 35 Pine Street, where David Berkowitz' vehicle was then searched. On the front seat, in a brown paper bag and wrapped in plastic a .44 caliber (Chart Arms Bulldog) revolver which was fully loaded was found. In the rear seat, a .45 caliber machine gun and several clips which were fully loaded with .45 caliber ammunition were found in a khaki colored gun sack. Letters and items of clothing were also found and all of which became the property of the New York City Police Department.

The assigned then proceeded to Apt. 7-E of 35 Pine Street, and entered with the key which was taken from David Berkowitz and entered the apartment, at which time, New York City Police Officers conducted a search and found one rifle, a shotgun, and boxes of ammunition. There were numerous writings on the wall along with personal papers apparently belonging to David Berkowitz which showed hatred for Sam Carr and Craig Glassman.New York City Forensic Technician under the direction of Lieutenant Luisi responded to the place of occurrence and processed both the vehicle and the apartment and all evidence was handled by them. The apartment was secured by Detectives Thomas Dugan and Andrew Cavallo of this Department, and the keys were left at the Detective Division.

David Berkowitz' vehicle, a 1974 Ford, was driven to the New York City Police Department Headquarters by Detective John Longo.

David Berkowitz was booked at the Detective Division by Detective Sergeant Frank Fernandes for Criminal Possession of a Weapon and turned over to the New York City authorities.

Here is Detective Zigo's search warrant application for David Berkowitz's car and apartment:

THE APPLICANT FOR A SEARCH WARRANT FOR THE PERSONS OF: David R. Berkowitz

AND THE PREMISES: 35 Pine Street Apartment 7E, Yonkers, New York

AND VEHICLES: 1970 4dr Yellow Ford Sedan, New York Registration No. 561-XLB

DET. EDWARD ZIGO, Shield No. 2419 of the New York City Police Department being duly sworn, deposes and says: I have information based upon.

1. *I am a Detective in the New York City Police Department, and am a public servant of a type described in C.P.L. Section 690.05*

2. *I have information based upon the following:*

   A. *On August 1st, 1977 I was assigned to investigate a shooting incident which took place on July 31, 1977 in the County of Kings, City and State of New York, in which one Stacey Moskowitz was killed and one Robert Violante was shot, as a result of which he lost sight in both eyes.*
   B. *I have examined the files of the New York City Police Department regarding this shooting as well as twelve other shooting incidents which have taken place in the City of New York since 1976. As a result of these shooting incidents, including the one on July 31st, 1977, six people have been killed and seven other persons wounded by gun shot. Based on my examination of the files of the New York City Police Department, and*

other information it is my belief that all of these shootings were perpetrated by the same individual. This individual has become known as the ".44 Calibre Killer" or "the son of Sam." This perpetrator is described as a male, white, 25 to 32 years of age, 5'8-5'9 tall, 165-175 pounds, Clean shaven, dark eyes, dark hair, high cheek bones. In all of the above shooting incidents a firearm of .44 calibre was used. It is believed to be the "bulldog" model .44 calibre revolver. A copy of a composite photo which was prepared and circulated by the New York City Police Department is annexed hereto as "Exhibit A."

C. *Your deponent in the course of investigation of the above described shooting incident which occurred in Brooklyn, New York, was informed by Detective Edward O'Sullivan Shield No. 646, Brooklyn Robbery Squad that a check of the records of the New York City Police Department records revealed that at 2:05am on July 31, 1977, summons No. 749069532 was issued to a Yellow Ford, Blk top, Registration in New York State, No. 561-XLB. This summons was issued in the "200" block of Bay 17th Street, Brooklyn, New York. This is a few blocks away from the scene of the shooting incident which took place on July 31st, 1977 at approximately 2:45am.*

D. *Your deponent cause a check of the New York Registration 561-XLB to be made. New York State Motor Vehicle Bureau computer reveales that this registration plate is registered to David R. Berkowitz, Date of Birth: June 1, 1953, at 35 Pine Street Yonkers, New York. The vehicle is described as a 1970 Ford, Yellow Sedan.*

E. *Your deponent was present at the Yonkers Police Head-Quarters and on August 10th, 1977 had conversations with various members of the Yonkers Police Department, and Mr. Craig Glassman, Deputy Sheriff-Investigator Westchester County. Your deponent was informed by these individuals whose identity is known to your deponent, that David R. Berkowitz is a "Male, White, in his 20's, about 5'10"-6', approximately 170 pounds, brown hair."*

F. *At 4:00pm on August 10, 1977, your deponent was present on Pine Street in Yonkers, New York and at that time observed a vehicle parked at the curb. Said vehicle was a 1970 Yellow 4 door Ford Sedan, with a*

Black vinyl top, with New York Registration plates 561-XLB affixed to it. Your deponent looked into said vehicle and observed a duffle-bag on the rear seat. Protruding from the duffle-bag was part of what appeared to be part of a rifle, possibly of a type, possession of which is illegal in New York State, (Article 265. New York State Penal Law). Your deponent further observed that the left rear door of said vehicle was open and further inspection of the firearm revealed that it appeared to be of a type which fires bullets automatically with a single pull of the trigger. Said weapon constitutes a machine gun under New York State law and possession thereof is a class C Felony under Section 265.03 New York State Penal Law.

G. *In addition to the above, your deponent observed a white envelope which had printed on it "Attention Suffolk County-NYPD and the press." Said lettering on the envelope appeared to your deponent to be the same as that on two notes which were delivered to a member of the press and which "take credit for" the shooting which are herein above described.*

H. *Your deponent further states that on August 10th, 1977 at approximately 8:00pm he was present at No. 35 Pine Street Yonkers, New York, and at that time observed a doorbell, located in the lobby of said address, and a printed label bore the legend "D. Berkowitz" and also bore the apartment "7E". Your deponent is further informed by Mr. Glassman that Mr. Berkowitz resides in apartment 7E of 35 Pine Street Yonkers, New York. Mr. Glassman has this knowledge because he also resides in said building.*

I. *Your deponent further checked a telephone directory for the County of Westchester and it revealed that Mr. Berkowitz resides at 35 Pine Street Yonkers, New York and has listed to him telephone No. 423-8908.*

3. *Based upon the foregoing reliable information there is probable cause to believe that certain property, possession of which is unlawful, constitutes evidence and tends to connect and demonstrate that an offense was committed, to wit:*

A. .44 Calibre Revolver, "Bulldog" model
B. Ammunition for said firearm
C. Handwriting samples
D. Documents, Writings, and other records such as telephone receipts, rent receipts evidencing dominion and control of apartment 7E of Premises 35 Pine Street Yonkers, New York and of a 1970 Ford Vehicle bearing New York Registration 561-XLB
E. Fingerprints and Palmprints, is located in apartment 7E of Premises 35 Pine Street Yonkers, New York.

There further exists probable cause to believe that the following property, possession of which is illegal, constitutes evidence and tends to connect and demonstrate that an offense was committed, to wit:

A. A long firearm, of a type which is capable of being automatically fired.
B. Ammunition for said firearm
C. .44 Calibre Revolver, "Bulldog" model
D. Ammunition for said revolver
E. Handwriting samples
F. Fingerprints and palmprints is located in a 1970 Ford Sedan bearing New York registration plates 561-XLB.

Request is further made that the warrant and order of contain a provision permitting execution thereof at any time of the day or night and that it further provide that entry to said premises and vehicle can be made without the executing officer being under the obligation of announcing his authority and purpose, in that because of the nature of the crimes being investigated and because of the potential dangerous nature of the items sought, to announce authority and purpose would constitute a substantial potential danger to the lives of the officer executing the warrant, or said property may be quickly destroyed.

WHEREFORE, I respectfull request that the Court issue warrants and orders of seizure in the form annexed, authorizing the search of David R. Berkowitz, premise 35 Pine Street Apartment 7E, Yonkers, New York and of vehicle: 1970

4dr Yellow Sedan, New York Registration 561-XLB and directing that such property herein described or evidence or any part thereof be found be seized and brought before the Court; together with such other and further relief that the court may deem proper.

No previous application in this matter has been made in this or any other court or to any other Judge, Justice or Magistrate....signed, Detective Edward Zigo, shield No. 2419, 10th Homicide Zone-N.Y.C.P.D.

I would like to go over the search, as some would argue if Detective Zigo had the right to enter Berkowitz's vehicle or not. According to this warrant application, which was written by Detective Zigo, he saw a sack on the back seat of Berkowitz's car with what appeared to be the butt end of a machine gun sticking out of it, all in plain view by looking through the back window.

A machine gun is what Detective Zigo described he saw on the back seat, and a machine gun is an illegal weapon for a civilian to possess in New York State. Detective Zigo left all evidence in the car and notified his superiors. The NYPD then had 35 Pine Street surrounded, waiting for Berkowitz to come out. At 8:00 p.m., Craig Glassman approached Berkowitz's car and was questioned by the NYPD. Glassman told Dectective Zigo that Berkowitz was home as he could hear him walking from his apartment below. Detective Zigo, after speaking with Glassman, proceeded to the Yonkers Police Headquarters to get the search warrant applications for Berkowitz's car and apartment. At 9:15 p.m., Berkowitz came out of 35 Pine Street and was apprehended with badges and guns drawn by Craig Glassman, Detective John Falotico, and Sergeant William Gardella. Detective Zigo then had to present these warrant applications to Judge Cacace at his home for the warrants to be issued. No evidence was removed from Berkowitz's car or apartment until after these warrant applications were signed.

Did Detective Zigo have the right to enter Berkowitz's car? He did not, and if Berkowitz would have went to trial, all evidence taken from the car would have been inadmissible in court. Zigo needed a warrant before entering, and we see clearly he entered the vehicle without that. The .44 caliber revolver was in Berkowitz's possession when he exited 35 Pine Street and was apprehended. The .44 caliber revolver would have been admissible in court, and that was the actual murder weapon needed to convict him.

To me, however Detective Zigo got into Berkowitz's car is irrelevant. If you were a detective and had leads on the "Son of Sam" that led you to this car, would you not go in after seeing a sack on the back seat with a machine gun bulging from it? Don't forget, Detective Zigo was briefed beforehand by the YPD and Wheat Carr, who gave him all the information Officer's Intervallo and Chamberlain had on Berkowitz, including Craig Glassman's letters that referred to Sam. Detective Zigo did his job, and at the end of the day, this car did belong to the "Son of Sam." So under the circumstances, may I ask why technicalities on how he did his job should matter?

Now I will go over some of the handwritten letters by Berkowitz which were found in these lost files.

Here is a letter that was found in Berkowitz's apartment on the night of his arrest. This letter is about the satanic cult David Berkowitz belonged to... and it wasn't at Untermyer Park:

The commander of Yonkers has the name "Captain Blood" and he supervises most of the murders. The highest temple of Satan is located at 18 Wicker St., Yonkers.

Here is a partial list of those with the highest ranks.

Jack Cassara-High Priest

Nann Cassara-High Priestiss and family-174 Coligni, New Roch.

"The Wicker St. Gang" with Captain Blood. 18 Wicker Street Yonkers.

The "House of Horrors"- "The Carr Gang."

Sam Carr alias "1st Lueitenant Tinker"

Francine Francis Carr

John Wheat Carr-"Johnny Rape Slayer" 316 Warburton Avenue

This here is your satanic cult…Jack and Nann Cassara, along with their family, are the "*High Priest*" and "*High Priestiss.*" "*Captain Blood*" and "*The Wicker St. Gang*" from 18 Wicker Street. "*The Carr Gang,*" *"1st Lueitenant Tinker"* Sam Carr, Francine Francis and John Wheat Carr. These were the people Berkowitz was blaming for making him commit the murders. Notice in this letter, Berkowitz writes John Wheat Carr…there is no John Wheat Carr. That name only existed in the phone book as Wheat had stated. There is no mention of Untermyer Park, all Wicker Street. This letter was written before March 15, 1977 or Craig Glassman would have been included in this cult. Who is "Captain Blood" from 18 Wicker Street…keep reading.

This next letter found in Berkowitz's apartment was written on March 8, 1977…the same day Virginia Voskerichian was shot and killed:

Today the Devil Dog at Wicker Street is in great pain. Apparently Joaquin Goncalo is low on blood. Yes, I'm right. The Dog is screaming for fresh blood and meat to quench his thirst and pangs of hunger.

I said to Joaquin, why all the suffering and pain? Why do you bring so much destruction into the world? Joaquin laughted, "to hell with the people of the world, the people of the world shall bow down to me and I shall conquer."

I said to him you evil beast and the Wicked Wicker Dog cried out saying "yes, we are evil, we are the Children of Satan, we kill the innocent, and praise the guilty." At this time the dog barked fierce cries and my head developed a severe pain. I was no longer permitted to speak to the people of Wicker St.

All day long the Devil Dog as been yelling in pain-there is no ceasing. I begged the Wicker street cult to leave me alone. I am there slave. Today the demon has not stopped for a moment. How much blood does he want me to spill for him? 3/8/77...9:15am

Okay, first thing I would like to point out, Berkowitz refers to the dog that is bothering him at 18 Wicker Street as the "*Devil Dog at Wicker Street*" and the "*Wicked Wicker Dog.*" King was the name of the dog at 18 Wicker Street. King was the "*Wicked Wicker Dog,*" also known as "*THE WICKED KING WICKER.*"

I now can see in this letter Berkowitz mentioning Joaquin Goncalo living at 18 Wicker Street. Who the hell is Joaquin Goncalo? Sylvia Neto helped me out with this one. I called Sylvia to ask her about this guy, Joaquin Goncalo, and she corrected me, "You mean Joaquim." I said, "No, not your father. The Joaquin who lived at 18 Wicker Street." She explained, "Yes, he lived on the third floor and his name was Joaquim with an M, same as my father's." "How was he" I asked, and she told me he was an excellent tenant, a very nice guy from Portugal and was married with a daughter.

I told Sylvia I was reading a letter written by Berkowitz and he repeatedly spelled Joaquim Goncalo's name with an N, Joaquin. She told me adamantly that his name was spelled with an M, Joaquim, not with an N. I hung up the phone with Sylvia and looked in the 1976 Yonkers phone book...sure enough, my hunch was right.

The Netos were not listed in the phone book that year as Sylvia told me her father did not list their number. Then I saw the name Joaquin Goncalo listed at 18 Wicker Street. The phone book had Joaquim

Goncalo's name misspelled as Joaquin Goncalo, just like in Berkowitz's letter. A reminder, the Yonkers phone books back in 1976 listed phone numbers by street, not last names. Wicker Street only had two houses on it, 18 and 22. The only name listed to 18 Wicker Street was Joaquin Goncalo..."*Captain Blood.*"

Berkowitz did not know of the Netos because all he knew were the names listed in the phone book. The Neto home was firebombed on May 13, 1976. This letter was written on March 8, 1977, almost a year later, and Berkowitz still did not know of the Netos. Berkowitz's target at 18 Wicker Street was Joaquim(n) Goncalo, "*Captain Blood*," because he was the only one in the phone book listed at that residence. Proof was how he spelled Joaquim's name in his letter with an N, Joaquin, as that was how it was spelled in the phone book. This is also why Berkowitz said there was a "*Joaquin the Joker*" living at 18 Wicker Street, he was referring to Joaquin Goncalo, a name that only existed in the phone book.

Berkowitz thought the barking dog King at 18 Wicker Street belonged to "*Captain Blood*," Joaquin Goncalo, because he was the only one listed in the phone book as living there. This adds proof to Wheat Carr's claim that Berkowitz used the phone book to come up with the name "*JOHN WHEATIES.*"

This next letter was sent to New York City Mayor Abraham Beame from Berkowitz while he was being held at Kings County Hospital after his arrest:

Dear Mayor Beame,

My name is David Berkowitz and I am writing you with the uttmost urgency. There is little time left in the world because demons (Sam Carr, 316 Warburton Ave., Yonkers), (Jack Cassara, 174 Coligni Ave., New Rochelle, N.Y. have taken a strong hold in the government.

I am a dedicated Gladiator who will fight the forces of darkness to the ends of the earth. However, I need your help. We must work together to help the public and warn them of "Sam" the terrible foe of people.

Sam Carr, John Wheat, Jack and Nann Cassara, and Craig Glassman all know each other.

According to the voices I heard one of them, a demon, stated that Sam Carr strangled young people and buried them behind Sam's house. These people are just bones now however I can hear them calling out my name and becoming me to join them. They are all bones now but I can hear them calling me. Surely Sam Carr killed them and drank their blood.

See, I told you Sam is a thirsty lad.

I, David Berkowitz am merely a tool for Satan the devil. But perhaps God has spared my life to an extent for a heavenly purpose.

Though I am suffering now, I want to help the people and warn them of the dangers of Black Magic and the hopes that others will see the light and trust in God.

Please help-warn the world of the terror that is in Sam. Please help me Sincerely David B

Look at "*Sam Carr strangled young people and buried them behind Sam's house. These people are just bones now*." Doesn't this sound very similar to the passage from the Borrelli letter? "*BEHIND OUR HOUSE SOME REST. MOSTLY YOUNG-RAPED AND SLAUGHTERED-THEIR BLOOD DRAINED-JUST BONES NOW*." How about "*Surely Sam Carr killed them and drank their blood. See, I told you Sam is a thirsty lad.*" Look back at the Breslin letter. "*BUT SAM'S A THIRSTY LAD AND HE WON'T LET ME STOP KILLING UNTIL HE GETS HIS FILL OF BLOOD*." This similarity in writing is good evidence to believe that the same author who wrote this letter to Mayor Beame is the same author who wrote the Borrelli and Breslin letters…David Berkowitz.

This next letter was David Berkowitz's first letter to Sam Carr, dated April 10, 1977, which Sam received on April 11, 1977:

Mr. Sam Carr,

This letter is to inform you that I am in the process of filing legal papers in Yonkers City Court to have one of your dogs removed from your property because he is a public nuisance. I have already spoken to the people of the humane society of westchester and they agree with my actions.

You're probably thinking that I am some kind of animal hater or I'm a cruel person but that isn't true. Let me tell you that I love animals very much. However, one of your dogs, and you know which one, is obviously very sick or is being treated badly. He howls and barks constantly for hours at a time and there is no reason for it. If he's sick, take him to a vet. If he cannot be left alone then don't leave him alone. And if it's because you mistreat him then maybe it's best you just give him up.

When my wife and I set up our home in Yonkers we wanted to live our lives in peace and happiness. Unfortunately your dog has prevented us from doing so. Our lives have been torn apart because of this dog. We can't sleep late in the day. We can't come home in the evening and relax, and we cannot keep our windows open at all. Even with our windows and storm windows closed, to include heavy drapes, the howling is so loud and constant that these barriers cannot keep the sound out. It's as if he were in the house with us.

In the past week, for example, we tried to arrange our work schedules so we could have a few days off together. We wanted to spend some quite weekdays, just the two of us, to sleep late, to make love, to read, etc., but the barking and howling continued and we had no peace. Today is Easter Sunday, I'm writing this letter now and as usual the dog has been going at it for the entire day-unbelievable!

My wife is about to have a nervous breakdown and I'm a bundle of nerves. We can't go on like this. The only thing we regret is that we did try to rid ourselves of this problem earlier. However, as I said, we are peaceful people and we don't like having to take such drastic actions. We were always hoping that the problem would alleviate itself but I can see that its going to be another miserable season.

No I cannot afford to move, our home is here.

Mr. Carr, every dog is expected to bark a reasonable amount, thats normal. Howling and crying all day long isn't and I think that dog is very sick. Furthermore, don't think that by keeping the dog leashed, licensced, and fed, that it's enough. The law clearly states that if a dog continuously barks when unprovoked it is a "public nuisance" regardless of the time of day. Keeping the dog on the property physically isn't enough if his barking GOES OFF the property to other homes and disturbs the peace of others. Matter-of-factly, I can hear that dog barking for blocks and blocks away.

We do hope that you will cooperate with us to solve the problem.

We wish to remain anonymous for personal reasons. Thank You.

The Carrs barking dog was truly bothering Berkowitz. He was not lying about the madness he was experiencing from the surrounding dogs. Remember, the last two places he lived at, he moved because of dogs. It was not a fake scenario he was making up. The barking dogs were driving him crazy.

Here is the second letter Berkowitz sent to Sam Carr dated April 19, 1977, which Sam Carr received on April 20, 1977:

Samuel Carr,

I have asked you kindly to stop that dog from howling all day long, yet he continues to do so. I pleaded with you. I told you how it is destroying my family-we have no peace, no rest.

Now I know what kind of person you are, and what kind of family you are. You are cruel and inconsiderate. You have no love for any other human beings. Your selfish, Mr. Carr.

My life is destroyed now. I have nothing to lose anymore. I can see that there shall be no peace in my life, or my families life until I end yours.

You wicked evil man-child of the devil. I curse you and your family forever. I pray to God that he takes your whole family off the face of the earth. People like you should not be allowed to live on this planet. (signed) *A Citizen.*

Both of these letters were important to show you. You can see Berkowitz was taking the Carrs' barking dog as a personal attack. I think he felt the Carrs were ignoring him and didn't care he was being bothered. This made Berkowitz even more agitated as the tourment continued. Also remember, at this time, Berkowitz had a post office job he started only a month earlier. His hours were 4 p.m. to 12:30 a.m., not normal working hours. I'm sure the dogs barking were affecting his sleep, as well as Glassman's loud television set, which also started a month prior to this letter. This scenario was real, and Berkowitz hated it.

Another reason these two letters are important is because these letters are the reason Berkowitz was caught when he was. If Berkowitz never sent these letters, Sam Carr would not have been able to match the handwriting with the get-well card that had been sent to the Cassaras. Hence, when Sam found out who was writing these letters, his campaign to catch David Berkowitz began.

In these stack of letters, there was one which was found in his apartment that was not sent. It was dated July 17, 1977 and was to be sent to Stiller, Miller, and Godzilla on 42 Broadway, N.Y. The letter was signed…Sincerely, Francis Carr:

Gentlman,

My name is Francis Carr and although I'm not as young as I used to be, I can still get into perverted sex scenes real good.

I believe I'm the one your looking for in your upcoming porno movie "Sweet Tootsie."

I can do all types of acrobatic stunts in bed and I will really copulate anything except turtles and mice.

I love bondage and sado masochism. Please contact me as soon as possible so I can audition. Thank you…Sincerely, Francis Carr

Berkowitz's letters were not the only form of harassment he caused the Carrs. Numerous obscene calls flooded the Carr's answering service switchboard while Berkowitz lived at 35 Pine Street. There was also a complaint from Sam Carr I found in these files which showed more of the games Berkowitz would play with the Carrs.

This was the Yonkers Police report regarding Sam Carr's complaint:

On August 5, 1977, Detectives Michael Lorenzo and Edward Oakley went to Mercy College, 555 Broadway, Dobbs Ferry, N.Y., relative to checking a fraudulent mail-in registration made out in the name of Samuel Carr. Sam Carr stated prior to dectectives that someone contacted him from Mercy College by phone and asked what courses he wished to enter in the upcoming semester, also if he was eligible for Veteran credit. The caller stated to Sam Carr that a registration mail-in was made out in his name, giving his phone number and address. Detectives checked with the Director of Veterans Affairs and the

Admissions Office at Mercy College and there was no record of Samuel Carr applying for anything at the college.

The Carrs were not the only ones Berkowitz would harass, he liked to play games with the police too. Look back in the Surlak/Cerasi reports. On May 15, 1976, Yonkers Police Officers were sent to 35 Pine Street to respond to an anonymous complaint of shots fired. I found reports in these files that stated the anonymous complaint was shots fired inside of the building on the 4th floor of 35 Pine Street. Officers spoke to three residents from the 4th floor and no shots were reported being heard. Berkowitz was having more fun than you think.

This next letter, dated the first Saturday of August 1977 (August 6), was found in Berkowitz's 1970 Ford Galaxie's glove compartment by Detective Zigo when he entered Berkowitz's car the day of the arrest:

> *I must get this job done. This is the last assignment, the last mission. Once it is finished I will be of no use to Sam Carr and I will be destroyed.*
>
> *I do not fear Death for I do not wish to go back to my apartment, ever. Never again will I have to give my life to Craig.*
>
> *However, I will do my best to come out of this alive because as one columnist said, "someone must pay for these horrendous crimes."*
>
> *From the Bronx to Water Mill, New York no soul shall be safe.*
>
> *I would also like to meet with the task force personally, not that I have anything to say to them but its only fair we meet face to face. I wonder if they will take me on a brief tour of their war room?*
>
> *Perhaps the hidden secrets of the Carr house will never be known. Those hideous blood monsters who lurk in the woodwork and under those rotting floor boards, yes, they will still live on.*

At this time Craig is awaiting anxiously by his T.V., ready to take command.

Bullets crackle in a quiet town. The sounds of running feet and screams of anguish fill the air. Huge streams of blood travel down curveous buttocks, bosoms bouncing, bullets flying into the night coldly seeking flesh and bone, yes, its terror in the night. Sergeant Craig is terror!

Who has brought the wrath to this town? Where is the "Great Lord Bloomingdale's" their Saviour. Why has God forsaken this place?

For truly there has never been peace in the Hamptons, inner peace I mean. They aren't a sensual people but they are filled with rage and jealousy.

So let New Yorkers everywhere gather together, gather to battle the unseen forces that roam their neighborhoods at night and seek to imprison their children in coffins. Let them hunt down the Son of Sam and the mysterious thereof.

Truly nobody knows what time it is. For the end of Sam is drawing nigh. Yet, the police continue to hunt and trap. The Inspector continues to work feverishly trying to unravel the mystery but, would he dare to believe that by surise of the next morning he will be holding that .44.

The curtain always closes quickly when the stars walk off or die.

In the aftermath the Hamptons chamber of commerce will have to count their dead and file a report. Reporters will be swarming the streets snapping pictures of dark red spots on the ground which symbolize where people once stood. Perhaps a big tall cop with an empty .38 will be playfully kicking in the ribs of the Son of Sam with his shinny boot. He'll be enjoying those sadistic delights and he'll be looking on with satisfaction at his prized catch.

In a short time things will be back to normal and if you go into a lover's lane at night you'd be able to here the sound of dozens of car springs squeaking in unison. Then you will know that there is peace in the world. (signed) *X.*

This was Berkowitz's last letter he wrote as a civilian, and I can see it was written on the same day he set fire to Craig Glassman's door, "*Bullets crackle in a quiet town.*" When Berkowitz set the fire to Glassman's door, he did so by lighting a bag of garbage filled with .22 caliber bullets, which did cause the bullets to fly "*into the night coldly seeking flesh and bone.*"

Berkowitz had plans to shoot more than one person at his next attack. "*Reporters will be swarming the streets snapping pictures of dark red spots on the ground which symbolize where people once stood.*" Berkowitz was going to commit these murders in the Hamptons, just like he told Klausner in his book. He drove there to kill, but it rained, so he chose to wait for another day. This letter was written on August 6, 1977, and was the night he drove out to the Hamptons for his grand finale. God rained down on his encore and ruined his plans.

I think this was going to be his last time committing murder as he knew the police were on to him. "*The Inspector continues to work feverishly trying to unravel the mystery but, would he dare to believe that by surise of the next morning he will be holding that .44.*" I feel he was prepared to die in his blaze of glory, "*The curtain always closes quickly when the stars walk off or die.*"

Berkowitz knew his time was up and couples in cars would be safe once again. "*In a short time things will be back to normal and if you go into a lover's lane at night you'd be able to here the sound of dozens of car springs squeaking in unison. Then you will know that there is peace in the world.*" Berkowitz was saying, once he was caught or killed, "*the sound of dozens of car springs squeaking in unison*" would be heard again, meaning, couples in cars would be safe once he was gone.

When Berkowitz started to kill, my opinion is he was originally motivated by his hatred towards God and women. His attack on Carl Denaro I feel was a mistake, his target was not men at that time. As the shootings went on, especially after his April 17, 1977 double homicide, I think killing men and women he assumed were having sex in parked cars became more justifiable to him. He now had their sin of sex out of wedlock as an excuse for his actions. He gained purpose and meaning for what he was doing, and with that came less guilt.

These files I obtained included both the Borrelli and Breslin letter, both of which were very very crisp and clear, like I had never seen before. I started to fold the letters in a way the two letters were side by side with their letters closely next to each other. I couldn't believe my eyes, are you kidding me? The H's were exactly the same, the I's were exactly the same, the G's were exactly the same, the T's were exactly the same. How could Maury not have seen this? I can say with 100 percent certainty that Berkowitz is the author of both letters.

In the back of this journal you will see more letters written by David Berkowitz which were found in these files...enjoy.

I started this journey looking for people who were connected to a satanic cult which supposedly included David Berkowitz. I spent the first half of this investigation wasting my time like all the people before me, looking for things that did not exist. When I finally decided to follow my own leads and focus on the actual people involved, as you can see, that's when I started to make some real progress.

I still had some questions I needed to be answered. Teresa Ramos said when the Netos' dog was shot, she saw a man running down to Warburton

Avenue with a rifle get into an off-white idling car. Who was driving that car? What about Tommy Zaino's story with the vehicles he noticed at the Moskowitz/Violante shooting? I still had some work to do.

I called Larry later that day to tell him I found some breakthrough material but to be patient. I gave him two letters written by Berkowitz to start out with and told him I was going to give him a little at a time. These files have been held from the public for over forty years, and I needed to make sure everyone was safe...I had to be careful. I then emailed Larry about the Borrelli and Breslin letters being both written by Berkowitz. I sent him pictures of the letters side by side, showing him how certain letters were identical. Larry couldn't see what was obvious and insisted there was no way they were both written by Berkowitz.

On April 10, 2022, Larry had one of his Zoom meetings again. Attending were John Rinciari, Bob Maitre, the podcaster guy, and Scarlett. Before we started the meeting, I Zoomed with Larry solo and asked if Bob Maitre had gotten in touch with Anthony Cerasi. Larry said no, so I called a friend of mine in front of him and asked my friend if he could have Anthony Cerasi call me. My friend told me no problem and I hung up the phone. I said to Larry, "You are talking to all these cops now, cops that actually worked with Cerasi. Why haven't you gotten any of them to talk to him?" I got no response.

The meeting was like the last, controlled by Larry and no one could express their thoughts. Before the Zoom meeting ended, Larry brought up the phone conversation between Wheat and Detective Justus. He wanted to know the exact date it occurred on. I had the entire conversation in my files, so I ruffled through them to get the exact time and date. Before I could do that, Bob Maitre pulled out a piece of paper with the phone conversation between Wheat and Justus. I asked Bob where he got that from and he said his friend who worked for the NYPD gave it to him. Nobody had these files but me and Detective Geiss...and Bob was friends with Geiss.

Larry started to ask why we had files he didn't see yet. I told him he was going to get these soon, as I told him earlier, I needed to release these files slowly. Larry then told Bob to send him everything and Bob did just that. Bob sent Larry all my files and Larry sent them to everyone in the Zoom meeting.

After the meeting, I called Detective Geiss and asked him why he sent the files to Bob Maitre. He apologized and told me it was a mistake. Bob was sorry as he didn't know I was the Paul Agostino who found these. He only knew me as Neo and didn't realize who I was at the meeting.

I accepted Bob Maitre's apology and told Geiss I was done with this. I didn't need this in my life anymore.

Detective Geiss then text my phone a few minutes later.

Detective Geiss: This is all you, keep your head up, everyone including Larry knows that. You know this stuff frontwards and backwards. After Joe Monaco got these files he had to let the higher-ups know because the shit you got was missing. Don't sell yourself short, everyone knows what you did. You know more about this case than anyone. I would not give up on it if I was you. You are really into this for all the right reasons. I will be in the office in the morning if you want to talk.

Larry didn't understand what Bob gave him was the files I found. He didn't realize those files were the same ones I was going to be giving him the next few days. He thought the files Bob gave him had nothing to do with what I found and realized, after I spoke with him, the podcaster guy now had access to do whatever he wanted with them...just great.

I emailed Larry the next morning.

Paul: No one has seen these files but Geiss and he did not mean for this to happen. You need to be grateful and stop fighting with everyone, no one wants to help you when you keep insulting people every chance you get. I can't expect people to help when you treat everyone like garbage. I'm not hiding anything from you, but at the same time, I can't lose people's trust. I'm not playing this game like that.

I called Larry that afternoon and talked him into calling Carl and Josh so he could give them these files. I could have easily given these files to them myself, but I again felt if Larry did, it would be a good gesture. Larry called both Carl and Josh that day not to share the files, but to gloat to them with what he had. The olive branch I once again tried to extend was smashed by Larry's arrogant ego. No worries, I sent everything to Carl and Max, and made sure they sent it all to Josh.

I then spoke to Josh about these files, he was open to them and my theories. I really wanted him to understand I was not against his work. Everything that happened the past year just came into my life and I was delivering it. Josh knew my intentions were good and whatever came out of what I was doing was honest. I told Josh he was the reason this all started. His documentary brought forth much awareness to people and myself. Without seeing his documentary, David Berkowitz would not have been a thought in my mind and would have remained a crazy guy from my neighborhood who talked to a dog that told him to kill.

On April 13, 2022, I was looking through some of Berkowitz's letters and realized I hadn't tried to contact the Goncalos yet. I also realized I needed to find someone who had information about Craig Glassman. Larry ruined the one true connection there was left with his daughter Shayna. I just wish I could have spoken to her first. I can guarantee things would have been different. First things first, Joaquim Goncalo, here I come. It took me about a half hour with Penny to track him down. He was still living in Yonkers about five minutes from my old house...knock, knock.

At this time, Larry was still pissed off about how Josh treated him when he called to give him the files I found. Larry didn't understand that when you talk to people with arrogance, they automatically don't want to be grateful.

When you talk to people in a way where you act like they owe you, especially from Josh's status in this case, it comes off as insulting. Why couldn't he just be grateful I got these files and use them to make peace like I intended? His ego this entire time has been disgusting. Josh wasn't wrong, it's how people have to act when such arrogance is upon them.

That night I got a phone call from the only Yonkers Detective involved with Berkowitz's arrest who was still alive, Anthony Cerasi.

Before I started getting into the case with Anthony, I was curious if he had seen any of Larry's shows. He said yes, but had to turn them off because of Larry's misinformation. He asked who Larry was, and I told him he was from the Bronx, an outsider.

First thing Anthony mentioned was he was lucky Berkowitz was not home when he knocked on his door the day of Glassman's fire because there were firearms Berkowitz had inside his apartment and he could have been blown away. We discussed Sam and Wheat, and the roles they played in Berkowitz's capture. He told me Sam was a pain in the ass but they were both good people and were essential in stopping Berkowitz when they did. I brought up Craig Glassman to him, was he involved with Berkowitz at all? "No way," he replied, "That poor guy had no idea what was going on until they went to his apartment for the fire and he showed them his letters." Anthony said the only thing Glassman did was help them identify Berkowitz when he exited 35 Pine Street the night of the arrest. He was the only person who knew what Berkowitz looked like. Glassman was not friends with Berkowitz at all, he was a Westchester County Deputy Sheriff who lived in Berkowitz's building.

Anthony asked me where I had gotten the lost files from and his personal reports. I told him I couldn't really get into that, but I brought everything back to Detective Geiss, where it belonged. He laughed and said those reports were his and he couldn't believe I found them. Before we got off the phone, I asked if he thought Berkowitz acted alone. He immediately answered, "Absolutely, no doubt." I thanked him for his time and we made plans to see each other soon.

On April 14, 2022, I found out how to open chat rooms on Larry's website. It allowed me to finally be able to talk directly with the people who were posting comments all year. I had been waiting a long time to talk with some of the many people who were along for the ride. It was also good for crowd participation, which I asked Larry to do from the beginning. I started to meet a lot of the people who posted during the year, Larry refused to participate.

My favorite of all the people who posted on the website was a woman who went by the name of Cookie. Cookie stuck out to me a while back when the website was talking about Shayna Glassman and how she visited Berkowitz in prison. Cookie posted if that were her, and Berkowitz did these things to her father, she would punch him in the face before she even sat down with him. I liked that...that is probably what I would have wanted to do also. These chat rooms worked out for me as I got to know some of the people who followed us all year.

On April 16, 2022, after reading all these files, there was something I needed to do. I needed to apologize to Wheat Carr for some of the things I had said in Larry's videos. I was wrong for assuming she was involved with Berkowitz and I needed her forgiveness. I knew there was still a chance her brother might have known Berkowitz, but I don't think Wheat, who had a major role in Berkowitz's capture, knew that her brother had known him, nor did her father.

Following all these false leads and theories in the beginning led me to believe Wheat was guilty. With the reports I had now, she was a hero who helped catch the biggest serial killer in New York history. These police reports are what everyone should be paying attention to. The police had absolutely no reason to lie or cover up for a sick lunatic. When I spoke with Detective Cerasi, he laughed at that notion. He told me no one at all knew this creep and there was no reason whatsoever they would have done anything in his favor. I have spoken to enough law enforcement on this case to stand by that.

Here was my email to Wheat.

Paul: Dear Wheat, I am writing to you with nothing but hope for your forgiveness. I am sorry if in any way I have disrespected you or your family as I went around Yonkers trying to find the truth...or what I think is the truth. Maury Terry did not do this right, and unfortunately, you and your family had to pay the price. I lived in Yonkers my whole life and have been everywhere in this city. I have been blessed to be acquainted with so many people, my loyalty to them has brought me here. I am honest, loyal, and my family and I have always been here for the people of Yonkers. I take pride in saying I am from there. I remember seeing your father at the Boys Club when I was little. My close friend, like a father to me, worked with your father for the City of Yonkers. Many times I rode my bike through the aqueduct stopping at your house, just looking. My family was always close to the politicians so I grew up around city hall. From Martinelli to Spencer, I saw the city change. I also have been employed by the City of Yonkers for the past twenty-two years, doing the same exact job as your father did. I have met Pete Intervallo, Sal DiMaggio, and many other officers you have come across because of my job. My access to the police and fire departments have helped me because of my years of loyalty to them. I have recently come across some Yonkers files given to me by a firefighter. I then went out to talk to the officers alive. Nowhere have I gotten you or your father guilty of anything. Your family was targeted like other families in the neighborhood...and I have talked to them also. No one knows the truth because no one from Yonkers besides Maury reported this. He was wrong and this kind of stuff I take hard and deep. We have one life, just one, it should never have to have this. He stained my city at the same time, was trying to stain my church, Sacred Heart. My loyalty to my church is why I did this. It has been all bullshit. I can only apologize for myself if I have assumed wrong during this year of nonsense. My information was coming from Maury and an outsider until I realized something was terribly wrong. I can not figure out what happened with your brother John, I just don't think at the time you did either, nor your father. Can I say your brother was an accomplice with the shootings, I can not, but I have talked to a few people who saw your brother with Berkowitz. I am just being honest, I'm not doing this to get anyone in trouble. I have realized that I'm doing this for you, the victims, my church, my city, my people, the police. I know you don't want this in your life, it has been nonsense, and you deserve the opposite according to all the police here in Yonkers. I have talked to many kids of the detectives that were on this case, not one of them says you were involved in a bad way. You and your father saved lives by helping catch Berkowitz and received nonsense because of Maury Terry. I don't know what went on with Berkowitz and your brother, if it was devil worship, then there lies your answer...I guess only Berkowitz could ever answer that completely. To me, if he knew him or not, I can not accuse your brother just for that. Reports I have gotten from North Dakota and Yonkers just have a troubled hurt man. I again would like to apologize to you if I have disrespected your brother during this. I may have said some insults about him that are just completely not needed. I am not a judge and I am far from perfect. Please accept my apologies, forgiveness is important. I will stand behind you and the police who have been railroaded with this case. When I started this, they had you as a possible shooter. I feel I have now even convinced Carl Denaro that you are innocent. I have talked to all these people in this world that Maury created, even Josh Zeman. No one is mad at me, they all know I tell the truth...I'm honest and I'm loyal.

Wheat: Please Note, I do not respond to anonymous emails beyond sometimes acknowledging receipt. I have received and read your note.

Holy shit, she responded! My email was set up as NEO YES THE ONE. I didn't know how to change it.

Paul: I apologize again...I have never used emails until recently. I did not know my name was not presented. My name is Paul Santo Agostino.

Wheat: Thank you for your transparency, as to "reports" I would note that some of the people who are believed to have supposedly seen John in places have given dates when it would have been impossible since he was not even in the country and in one case was not even home at the time of supposed sightings. But again, hard to prove a negative. Other than John did not even live in New York, and New York City cleared him because the USAF supplied evidence of where he was at the time of most of the shootings. There are so many inaccuracies out that can never be corrected, there really is no point to even try, people will believe what they wish to believe particularly when it is presented to them in a seemingly factual manner. As to Carl, I have only ever wished him well. He went through a horrible experience and has been misused ever since. It is sad that he never got the kind of help that would enable him to have had a better life. As to forgiveness, not mine to give, but interesting you ask for it on Easter weekend. Peace of the season, Wheat.

Paul: It is yours to forgive and it means a lot to me. I have opened many peoples eyes to see what I see. A year ago everyone thought you, your father and the police were crooked, that you all were hiding things. I have proven Maury wrong about you and your family and people are believing me. Maury said you shot a clock out at the Candlelight Inn on Central Avenue. I went up there and talked to the owner and he told me Maury was full of shit. Maury accused Robert "Tocco" Grady of being with Berkowitz. I found him and proved Maury wrong. Maury had the nerve to accuse a friend of mine's uncle of being a devil king. I with embarrassment proved that wrong. I presented, with the help of the active Yonkers Police, records proving you were a part of the investigation. The records show you were talking to detectives. Where was this the whole time? I'm doing what is right and vindicating you and the police. I owe you that at the least...and these kids here, whose fathers who were detectives that got shit on for doing their job, the wives of these detectives deserve honor restored to their husbands. I've changed a lot so far, they can't beat the truth.

Wheat: Christ died on the cross so that our sins can be forgiven. If you feel you have wronged my family, then consider yourself forgiven. I suppose if I can learn to forgive certain members of YPD, someone misled by the Terry family deserves that as well. I wish you good luck in your endeavors, who knows, you might be the one who finds all the records proving, disproving all the unfounded allegations. Time to go do other, happier things for the rest of the day. Peace of the season, Wheat M. Carr.

Yessss!!! I needed that.

Paul: Thank you...your forgiveness to me is priceless. God bless you Wheat and have a Happy Easter.

I needed her forgiveness before I ended this journey. I did this to make things right and all my wrongs should be accounted for.

Wheat said John was not in New York City when some of the shootings occured. That was verified by New York City law enforcement, as the United States Air Force supplied evidence of where he was at the time of most of the shootings. I believe her, but what about Albie and Caveman seeing John and Berkowitz together? Albie heard John threw the rocks at the Netos' house. He heard, he didn't see John or talk to him about this, he heard. I will take people's word for things if I don't have evidence or proof to combat it with. I have no reason to think they were lying, but Wheat was at the center of all this and her involvement in this case proves to me that she is a credible source.

The next day Larry and I did a show presenting some of Berkowitz's letters to his audience. We went over the threatening letters sent to Sam Carr and as Larry was reading them to a live audience, I realized he was missing two pages of the first letter. I had them, as he was never given the original files from me. He had what Bob Maitre gave him and they were missing some pages from the files. Bad preparation, I had to read the letters in their entirety to the audience.

On April 20, 2022, I called Larry to tell him about my emails with Wheat and how adamant she was about her brother John not being involved. This conversation with Larry did nothing, he still thought Wheat was guilty.

I emailed Larry later that day to remind him to stop insulting the Carr family.

Paul: Please remember to not call John Carr "Jelly Head John" anymore, respect the innocent until proven guilty. Wheat has been through enough already. Also, I talked to my friend who worked with Sam Carr and he told me no one ever thought the Carrs were involved with this in Yonkers. It looks like Maury found out John Carr was in a satanic cult and just tied this all to Untermyer Park. It's upsetting, Carl and Wheat are who I care about at this point.

The next day I found where Joaquim Goncalo was living and knocked on his door. Joaquim's wife answered and could hardly speak English. I tried to talk to her about her husband and David Berkowitz, but it was difficult. I asked if she had any children I could speak with as she said Joaquim was sick inside the house. Joaquim's wife then gave me her daughter's phone number. I called Joaquim's daughter and had an extremely nice conversation with her. This family was exactly like the Netos, an immigrant family that came to America to work.

I asked Joaquim's daughter if she ever heard of David Berkowitz. She only heard of him because he lived near where she grew up, but nothing besides that. I asked if her father had ever mentioned anything to her about Berkowitz. She replied, "Never." She then asked, "What is this all about?" I explained her father was mentioned in a few letters written by Berkowitz that were found in his apartment forty-five years ago. "Oh my God" she said, she never heard of any of this, her father never told her anything about David Berkowitz. I asked, "Can I speak with your father?" She was sure I could, but he was not feeling well at the moment, and would call me back after she talked to him. She assured me her father was a hard-working man and did not know David Berkowitz or anything about what was being written in his letters.

Joaquim's daughter called me later that evening, her father had never seen David Berkowitz until he was on the television after the arrest. He had no idea what I was talking about and he never heard he was mentioned in Berkowitz's letters.

The Goncalos were exactly the same as the Cassaras, the Netos, and the Carrs...families that were brought into all this by a sick person who created a satanic cult in his mind using the people around him. There was no satanic cult in which Berkowitz belonged to, there was only a sick person with a sick imagination that had run wild.

CHAPTER XVII

END OF THE NONSENSE

April 22, 2022, I was going to be working at a sports memorabilia show that weekend at Hofstra University in Long Island, New York, so I called Carl and asked him if he was free for dinner. He told me to come by his social club when I was done with the show and he would take me around town. Hofstra University was only fifteen minutes from where Carl was living and I thought this would be a perfect time for us to finally meet.

When I got off the phone with Carl, I checked my voicemail and Tommy Zaino had left me a message. I called him back and he wanted to know if I could get him hockey playoff tickets for the New York Rangers. I made a few phone calls and I couldn't get playoff tickets, but I did have a friend who could get me tickets for the Rangers' last home game. When I called Tommy back and told him, he said he had tickets to that game already and just needed playoff tickets. Tommy wanted to get together, so I told him I was meeting Carl that weekend and suggested he join us. He and Carl had some problems in the past, but I wanted them to forget about whatever went on previously and make peace. He agreed and said he liked Carl, he would love to see him again. I thought this was a good thing for them to talk, as they both lived with being a part of this madness Berkowitz created, and I wanted them to be friends again. Putting them together was important to me. They hadn't seen or spoken to each other in a long time

I called Larry later that day to tell him I would be working at a sports show in Long Island and was meeting with Carl and Tommy for dinner. He got angry and asked why he wasn't invited. Are you kidding me? He just spent an entire year abusing Carl, and he was asking why he wasn't invited? Why would I even think he would want to come? Besides, it wasn't like we were having a meeting, I was working and then getting a bite to eat while I was in town.

Larry asked why Tommy Zaino was going. I told him I mentioned to Tommy I was meeting Carl for dinner and asked if he wanted to join...what's the big deal? Larry started complaining that Carl was going to mess everything up and talk bad about him to Tommy. We were not meeting to talk about him, we were meeting to eat and drink.

I asked Larry, "What is Carl going to mess up?" He replied, "Tommy and I are going to write a book together and Carl is going to mess my relationship up with Tommy by talking bad about me." I asked him why he was talking with Tommy for months now and he hadn't been brought on board. His answer...he was cultivating him...cultivating? Tommy Zaino is a street guy, you take him to Yankee Stadium and bullshit...what was he cultivating?

Truth was, Tommy was just another person of value for Larry to use. I got off the phone with him and knew I had enough. Now this kid was going to tell me who I could hang out with? Larry was also complaining that he should be meeting Tommy first. What the hell was he doing for the past two months? What was stopping him from going to see him?

Larry called Tommy later that evening and gave him a hard time about meeting with me and Carl. Not only did he bother Tommy, he emailed Carl, calling him a snake and would appreciate it if he didn't talk about him to Tommy. I knew this because they both called and asked me what Larry's problem was.

Larry then sent this text to my phone.

Larry: I wish I had been invited to the meeting with Tommy. I was hoping to clear a pathway to working with him and now I feel excluded. Tommy just told me he is going.

Paul: I am going to Long Island for a show. Carl is about fifteen minutes from there, he asked me to stop by. I was getting Tommy Ranger tickets and told him I was meeting Carl, he wanted to join. What's the problem?

Larry: Just letting you know how I feel about it, no big deal. I felt that I should have met him first.

Paul: Then make an effort, you've had two months.

Larry: I'm not making an effort? I've been cultivating this guy.

Paul: For what? He is street. I'm getting two guys together who were victims to be friends again. What's the problem with that? This isn't a meeting, we are not talking about you. I'm going to be in the area getting something to eat. I have to ask your permission to see people, is that what you're saying? I have other people meeting me. This isn't about Son of Sam.

Larry: I would have preferred to meet Tommy first and I thought that was understood since he was my contact.

His contact? I called Larry out of nowhere with all of Tommy Zaino's contact information. He never even discussed getting a hold of him. He didn't look for Tommy, I did. Letting him call Tommy was a big mistake as you can see. Months had gone by and he produced nothing...he was too busy cultivating.

Larry didn't want anyone talking to each other, as it was all part of his plan to make him the center of attention and not expose his true role in all this. He didn't want people to figure him out...but I did, and I was tired of his nonsense. I was honestly trying to hang out with two guys who were involved in this tragedy and put them together to maybe help heal them. Larry was horrible with people and his motives were selfish. He was extremely ungrateful and I was wrong to have helped him.

Paul: I brought him to you, you never even asked for him.

Larry: Ok, he is all yours then.

Paul: No one is mine, I'm just hanging out. You can have it all. You pulled your bullshit again the other day, you gave credit to someone else for finding Sal DiMaggio...how is that? He was given to me through Frank Carozza. I bring in information and you give credit to other people. You have this imaginary team you want the audience to think is helping you, it's only me and you know that. They both wanted to hang out and making peace between these two is what's important to me, not your nonsense.

Larry: Carl and company are snakes in the grass.

Paul: Carl has not said one bad word about you ever, I told you that.

Larry: I would have advised against a meeting at this time. Later would be cool. Carl is gonna meet him before I do. I just find that wrong.

Carl had no intention on bothering Larry. He already knew Tommy, and from what they both told me, they wouldn't mind seeing each other and having a reunion.

Paul: I am in town this weekend and they should make peace if they want to. I am working all day at the show and then meeting some friends of mine also down there to get something to eat.

Larry: I just have a bad taste in my mouth. I personally am not on a save the world mission with this as much as you are and that is cool. What you do is important. Have a good time at your meeting.

Paul: It is not a meeting for the last time. I am working and getting something to eat.

Larry: It's cool, maybe I'm overreacting.

If Larry had any manners or respect for anybody but himself, he would have been invited. He's done nothing but cause problems with everyone he came in contact with during this entire journey. There were so many more incidents of him disrespecting people I could tell you about, so many lies, so much manipulation, but I would not have enough space in this journal to cover them. Truth is, Larry put nonstop hurdles in my way this entire time I investigated. His conspirator mind was set on accomplices, now he can continue to look for those accomplices on his own. That was the last conversation I had with Larry as I realized what I was dealing with, an outsider I should have never let in.

The next day I worked at the sports show and was looking forward to meeting Carl and Tommy. At about noon, Tommy called me and canceled. He wanted to come but it was a little too far and he was stuck at work. He was sorry and hoped we could catch up soon. Larry's maniac call to Tommy definitely bothered him. Tommy did want to come, I could tell, but Larry said things to him I'm sure made him not want to cause problems. Yeah, I wish I could have put Carl and Tommy together, but this kids selfish motives once again got in the way.

I finished my sports show and put Carl's location into my GPS. I arrived at his social club and walked in through the front bar to a back room where Carl was hanging out. When he saw me, he had nothing but a big grin on his face. I could see he was happy to meet me. We shook hands and he said, "NEO." I smiled back and corrected him, "No, it's Paul, how are you Carl?"

Carl and I sat down at the bar and talked about a lot of things, very little to do with the "Son of Sam" case. That was not why I was there. I was there to meet a person I wanted to help heal from a life he did not choose. We talked more about him and what he had been through.

Carl spent a good part of his life trying to find answers about who shot him, his life had no escape from that. He was a great guy, stuck in Maury's findings for years, not knowing a way out. He didn't hate me at all with what I was doing, which was proving Maury's theories wrong. Deep down inside, I felt he believed what I was finding was only the truth. It was important to me he knew my intentions were good. I didn't do all this to hurt him or Maury, that was never my intention. I went out to talk to people to get more insight on what Maury had done, and what Maury had done, I cannot explain, but it wasn't real. When this first happened to Carl, he thought Berkowitz shot him. Then along came Maury, and his life would never be the same.

Carl took me to an Italian restaurant named Poppy's, and his choice of what to order was on point, delicious. His girlfriend joined us and she was an extraordinary complement to him. You could tell she kept his wild side grounded. Us men like to party at times and we can get out of hand. She definitely was good for him. She was a classy woman who I could see really, really loved Carl. I was so thankful to see he had that. They were perfect for each other. I was grateful for God's work.

After dinner, Carl took me to a bar where a live band was playing and we threw back some drinks. I felt extremely comfortable with him. He knew everyone in the bar, and they were all happy to see him. As I listened to the band play, I watched Carl enjoying himself with his friends and began to think to myself... what did I do? Why didn't I just mind my business? I started to feel down watching Carl, knowing what Larry had put him through over the past year. He just wanted answers and I felt I got them for him, but the way Larry shoved my findings in his face, it was complete disrespect. Larry ruined everything with his ego and made a mess with all his non-needed arrogance towards Carl.

This was why I wanted Carl involved from day one, so he could have been a part of it all, not have to fight with Larry about what I was finding. If Carl was involved from the beginning, it would have been "our" findings, and I feel he would have accepted everything "we" found in a better manner, Josh also. Carl and Josh didn't want to fight. They just didn't want to accept what I was finding from an egotistical bully. What I felt sick about was I was giving Larry the bullets to put in his gun to shoot them with.

I ended the night giving Carl a hug, telling him I would see him soon. I left the bar in a depressed manner, sorry for what he had been through because of what I did. Then my faith in God reminded me that only God can choose who brings balance...NEO YES THE ONE.

April 24, 2022, Larry sent me an email as I stopped answering his phone calls. He now knew I was done with his nonsense and was thanking me, telling me he had the best time of his life. It seems Larry's best times were my worst, which is exactly why I needed to get away from him. This email was his last desperate attempt to keep me around...I had value he needed. I went no-contact with Larry and blocked his phone number and emails. My motivation to succeed prevented me from seeing what Larry was truly all about. We were only bonded by the case, not by friendship.

Penny had already gotten tired of Larry and stopped watching his videos a month earlier. She was the one who kept me grounded this entire time, having me ignore his selfish attitude and go forward with the case. When she wanted no more of Larry that last month, I was dealing with him alone. That didn't last very long as you can see. If it wasn't for her, I would have stopped giving him information for content a long time ago. Penny felt bad this whole time with the way Larry treated Carl. She couldn't stand his relentless insults to people as his ego grew worse and worse from our success. No contact was the only way, I just walked away. I wasn't going to bother him, I didn't build him up to knock him down.

April 27, 2022, Carl noticed what I did and reached out to me by text.

Carl: What happened, did you drop the hammer on Larry? He was very unnerved on his show.

Paul: I realized a lot when I went to see you. He was never my friend and I just wish him the best. I tried, but he is not my kind.

Carl: I hear you, we all got fooled, you, me, Max, Jess, Mason, the podcast guy, and the list goes on. Don't feel bad, he just uses people.

Paul: This could have been something good, I'm just disappointed. I can not help someone who is a bully. I gave him everything he could ever ask for as he treated people like garbage. I can't no more...I love people.

Carl: I have the same lament. We have so much information that he could have used but his bombastic personality got in the way. He can't help himself.

Paul: I can only help myself by going no contact with him.

Carl: We all win as soon as we step away.

So, we have Detective Borrelli, who was on this case, saying Berkowitz acted alone. Borrelli also claimed every detective and doctor who interviewed Berkowitz, also said he acted alone. We have a pastor who knew Berkowitz, and is still in contact with him, saying he acted alone. We have a decorated Yonkers Detective in John Geiss who also felt Berkowitz acted alone. Even Detective Cerasi, another detective who personally dealt with this case, was sure Berkowitz acted alone. Every witness to the shootings, except for Tommy Zaino, said there was only one person they saw at the crime scene. Tommy also said it wasn't Berkowitz that night in Brooklyn, and Berkowitz confirmed that. I wish I could have spoken to Tommy more about this incident. Letting Larry handle him was a mistake.

CHAPTER XVIII

THE FLYING MONKEY

A few days went by and some people from Larry's website decided to start a "Son of Sam" Facebook group, which did not accept Larry as a member. Alicia, also known as Leash, started the group with Scarlett. I liked Leash a lot, as she participated with her online posts frequently. Early on in the investigation, Leash communicated with Wheat Carr by email and shared their conversation with the audience. I posted right after she did that and thanked her. Nothing was really in the email from Wheat, but I always wanted to thank those who contributed. I loved when people got involved.

Leash and Scarlett got a hold of me through email and asked if I would join their Facebook group to talk about the case. I didn't have a Facebook account and knew nothing about it. I told Penny about this and she was against it, saying Facebook is too much drama, stay away, it would be nothing but trouble. I didn't listen, made a Facebook account, and started making friends instantly.

I really wanted to walk away from this, but I liked these people, and they were asking me for my help. When I talked to Scarlett in the chat, she said she was helping Larry since the beginning with all of his articles. That's funny, Larry never mentioned her to me until I asked him to get her to help out with the Zoom meetings. I thought she just posted on his website.

Another person I met in the chat was a lady named Sharon. This was the woman who Larry told me to stay away from, he insisted she was a mole for Carl. She was also helping Larry from the beginning with information. Larry kicked her to the curb a few months earlier for no reason besides talking to Carl. Sharon was the lady who told Carl she could get files on this case for five thousand dollars. She actually asked Larry for my help to get the files and he said no. Sharon knew Detective Cerasi and tried to put him together with Larry, but Larry arrogantly didn't want to talk to him. How could this kid blow off Cerasi? Now it made sense why Cerasi didn't want to talk to him.

All of these people had no idea what I did. As you can see, Larry gave a lot of credit to his imaginary team of researchers. So many people were used by this kid, and most of them were discarded when he was done.

I emailed Scarlett the missing pages to Sam Carr's letters that Larry didn't have and told her to give them to him. I told her not to tell him I gave them to her to give to him. I didn't want Larry to know they were from me, but I wanted him to have the pages I knew he was missing. This is something I knew Larry would never do for me, but that's okay, not even he can change me.

On May 15, 2022, I attended a meeting held by Carl at his social club. There were about fifteen people there, all were welcoming and cordial. We discussed Carl's visit with Berkowitz and some accused cult members. I could tell some of the people there had seen my research, they knew I was not behind Maury's theories. There was no arguing, and no enemies were made at this meeting. I understood them and respected their points of views, they did the same with me.

These people were not wrong, they believed in Maury and trusted him. It's not their fault no one ever fact-checked Maury's work, no one ever felt they had to. These people believed Berkowitz, like we all did when he told Maury he didn't act alone. Berkowitz told the world he did not act alone. How do you contest that without any proof all these years? This wasn't just Maury's fault, Berkowitz led him on, claiming Michael and John Carr were involved and a satanic cult was behind everything. In the beginning, I believed all of this too, but I had something that none of these people had... Yonkers.

No one went through Yonkers with this case like I did, not even Maury, no one could. It amazes me no one from Yonkers ever looked into this, but understand, no one from Yonkers ever believed Maury to care to. Maury's theories only worked on outsiders. My advantage was Yonkers and it's people. No one else had that, including Larry. The bottom line is, these people are not wrong for believing Berkowitz and Maury, no one ever showed them any information to believe otherwise.

The meeting ended well and I met a lot of good people that day. They accepted me and what I had to say. It was a start, but I could see I had a long road ahead of me if I was going to try and push that Berkowitz acted alone. I remember when Detective Geiss first told me this, it was like something you just didn't say. Carl was mortified when I told him Geiss thought this. No one ever thought this, and if you did, you were considered crazy. Times have changed, and the right information is now in front of us…Berkowitz acted alone.

I got home from the meeting and Leash had messaged Carl to join their Facebook group. I told her if she really wanted Carl in their group, I could talk to him, it was up to her, I wasn't going to make that decision. Leash was ecstatic to have Carl Denaro be a part of her "Son of Sam" group.

Leash was now giving me the opportunity to break down this division in the community Larry had made. I would now be able to get Carl in this community and I was sure others from his group would follow. I knew exactly what I needed to do. Carl has been wanting me to join his Facebook group for a while now. I always told him I didn't do this internet stuff and didn't know how to get on Facebook. Well, I was on Facebook now, and all I had to do was tell Carl I would join his group, but in return, do me a favor, join Scarlett and Leash's. Carl agreed to this, and by the end of the day, I was a member of the Maury Terry Facebook Group. I didn't mind this at all. Now I would be able to reach his people with the information I had and let them see the truth.

That night I sent Carl a text.

Paul: I again apologize to you Carl. Larry has insulted you terribly and it was because I let him in.

Carl: Let him go, he is a pathetic little man.

The next day, like I thought, people from Carl's group started joining Scarlett and Leash's Facebook page. These people were coming to learn more about the case, not to argue.

On May 17, 2022, I began sharing all my documents, files, and audio interviews with people from both Facebook pages. This was all I ever wanted to do, find information and share it. This went on for days as I answered people's friend requests and questions. As a sign of unity, I asked Carl and Max if I could give Scarlett some material to post on her page so the group could have some discussion. Carl and Max agreed to let me share the North Dakota documents on John Carr that they gave me a few weeks earlier. I sent the documents to Scarlett and told her to post them whenever she wanted, just say they were from Carl and Max.

A few days went by and Scarlett still had not posted the North Dakota documents I gave her. I didn't think anything of it as I was spending my days reaching out to people in both groups, sharing information about the case... and then it happened. Larry released a video and told his audience he had a whole bunch of new material to discuss. It was all my work, and all the material I shared with the Facebook groups, including the North Dakota documents Carl and Max had given me. Larry claimed an anonymous emailer sent him all this new information and he now had weeks of content. Scarlett gave him everything I was sharing with both groups. Those North Dakota documents were meant for her Facebook group, not for Larry to do shows with. I should have listened to Penny.

I left both Facebook pages as I could see my no-contact with Larry would not work if I stayed. Larry began doing shows spewing hatred against Carl, hatred against me, calling me a backstabber. He was blaming me for all his bad relationships with people. He did this in order to succeed in erasing what I had done to claim for himself. He was going to play me, and to do that, he first needed to ruin my reputation.

Larry had a platform, and I did not. New people were coming into the mix as the old were gone. He was going to continue as if I never existed. He began to lie about how everything happened, how everything was found, and began taunting me through his videos. Larry used the North Dakota documents to completely trash Maury, Carl, and Josh.

Larry was now telling his audience Wheat and John Carr were innocent and Berkowitz wrote both the Borrelli and Breslin letters. All of sudden, his conspirator ways were no more and he could prove Berkowitz acted alone. He was stealing everything I ever said and did, using my files as if he had found them.

He erased every video I was in, stole my thoughts, my theories, my conclusions, my words and began making videos literally playing me with no shame. I never told him to quit, but if Larry thought I was going to sit here and watch him lie about everything he didn't do, that was not going to happen.

I don't like liars, I despise them. Lies are what got me into this in the first place, and lies are what are bringing me back into the picture. I preached to this kid the entire time not to worry, the truth of things can never be beat. When you have the truth, things will always end up right and prevail. This is when I knew I had to write this journal. It was my only way, the old-school way, to be able to tell my side of this story. I had the truth, therefore he can not win this war he just started. He has asked for the Jedi to return, the one who brings balance...NEO YES THE ONE.

Weeks went by as Larry continued his smear campaign against me. I gave that kid everything, and now I was the bad guy. Countless lies and manipulation became Larry's weapons...I've already showed you how weak those weapons are.

CHAPTER XIX

THE HOLY GRAIL

June 22, 2022, mark this date on your "Son of Sam" timeline. An unknown person released all of the New York City Police Department records on David Berkowitz. It was presented online and contained everything law enforcement did regarding the "Son of Sam" case, letters to and from Berkowitz's doctors, the Queens District Attorney investigation from 1979 when the case was reopened, and a ton of handwritten letters by Berkowitz.

First thing I did was print every single page of it, over nine hundred pages, and brought them to the Yonkers Detectives to put in their files. That was always one of my goals. I hated it when I went to the Yonkers Records Department and they told me they had no files on this case...now you do. I then bought a fresh pack of *Davidoff* cigars and dropped them off to Chief Monaco. What was in those files, helped me confirm what I had figured out. Berkowitz acted alone, and was not part of a satanic cult at Untermyer Park. The Carrs, all of them, were innocent. These files were exactly what I needed to finish my investigation and conclude my journey. The unknown person who did this, did an extremely amazing job...thank you J.C.

This incredible website had two parts. The first part included over forty audio recordings of the Queens District Attorney interviewing people such as Donna DeMasi, Joanne Lomino, John Comparetto, John Diel, Judy Placido, Maury Terry, Nann Cassara, Nathan Berkowitz, Patrick O'Shaughnessey, Richard Sperrazza, Rose Mary Keenan, Salvatore Lupo, Tommy Zaino, Wheat Carr, Sam Carr, Frances Carr, and many many more.

The second part included investigative files consisting of eight folders. "*Arrest Reports*," "*Berkowitz Letters*," "*Forensic Analysis Reports*," "*Maury*

Terry Files," "*Psychiatrist Letters*," "*NYPD Reports*," "*NYPD Victim Reports*," and "*Yonkers Police Reports*."

I would like to go over all of these recordings and files with you, but that is impossible, the material is just too much. I will go over what I think is necessary to show you, what I needed to end this. This is the fourth quarter... the ninth inning...enter the sandman.

I listened to all of the audio recordings and I'll discuss a few of them. These are not the recordings in there entirety, as I use what I think is important to hear.

Donna DeMasi, Son of Sam victim who was shot on November 27, 1976, interview conducted by Herbert Leifer, Assistant District Attorney, Queens County Attorney's Office, 1979.

On November 27, 1976, Donna DeMasi and Joanne Lomino went into Manhattan that night to see a movie. When the movie was over, they took a bus home to Floral Park, Queens, and walked from the bus stop to Joanne's house a few blocks away. As they approached Joanne's house, they noticed a man standing on the corner at the end of their block. They hung out on Joanne's front doorstep to wait for the man to pass so Donna could continue to walk home. A few minutes later, the man they saw at the corner walked on the grass of Joanne's house, asked for directions, then began to shoot Joanne and Donna right where they stood. Donna says the man was directly under a streetlight when he shot them.

Herbert Leifer asks Donna if she got a good look at the shooter. Donna says she did, but Joanne did not, as her back was turned when the man started shooting them. Leifer asks Donna for her opinion, "Since the arrest of David Berkowitz, they have pictures of him on TV, pictures in the newspaper, is that the same person that you seen that night?" Donna replies, "I also seen him in court and that was him, that was him. I don't believe it was anyone else." Donna then says, "What I remember about him was his eyes, he had very weird looking eyes. That was the main thing that stuck in my head." She also recalled, "When I seen him that day in court, that same eyes came back to me."

Leifer places a picture of David Berkowitz in front of Donna and asks, "Does that look like the person who shot you?" Donna replies, "Except for it looks like he gained more weight, I don't know, he didn't look that big." Leifer questions Donna, "How about his hair?" Donna answers, "No, but his face does, his face really does. I had no doubts in my mind when I seen him in court, 'cause when he turned around he was screaming out and yelling Moskowitz and screaming I'm going to get you yea I'm going to do this and do that. It looked just like him." Leifer then asks, "Did the voice sound the same?" Donna quickly responds, "Yeah," and goes on to say, "The main thing that really stuck in my head was his eyes. It was the same exact eyes he had when I seen him."

Donna DeMasi was the only victim of this attack that got a clear look at Berkowitz. He did not sneak up on them while they were in a parked car like most of his victims. He walked up to Donna and Joanne under a streetlight and started to speak to them. This eyewitness in this recording is saying the man she saw shoot her and her friend that night was David Berkowitz…with no doubt in her mind.

Nathan Berkowitz, adopted father to David Berkowitz, interview conducted by Herbert Leifer, Assistant District Attorney, Queens County District Attorney's Office, 1979.

Nathan Berkowitz says this in his interview, "Now let me tell you something, according to what I read in the paper they feel that there was a cult involved in this. David has never mentioned this to me and I'm very close to David. He's never mentioned this to me. Whether there is or not, he's never mentioned this to me, you understand? I don't know anything about it. As far as I know, as far as what I know and what I have, letters from him, my impression that he did all these himself. Ya see, all these things himself, because the boy was sick, really sick. I got several letters there, that if I wanted to sell them, they would be worth a lot of money. Those letters are every indication of what he was under, but as far as knowing whether he was hooked up with anybody, I have no idea whatsoever."

Herbert Leifer asks Nathan later in the interview, "Did he ever talk to you about the Carr family?" Nathan replies, "No, he never told me anything about the Carrs."

Curious how Berkowitz was while living on his own, Leifer asks Nathan, "How did he sound when he came to visit you when he was at Barnes?" Nathan recalls, "Normal." Leifer continues, "No change in his personality?" "No," Nathan firmly answers, "In fact everybody that knew him was surprised about this whole thing because he acted just like anybody else would."

Leifer questions Nathan, "Did he like dogs?" Nathan says, "We had a dog that he was crazy over. He never seemed to shun him, but I'll tell you what bothered him a lot, all his life, any little loud noise used to annoy him. If I used to speak to him in just a little above the natural toned voice, he used to put his hands to his ears. He couldn't stand loud noises."

Nathan Berkowitz was the closest person in his son David's life. Nathan spoke to David after his arrest, and there was never a mention of any cult being involved. Not only was Nathan positive David committed these murders, he even thought David did all these murders by himself because he knew David was sick. Nathan also discusses with Leifer David's problems with handling loud noises all his life.

After his arrest, why wouldn't Berkowitz tell his father he was influenced by a cult or anyone else? Because there was no cult, he told his father the truth in the beginning. It was only after Berkowitz met Maury would his cult stories begin. Berkowitz didn't keep information from his father to protect him, he hadn't started to make up his cult stories yet. There were no people involved with him, Berkowitz acted alone. Once again, "*according to what I read in the paper they feel that there was a cult involved in this,"* Maury's articles are what influenced peoples' opinions.

Wheat Carr, sister to John Carr and daughter to Sam Carr, interview conducted by Herbert Leifer, Assistant District Attorney, Queens County District Attorney's Office, October 26, 1979.

Wheat Carr begins her interview, "At the time that John committed suicide. He had come home in January, this is 1978. When he arrived home, he told my mother and I, and this is within an hour after he got there, and we're sitting down and he came home because he was scared. It was, he said that he had been approached again about selling drugs on campus and he just didn't want any part of it, and he believed that that was, that these people were very serious, he didn't know exactly who they were, but he was very concerned about it." Wheat recognized her brother had drug problems and wanted to help him get his act together. John was going through a divorce at the time and lost everything. When her brother got back to North Dakota, he opened up a post office box, a bank account, and was going to straighten out all his school situations. She said he did all this on the day he supposedly shot himself.

Wheat says to Herbert Leifer, "It doesn't sound to me like someone who eight hours later was going to blow their head off, it really doesn't." Wheat then questions how her brother was found dead, "He supposedly sat down on a bed, put the gun in his mouth, and shot himself, but he was found face down on the floor with the back of his head blown off I guess, with the gun balanced across his heels somehow with either end of the gun not touching the floor."

Wheat did not think her brother John killed himself. Remember, during that time before his death, John was telling Wheat he was very concerned about the people who approached him on his college campus for dealing drugs and was very paranoid from this. This gave Wheat the impression something else had gone on to cause his death. Also, Wheat said there was blood found in another room of the house other than the room John supposedly shot himself in. She questions Leifer again, "How could there be blood in another room? You can't tell me that someone who just blew his head off is going to just get up and walk around." John told his sister people were trying to kill him, so she had every right to think the way she did.

Wheat then says, "John was home June of '77 and he was home at the time that we found out who David Berkowitz was. In other words, that's the point Mrs. Cassara came to us about the postcard, the get-well card her husband received, and put together the thing about the tenant and all of that, and then my father saw the sketch and that was when he first went to the police and they said he was nuts, that the handwriting was so different from the infamous letter, the 'John Wheaties' letter."

Wheat was not denying her brother was likely into drugs, and with that came the crazy, messed-up things he was around. Wheat honestly tells Leifer, "So, you know, John's involvement in the occult, I'm not going to deny, there's no way I can deny it, I'd be stupid to deny it, John was very heavy into drugs, but this last time I truly did believe, you know when somebody's saying I want to get out and they don't mean it. There's a fine line between saying, oh I wish I could stop this, I hate what I'm doing to myself and saying I have to stop it, I want to stop it. I wish and I want are two different things, very fine line. He had gone from I wish to I want. I believe that, this last time was the first time I ever believed it." Wheat really believed her brother wanted to change his life and was trying to be positive during the time he supposedly commited suicide.

Wheat goes on to say, "I'll tell you the truth, I don't even care if my brother comes up totally dirty, I just want this resolved." It had been two years since the arrest of Berkowitz and there was no evidence at all tying her brother John to these shootings, or to Berkowitz for that matter. Wheat just wanted all this nonsense to end, as she had nothing at all to hide.

During this interview, Wheat admits her dog Harvey definitely used to bark a lot, but insists he was such a nice dog, he loved people. One thing Wheat clarifies again, is the truth about the origin of the name "JOHN WHEATIES." Like she said in her email, and I backed it up with Joaquim Goncalo's name being spelled with an N, Berkowitz used the phone book to get that name. Wheat explains, "The other thing I don't know if anybody ever cleared up, the 'John Wheaties' thing. Obviously Wheat is my name, not John's name. I think I was about twelve, which would have made John about sixteen, at the age when children get a lot of phone calls from their friends. In order to avoid having calls go through the switchboard, we may have been even younger, I don't know, my mother listed a telephone line so that our friends could call us. The telephone company charged you at that time an extra dollar to have two listings, so she listed it John Wheat Carr, this way everybody knows John or Wheat and they could call us on this phone if they looked it up in the phone book. The first threatening phone call we got from Berkowitz came on that phone, and the rest of them came on the switchboard."

Leifer asks Wheat, "Did anyone ever call you Wheaties?" Wheat replies, "Only in an obscene fashion...Wheaties, breakfast of champions." Leifer questions Wheat if she ever called her brother Wheaties. Wheat's answer is, "No, my brother was John or JC." She goes on to say, "That letter was a dead giveaway. That is the letter that convinced two cops, one detective, and one dispatcher and one civilian that it was the same person. It all made sense. Everything in that letter points to exactly where he is." They were right, the four clues were all pointing to Wicker Street, where Berkowitz was, where the demons were.

October 12, 1979 was the first time anyone would publicly connect her brother John to the "Son of Sam" shootings. That day, Wheat entered a store and saw in the newspaper her brother was being connected to Berkowitz and these crimes. The article was titled: "*NYC Police Reopen 'Sam' Investigation*." This interview here, with Leifer and Wheat, was part of the reopening of the investigation as it was conducted only two weeks from October 12, 1979, on October 26. The article in the newspaper stated the key questions the police were focusing on were:

Was John Carr an accomplice in the "Son of Sam" killings? Was John Carr involved with David Berkowitz and others in occult activities? Did John Carr commit suicide as originally believed or was he murdered by other conspirators because of his knowledge of the "Son of Sam" killings?

Wheat said she got hysterical in the store when she saw this article. She may have entertained questions of her brother's involvement before, but this was the first time she saw her brother's name in the newspaper being publicly accused of crimes with Berkowitz. This was the first article ever printed by Maury Terry accusing John Carr of being an accomplice to the "Son of Sam" shootings.

Nann Cassara, owner of the residence in New Rochelle who rented an apartment to David Berkowitz in February 1976, interview conducted by Herbert Leifer, Assistant District Attorney, Queens County District Attorney's Office, 1979.

Nann Cassara in the beginning of this interview does not want to speak to Herbert Leifer. She had been reading about John Carr's alleged involvement in the newspapers and was not comfortable speaking about the incidents involving Berkowitz.

Leifer asks Nann, "When you received the get-well card with the return address, Sam Carr, you then contacted Sam Carr?" Nann replies, "Right." Leifer goes on, "As a result of your discussion with Sam Carr, what caused you to read back or check back in your diary with regard to your prior tenant?" Nann explains, "Because I went to see Mr. Carr and he showed me the letter, letters that he had gotten. They were anonymous letters, threatening him, and I compared the handwriting to the card and I knew it was the same person wrote it. I went home that evening and my son and I were reading the letters that we got, photostatic copies of Carrs' letters, we were reading the letters and my son says, who could connect the two of us together, has to be somebody we both know, and we didn't know each other so he happen to think back over a tenant I had the year before that up and left because of my dogs barking, and he says these letters are all about a dog barking, about dogs barking, and he says, don't you remember this guy we had live here a couple of weeks and he went crazy because my dog woke him up barking and he left? Then I looked back in my rent receipts and I come across David Berkowitz, so then my husband looked up David Berkowitz in the phone book and found he lived right near Carr." Leifer then asks Nann if she told Sam Carr about what she had found out. Nann replies, "Oh sure, Sam Carr knew all of this."

Leifer continues, "Did Mr. Carr ever mention to you having met David Berkowitz or gone up to see him?" Nann answers, "No, no, he didn't know him, he had no idea at the time I talked to him. He thought that probably it was a colored situation, it was a black situation, somebody was threatening him because they were trying to force him out of the neighborhood, because the blacks were taking over that area. He thought it was probably somebody that was black was doing it." Nann then says Sam Carr told her, "Go to the FBI, go to the police, this is a very dangerous situation. I said well, I have gone and they are not doing anything, and I said I turned over all the information to the New Rochelle Police, who said they turned it over to the Yonkers Police. What more could you do? Now another person's been killed. Then he said well, tomorrow morning I'm going to the Brooklyn DA's office, which he did. I think he took the information and went there."

Leifer questions Nann, "Did they ever mention that they knew the name Berkowitz before you mentioned he was a tenant of yours?" Nann replies, "No, he never did. My husband was very excited when he saw that he lived right in back of him. When he saw in the phone book where he lived, he knew the apartment building."

Nann admits Berkowitz was very neat and an ideal person to have as a tenant. She never heard a sound out of him while he lived there until the morning he went berserk over their dogs barking. Leifer asks Nann to describe to him David's outburst that morning. Nann begins, "Well it sounded as if someone fell out of bed or kicked somebody out of bed. It was a Saturday night and I felt, well, he's a young fellow and he's very quiet, so probably he has to have some kind of outlet and maybe he went out and he got drunk and probably brought a girl home, I don't know, but I jumped out of bed because there was a mouth talking and I thought he had somebody that he was talking to. Then he burst out of the top-floor room and went running down the stairs and out into the driveway, which is on the side of the house where he comes in, and he was walking up and down, shaking his fist at the house and raving. This is four o'clock in the morning. It was a very strange thing to happen unless he was on drugs or you know, it was very unexpected when we never heard a sound out of him while he was up there. Then he ran back upstairs and he got a can of beer and he went running down the stairs and my nineteen year old son at the time came out and he says hey what's the matter, and he mumbles something about the dogs again and he got in his car and drove away."

Nann, during this interview, continues to mention she thinks John Carr knew Berkowitz, but she didn't think Sam knew they knew each other. Leifer asks Nann, "What makes you think that his son knew Berkowitz?" Nann's response was, "Because of what I read."

Nann then tells Leifer, "Berkowitz knew my daughter and her name and she never laid eyes on him as far as she knew. She's married and out of the family." Leifer questions, "How would he have gotten her name?" Nann answers, "I don't know because he wrote to me, do you have the letter I had got from him? Something about Queen of the Gunhill. That was in the letter that he wrote to me after he left. He went on to talk about my children, and they got very insulted because they didn't know him. It was just a very strange thing he knew her so he must have been watching."

How did David Berkowitz know Nann Cassara's daughter's name? Does this sound familiar to you? What Berkowitz was doing to the Cassaras sounds very similar to what was going on with the Netos. Maria Neto told me a man would call the house asking to speak with Sylvia. Sylvia was twelve at the time. She did not know David Berkowitz, just like Nann's daughter didn't. Maria had no idea who the caller was, but the caller even knew what school Sylvia attended. "Queen of the Gunhill?" The Netos were also receiving phone calls about a queen. We now see Berkowitz would mention the children's names to the parents he was harassing, and the references with a queen to both parties is just too coincidental.

This Nann Cassara interview was important to show you. It wasn't just at Wicker Street or Barnes Avenue that Berkowitz had a problem with dogs. The problem was with him, not the dogs. Remember, Nathan Berkowitz said his son always had a problem dealing with loud noises. It was David's problems, not the dogs that caused him grief.

This interview also explains again how the Cassaras and the Carrs found out it was David Berkowitz who was harassing them, which led Sam Carr to later believe Berkowitz was the "Son of Sam." Nann recalled how her son went up to Berkowitz the morning he went berserk and spoke to him in the driveway. That is the same story her son Steven told me when I knocked on his door that day. Also during this interview, Nann was questioning John Carr's involvement even after knowing the Carrs were innocent and victims of Berkowitz's games like she was. Nann said, "*Because of what I read*," (in the newspaper) she thought John Carr might have known Berkowitz...she was reading Maury Terry's articles. Proving, even those directly involved, were mislead by Maury's information.

Tommy Zaino, witness to the Son of Sam attack in Brooklyn of Stacy Moskowitz and Robert Violante on July 31, 1977, interview conducted by Herbert Leifer, Assistant District Attorney, Queens County District Attorney's Office, December 5, 1979.

Herbert Leifer begins this interview with Tommy Zaino by asking him, "Just tell us in your own words as best as you can recall, starting from the time you arrived at the scene, give us the location you arrived at, where you were, what kind of automobile you were in, if you were in one, and what you saw." Tommy begins, "I got there about, I can't remember the time exactly. I think it was like about ten after two, around there, and I hung out there. We parked under the streetlamp on Shore Parkway between, I think it was Bay 17 or Bay 16 in between there, right next to the highway. I was under the light for a while and then I just happened to pull up til it was a little darker and a little while after that somebody parked behind me. I seen headlights from the mirror, just a reflection, then I happened to look through my mirror. I don't know why I looked 'cause I wasn't doing anything, I was just hanging out. So then I look through the mirror and I seen a guy hanging out near the entrance of the park in between over there. Right before that I had seen a lady walking a dog. They all walk their dogs and when I seen this guy, I looked and thought maybe he was walking a dog 'cause he was near the fence and then he just came out of the fence, off the sidewalk towards that car that was behind me, and it looked like he was getting into the car 'cause he had, I think he touched the handle of the car. Pretty sure he got like really close to it and then he just went into a stance and fired into the car."

Tommy said after the man fired four shots into the car behind him, the man ran back into the park the same way he came out. Tommy is asked, "When you saw him later on, once they caught him, did the fact that his hair was apparently different from the night you saw him bother you at all?" Tommy replies, "No, I can remember somebodies face even if their hair's messed up, his hair could have been all messed up." Tommy is then asked, "At this point having seen photographs of Berkowitz both on TV and in the press, do you feel it's the same person that pulled the trigger that night?" "Yeah," Tommy answers before the person asking him that question could finish. "Even though the difference in the hair is as great as it is," Tommy is asked and replies, "I still say it's him." Tommy is then asked for his opinion, "Are you satisfied that that was David Berkowitz?" Tommy recalls, "I seen him. When I first seen him, something that night, I remember the first night when they caught him. I was still in the hotel and I seen it on TV, it was splashed. You know he was downtown, and I seen him. I looked at him and you know, I knew it was him."

A detective questions Tommy, "What happened after the shooting? You say he ran in the park, what did you do?" Tommy explains, "I took off. I got the car started and went right around the block and I went to the front of the park like, and looked to see if I seen any headlights start coming. I went down to, I think, 18th Avenue, a couple blocks down, and went right to the 62nd, to the police station there and I told them. They looked at me like I was a nut. Everything was just going through my head right now and I told this guy, I says, I think people got shot. He looked at me and I took off and got back there before anybody was there. There was just some lady there with a couple of blankets and stuff. She didn't want to so I got out and handed one over to them. He was by then, you know, I seen it, I seen the girl in the car. Robert was out of the car by then. He was on the floor." Leifer interrupts, "Did you know Robert personally?" Tommy says, "I seen him around." Tommy is then asked if Robert saw anything. Tommy's response was, "All I can say is that he told me that it was fast when it happened, but the guy he seen before was the same guy. He knows the guy that he seen is him, it's no doubt about that." Tommy's then asked, "Did you see a Volkswagen go by there?" Tommy replies, "No, but I heard a Volkswagen motor go by." Leifer asks, "Were there any other cars parked there besides yours and his?" Tommy says, "Not that I seen. I talked to a couple of people that happen to be there that just split right after that that I didn't even know. They didn't want to get involved. They were down further though. They didn't see nothing, they just heard everything and they took off."

During this interview, Tommy did not see a yellow Volkswagen bug parked in front of him with a woman inside or a white van parked behind him like he had told me. Tommy also told me he didn't think it was Berkowitz who shot Stacy and Robert. I think this interview was done before Maury had spoken with Tommy, making him believe, just like Mrs. Moskowitz, and many others who read his articles, Berkowitz did not act alone. Tommy mentioned to me he liked Maury and they had a good relationship. I feel

Maury influenced Tommy after this interview and that is what caused Tommy to repeat the stories he did to me. Tommy's visit with Berkowitz also had Tommy confused.

Maury had you believe Tommy Zaino, the witness, told him about all these things that went on at the Moskowitz/Violante shooting. I can now see two interviews with Tommy (interview with Brooklyn DA on August 5, 1977) which happened before Maury's interview with him that tell me different. I don't believe Tommy told Maury what he saw, I believe Maury told Tommy what he saw.

This is why when looking into this case, it is important to pay attention to the evidence before 1979, before Maury was able to print his newspaper articles, before Maury teamed up with David Berkowitz. This was one of the doors in my investigation I had left open for accomplices because of what Tommy told me. Berkowitz acted alone for this shooting. Tommy Zaino and Robert Violante both saw it was him...door closed.

Maury Terry, journalist and independent investigator, interview conducted by Herbert Leifer, Assistant District Attorney, Queens County District Attorney's Office, 1979.

Maury Terry during this interview says to Herbert Leifer, "Berkowitz was in North Dakota on a couple of occasions, did you have that?" Leifer quickly answers back, "Nope, I never had David in North Dakota." Maury comes back with, "Okay, according to what I saw he was." Maury claimed he saw a letter from Berkowitz to another person saying he was in North Dakota, but he would not tell Leifer who Berkowitz sent the letter to.

Leifer reminds Maury that when Maury was in North Dakota, he found no one that could say Berkowitz was there. He goes on to tell Maury when he went to North Dakota himself, not one person he spoke to could identify Berkowitz or knew him. Leifer said he even showed all the people he spoke with Berkowitz's picture, and nobody recognized him.

Maury explains to Leifer that Berkowitz got in to the cult after returning from the service. He joined a Baptist revival group while he was in the service, and when he came home, his parents disowned him because of his newfound Christianity. Then more or less, as a reaction of that, he drifted into this cult thing. "Wheat was the one he met first. Okay, Wheat provided the introductions for him to John and Michael, who were both satanists and cult members along with others," Maury claimed to Leifer.

During this interview, Maury goes on a rant. "I'm sick and tired of people not believing me when I tell them things. I am really sick and tired of it."

Maury points out to Leifer that Berkowitz has enjoyed the stories he and his colleagues have been writing in the newspapers. Berkowitz particularly enjoyed the story on the Stacy Moskowitz murder...how he didn't do it. Maury goes on to say, "From what I've been able to learn, he started getting on this. He was following what we were writing very carefully 'cause people are sending him all this stuff 'cause I had no idea that he was getting the *Gannett* stories but he is, and he was following it all with great interest, and then like September and October, and the last couple months when we started to come out with some of the real heavier stuff is when he decided he was going to get involved."

Maury then goes on another rant about how no one wants to believe him. During this interview, Maury was not being cooperative with Leifer about information he had.

At the end of the interview Leifer says, "Let me ask you, do you think there is any possibility that your friend might meet with you and me?" Maury quickly answers, "No," without hesitation, and gives Leifer an excuse why. He tells Leifer if he were to make any efforts to go and see Berkowitz, Berkowitz might kill himself.

To me, in this interview, Maury Terry sounds like a gatekeeper to David Berkowitz. Maury holds back information from Leifer and felt that if anyone, but him, went to see Berkowitz, it would ruin everything. Why wouldn't he help the law enforcement he begged so desperately to reopen this case?

Maury claimed Wheat Carr was the one who met Berkowitz first, introducing him to her brothers, which led to him joining this so-called cult. I think we can agree by looking at all this new information, that is completely wrong...Wheat did not know David Berkowitz.

Leifer and Maury both went out to North Dakota, and Leifer said he spoke to a lot of people with a picture of Berkowitz in hand. No one knew or ever saw Berkowitz there. Maury agrees, but then tells Leifer he has information from a letter that was sent to someone from Berkowitz proving he was there, but couldn't reveal who Berkowitz sent the letter to. Is this how you do an investigation? You beg for the case to get reopened by the Queens District Attorney and then withhold evidence from them? Why have them reopen the case and then not help with information to solve it? I don't get it, holding back information and not wanting them to talk personally with Berkowitz doesn't make any sense to me.

Maury bragged about how Berkowitz enjoyed his newspaper articles on the case and was getting involved because of his investigative work. This interview was done two years after Berkowitz's arrest, and you can see, it was only after Maury Terry began writing his newspaper articles did Berkowitz then start to change his story. Only then did Berkowitz begin to nod his head yes to everything Maury speculated.

Remember, Berkowitz was in prison with no life again, alone. What Maury did was bring him the attention he always wanted in the first place, resurrecting his life while behind bars. If you were Berkowitz with no life in prison, and all you had to do was go along with Maury's theories to have people's attention again, wouldn't you do the same? Especially if it showed you in somewhat of a better light than before. People still to this day write to Berkowitz, send him money and gifts, wanting to know what really happened. Attention was always Berkowitz's goal, and Maury gave that to him.

I do feel Maury started looking into this case with good intentions. His evidence was formed from very strong coincidences that he came across at first, but these coincidences could never be concluded with any real, solid evidence...not until Berkowitz confirmed his assumptions, giving him reason to believe he was on the right path. Why would Maury think Berkowitz was lying to him? Berkowitz, by using Maury, was able to play his games again. His lies to the outside world is why we are still talking about him right now.

For Maury, I think by the time he realized the games Berkowitz was playing, there was no turning back. Maury became the face of "Son of Sam," doing interview after interview. All his years of work on this case was bringing him his income. I think Maury had to keep the story going in order to survive, this case is all he had and fabricating the truth is sometimes a survival skill some people must use in order to stay alive.

These audio recordings I have just gone over with you are only a few from this amazing source of evidence. Before I end this part of the journal, I would like to point out, Patrick O'Shaughnessey was among the many interviewed in these recordings. He was interviewed by George Byrd, Criminal Investigation Division–Homicide Bureau, Queens District Attorney's Office. I thought Maury said O'Shaughnessey disappeared, quit the police force, and enlisted in the Marines when he was asked to be interrogated by the Queens D.A. That is false, O'Shaughnessey fully cooperated with an interview and obviously was cleared of any wrong doing.

Richard Sperrazza was another person Maury made accusations against who was also included in these audio recordings. He was cleared the same as O'Shaughnessey. In fact, on August 13, 1977, Sperrazza was interviewd by Inspector Timothy Dowd, who stated it was the opinion of the N.Y.C.P.D. Task Force that Richard Sperrazza was not a party to any of the criminal acts committed by David Berkowitz.

The second part of this website contained eight folders of investigative files. One folder, which was labeled "*Berkowitz Letters*," is a gold mine of more handwritten letters by Berkowitz. I would now like to go over some of these letters to show you more evidence that Berkowitz acted alone.

This letter was written by Berkowitz while he was being held at Kings County Hospital after his arrest. It was postmarked September 16, 1977, and was written to Steve Dunleavy, an editor for the *New York Post*:

Dear Mr. Dunleavy,

Despite the fact that you are no good and that Mr. Carpozi Jr., has quoted me as saying many things which I did not say, I still need you as a messenger to reach the world. Please listen.

That letter to Breslin, I was forced to write. Breslin wanted to get up here so he need a letter. I was almost forced to write it.

Why did I want to speak with Breslin? It was not because I like him.

I know that he is just a greedy reporter but I need a messenger to earth.

Listen, I'm pleading with you to understand the forces of darkness and evil.

Sam Carr is one of the devils of Satan. I cannot make myself any clearer. That dog was not a dog but I demon from hell. I happen to love dogs.

Sam, is a force and person beyond the wildest imaginations of people. He is not human! I have seen them, Carr, Cassara, Glassman, as they really are.

I have seen them as demons not as humans. Their humaniss is only a front. They are here on earth to destroy it.

I have tried to tell the police (a letter). I have tried to tell the world (letter to Breslin). What more do you want? Why can't the earth wake up?

I am doomed now. My fate has already been decided. There are other "Son's" out there—God help the world. That is why in a sense I have given up in court because I am doomed by fate only not because I'm tired or depressed.

Please, I am writing quickly if a guard comes and finds me with a pen they'll kill me.

This is all a plot!

They are just trying to make me like a cold blooded killer or a nut.

The victims, the survivors are crying for blood, my blood. They have blinded themselves to my message the world must understand.

I tried to destroy the demons by killing them: molotov cocktails—18 Wicker Street—316 Warburton Avenue—Craig Glassman bullets in the fire to kill him.

The people, you too, are trying to make me look like a cold blooded killer. This I can understand but that is what Sam wants. He doesn't want to be exposed and now, everything is going his way.

You are fools.

Adolf Hitler was controlled by Sam's father-Satan.

Craig Glassman I didn't like him. I only had a file on him. I had no admiration for him. But he was one of the "Sons." Didn't you see the other crimes in my folder?

These were also Sam's doing. What about my folders on major disasters? Those were Sam's work. The train crash, the airplane crash—earthquakes.

People are to eager to destroy me but I have a message they must listen. I don't know why I'm writing you. I don't like you. Your paper wrote all those lies. They spread deciete against me with erroneous reports. You guys broke into my house. I should really kill you but I need you.

I need a messenger. Please, Please Listen to me for once. (signed) *David Berkowitz*

When I killed, I really saved many lives. You will understand later.

People want my blood but they don't want to listen to what I have to say.

I talked to the cops with dignity and respect when I got caught. I'm no wise ass like (name redacted) *made me out to be. Your just making it worse for the world and better for Sam.*

I need you now Dunleavy.

I must be released from here. Put me in touch with Inspector Dowd, Detective Jim Fox—he stayed with me—he knows about Sam he will listen. (signed) *DB*

The first part of this letter that sticks out to me is, "*I have tried to tell the police (a letter). I have tried to tell the world (letter to Breslin).*" Berkowitz is admitting here that he was the person who wrote the letter to the police, the Borrelli letter, and the letter to the world, the Breslin letter.

In this letter, Berkowitz is trying to use Steve Dunleavy as an outlet to the public to continue his games for his desperately needed attention. When Berkowitz talks about being forced to write Breslin, he is not referring to the letter he had written him in June of 1977. He is referring to a letter he sent to Breslin from Kings County Hospital before he wrote this to Steve Dunleavy. Berkowitz was desperately trying to remain in the media. He not only wrote Dunleavy and Breslin from Kings County Hospital, but as you have read, he sent a letter to Mayor Beame. The Carr family and Craig Glassman also received letters after his arrest. Berkowitz needed his attention and these people were his only way to reach the outside world at that time.

Now let's talk about the line that had Maury thinking there were more people involved with these crimes, "*There are other 'Son's' out there-God help the world.*" During the shootings, Berkowitz was sending letters to Craig Glassman, calling him his master, and accusing him of being one of Sam's servants. In this letter, "*Craig Glassman I didn't like him. I only had a file on him. I had no admiration for him. But he was one of the Son's.*" He is calling Craig Glassman a son of Sam, a person who serves Sam in his made-up satanic cult. We know now that Glassman had no involvement with Berkowitz, he was one of the people who helped catch him. There were no other "Son's" as it was all part of Berkowitz's wild stories about serving Sam Carr. There was another son of Sam according to Berkowitz that I know about...I'll explain in the end.

Another part of this letter explains why some of Berkowitz's targets were women in parked cars with men, "*When I killed, I really saved many lives. You will understand later.*" As I mentioned earlier, I think Berkowitz's main targets initially were shooting women, but it soon led to targeting men and women in parked cars that he assumed were having sex. This helped justify to himself his reason for killing. Berkowitz's justification for these murders was he was saving unwanted lives from being born into the world. He was saving the world from having another person like him. It was better for him to shoot women being irresponsible with sin, having sex out of marriage, as it allowed him to put blame on his victims for what he was doing. Again, I think after the April 17, 1977 double homicide, he was going to stick to that recipe as it gave him less guilt, and gave his meaningless attacks purpose.

By the way, if you had any doubts who firebombed the Neto and Carr houses, and who set fire to Craig Glassman's door, have no more. Berkowitz admitted in this letter he was responsible. "*I tried to destroy the demons by killing them: molotov cocktails—18 Wicker Street—316 Warburton Avenue—Craig Glassman bullets in the fire to kill him.*"

This next letter written by Berkowitz was found in his apartment the day of his arrest. It is dated Friday, February 25, 1977:

> *Today is Friday, blood day. Today I spill blood for the people of 18 Wicker Street and 22 Wicker Street, "The House of Joaquin Blood," and "The Horror Hotel."*
>
> *My ears are ringing because the dogs are hungry and they are screaming loudly in pain.*
>
> *Joaquin never feeds his dogs nor his mother any food. He relies on me to hunt for him and kill his dogs food.*
>
> *He likes his meat fresh and he loves warm blood. Joaquin and I like to hunt for food in Queens mostly because the hunting is good and Queens girls meat tastes best-maybe its the water they drink.*

I would like to point out again that the Neto family were sole owners of the house on 18 Wicker Street, not Joaquim(n) Goncalo. The dog that was barking and bothering Berkowitz was King, who was the Netos' dog, not Joaquim(n) Goncalo's. As I stated previously, the only reason Berkowitz thought it was Joaquim(n) Goncalo's house and dog was because Joaquim(n) Goncalo was the only one listed in the phone book at that residence. Berkowitz never mentions the Netos in any of these letters because he did not know they lived there. Another thing to note is...where is Michael Carr in all these letters? If you look in the 1976 Yonkers phone book, Michael Carr's name can not be found.

"*My ears are ringing because the dogs are hungry and they are screaming loudly in pain*," here Berkowitz is talking about "*THE WICKED KING WICKER*," King at 18 Wicker, and "*THE DUKE OF DEATH*," Duke at 22 Wicker.

Look at the last line in this letter, "*Joaquin and I like to hunt for food in Queens mostly because the hunting is good and Queens girls meat tastes best-maybe it's the water they drink.*" Does that sound familiar? Look back at the Borrelli letter, "*PROWLING THE STREETS LOOKING FOR FAIR GAME-TASTY MEAT. THE WEMON OF QUEENS ARE Z PRETTYIST OF ALL. I MUST BE THE WATER THEY DRINK.*" These two lines are practically saying the same thing using similar phrases.

This next letter was also found in Berkowitz's apartment on the day of his arrest. It is dated April 27, 1977…the same day Harvey, the Carr dog was shot:

> *On Wednesday April 27, 1977 Francis Carr ignites terror in Yonkers. At 7:55AM, fat Francis the lesbian unleashes the that howling maniac The "Blood Monster."*
>
> *A quiet neighborhood is destroyed. Francis is the queen of the demons and she with her cold loveless heart and soul ruins the lives of the people. God help us and protect us from the Carr family before we, are all driven mad.*
>
> *Oh God I'm going mad. Why Sam do you hate people so much that you let loose that terrible monster upon the people? They say that noise drives people crazy maybe its true and Sam Carr you are evil.*

At this point, Berkowitz had already sent two letters to the Carr house begging Sam to shut his dog up. Berkowitz was awoken by Harvey at 7:55

a.m. Harvey was shot that very same day at 9:30 a.m. Is there any doubt now as to who shot the Carr dog Harvey?

As for the witness who saw a blonde haired man running south on the aqueduct with a rifle after the shooting, I only have one explanation. We know it was 100% Berkowitz who shot Harvey, and he does not have blonde hair. So if this witness saw a blonde haired man, it had to be Berkowitz wearing a wig.

Here is another one of Berkowitz's letters that was found in his apartment on the day of his arrest:

The time as come and the time is now- I cannot go on like this, disobeying the calling of my master.

Day and night with the howling of the Demon Dogs chanting the Death Call. The Death Call that summons me to kill, to sacrifice for the master whom, in all honesty, I despise.

It took me all this time to realize who I am and what I have come here to earth for. I had premonitions of my destiny since childhood but I was afraid of what I saw.

Through the years I have tried to fight against my brethen, the children of Anti-Christ. However, Satan is much stronger than me, more determined and perhaps more desperate. How can I disobey my own father?

I have disobeyed my master quite often. Trying to be a good person, trying to love people, to make friends, to help someone-someone who needs me for nice things. I wanted to be a good man but in reality this is not possible since, in my soul I am thouroghly evil.

"Deliver me the souls of those chosen to die," commands the Demons of 2150 Holland Avenue. The Demon Dogs cry out in the alley way;

"David, David kill someone today for us." "Bring us their blood and souls so that we may dine and bath in their death."

Although my mission is comparatively minor, it has taken Jack Cassara and Satan over twenty-two years to form me into the soldier/servant that they so desire.

2150 Holland Avenue was located near Berkowitz's Barnes Avenue apartment in the Bronx. Berkowitz's apartment window at Barnes Avenue faced 2150 Holland Avenue and the alleyway where these demon dogs could be heard barking. One of these dogs was shot and the owner of the dog never caught who it was. As I stated prior, Berkowitz admitted to shooting this dog. Berkowitz could not escape barking dogs, so he would silence the dogs in order to free his mental pain. Mental pain that drove him mad and pushed him over the edge to go and kill.

Notice, *"it has taken Jack Cassara and Satan over twenty-two years to form me into the soldier/servant that they so desire."* This letter had to be written before June 1, 1976, as the letter states he is twenty-two years old at the time. It also had to be written after February 18, 1976, as Berkowitz did not know Jack Cassara until then. The "*Demon Dogs*" and Jack Cassara are who Berkowitz is blaming for his madness at this point. Wicker Street had not yet affected his false narrative.

This last letter was found in Berkowitz's apartment on the day of his arrest:

This is a WARNING to all police agencies in the Tri-State area.

For your information, a Satanic cult (devil worshipers and practioneers of witchcraft), that has been established for quite some time has been instructed by their High Command (Satan) to begin to systematically kill and slaughter young people or people of good health and clean blood.

They plan to kill at least 100 young wemon and men but mostly wemon as part of a satanic ritual which involves the shedding of the victims innocent blood. In this ritual, the victims are chosen at random and their blood is spilled. At this time, demons in the spirit (cannot be seen by humans), gather around the wounded or slain victim like a flock of vultures to suck, and drink the blood that has been spilled.

WARNING: The streets shall be run with blood.

I David Berkowitz have been chosen, chosen since birth, to be one of the executioneers for the cult.

He who hath eyes, let him see the dead victims.

He who hath ears, let him listen to what I say.

I David Berkowitz recieve no reward for my services. My services are performed in honor of my master-High Priest, "General Cosmo, Jack" Cassara.

WARNING-at this time there are people, or at least they appear to be people, but they are not. They are demons who have taken on human form.

These people are extremely dangerous and furthermore, they possess powers of super-human nature and have at their disposal tremendous powers.

Please, who will hear my word and believe it? Who will act before it is too late?

A Clue: The houses in Westchester County-Yonkers-Hastings-etc., the "old" house's. The secret lies in their history.

Many of the houses in Yonkers, the ones rich in history, hold many secrets of the past.

Some of these houses have spirits dwelling in them. These spirits are not good.

In this letter we see a word Berkowitz uses that is also in the Borrelli letter, "*wemon.*" "*They plan to kill at least 100 young wemon and men but mostly wemon,*" and in the Borrelli letter, "*I AM DEEPLY HURT BY YOUR CALLING ME A WEMON HATER.*"

"*At this time, demons in the spirit (cannot be seen by humans), gather around the wounded or slain victim like a flock of vultures to suck, and drink the blood that has been spilled.*" This is Berkowitz's rough draft of *"THE TWENTY TWO DISCIPLES OF HELL."* In the Klausner book, Berkowitz speaks of demons that would be surrounding his victims, waiting to snatch their souls after he killed them. These "*demons in the spirit* (*cannot be seen by humans*)" are your twenty-two disciples of hell that Maury thought were people. Demons that would rest at 22 Wicker Street.

We now know that the "*People, or at least they appear to be people, but are not,*" are people like Sam Carr, "*Captain Blood*" Joaquim(n) Goncalo, and "*The High Priest*" of the cult, "*General Jack Cosmo*" Jack Cassara. There was no satanic cult, it was all part of Berkowitz's fictional stories about serving demons.

I have talked to members of these families that Berkowitz used as part of his satanic cult, and they all have no idea what he is talking about. They were all hard-working families who did not know him. Berkowitz put all these people in a world of his own. It was letters like these that caused Maury to look and question about a cult that was involved with Berkowitz. Maury did not see all of Berkowitz's apartment letters. We have more information now than Maury had, and we now can see the imaginary satanic cult that Berkowitz created.

All these letters written by Berkowitz help you to see what was really going on in his mind...it was not reality. Berkowitz's satanic cult was made up of people who did not know him. I don't think Sam Carr would have been running around to every precinct he could, trying to alert them that Berkowitz was the "Son of Sam" if he was involved in his satanic cult. Craig Glassman was also part of his imaginary cult, and he is now being shown to you as vital in the capture of David Berkowitz.

I included a few more of Berkowitz's letters from these files in the back of this journal...thank J.C.

The next folder I would like to go over is the "*Psychiatrist Letters*," specifically letters David Berkowitz sent to Dr. David Abrahamsen after his arrest. I will use certain parts of these letters to show you why Berkowitz did what he did...alone.

Before I dive into the letters to Dr. Abrahamsen, here is part of a letter written by David Berkowitz to Harold McGraw Jr. in February of 1979. McGraw was the owner of the McGraw-Hill Book Publishing Company, that at the time, was publishing Dr. Lawrence Klausner's book on Berkowitz:

> *I've let people step on me just once to often and now I've had enough. It's time for the truth to come out-not a story about demons, talking dogs and legions of Satan's henchmen, but the real truth behind the crimes I've committed. These crimes more popular known as the son of sam shootings.*
>
> *I've told people time and time again that I was driven to kill by demons. Quite frankly, this is fictitious, it is invented, it is a lie. There were no real demons, no talking dogs, no satanic henchmen. I made it all up via my wild imagination so as to find some form of justification for my criminal acts against society.*
>
> *This is what you might call a 'mental justification' used simply to cover up a guilty conscious. I attached a cause to my actions in order*

to condon them. However, I must tell you right now so you know without a doubt that the story of Sam Carr and the demonic army is-BALONEY!

By the time you get this letter, the public will know the truth. They will know that there were no "demons" driving me, just me, myself and I.

David Berkowitz communicated with Dr. Klausner after his arrest to tell the world his demon stories...stories that, at this point, he was tired of lying about. Here Berkowitz writes to McGraw confessing that everything he had told Dr. Klausner was *"fictitious."*

Here are passages I took from all the letters David Berkowitz sent to Dr. Abrahamsen. I grouped them accordingly, in no specific order, to make more sense, and to better explain what Berkowitz was writing about.

"Sam Carr and the demons..." Yes, it was all a hoax, a silly hoax, well planned and thought out. I just never thought this "demon" story would carry out so much.

At the time I was committing the crimes, the Son of Sam shootings, I felt guilty unconciously. Therefore, I needed to somehow justify everything in my mind, condon it, and somehow mentally convince myself that there was meaning, purpose and justification for my acts.

This is where the "demon" story came into being. It gave me the mental motivation and mental justification I needed at the time. However, deep down inside I knew I was the real "demon" so to speak. It was just me, myself and I.

This is the reason I pleaded guilty, because I was. And the going berserk in the courtroom was an act too. I was trying to convince people that I was totally possessed. it was a desperate attempt. But it was just a case of pseudopossession, imaginary possession. Lets say I needed to be possessed. I wanted to be possessed.

The idea about demons came to me when I attended a Baptist church in Louisville, Kentucky when I was in the service. All the sermons were about demons, sin, Hell, eternal damnation, etc. I believe this also had a bad affect on my life and mind.

My involvement with Christianity while stationed at Fort Knox has had a tremendous impact on my life and thoughts. More than most people realize. There isn't a waking moment that goes by that I'm not thinking of god and the devil, good and evil, heaven and hell, and my usual sex fantasy's. I've always felt guilty but after reading my bible and listening to endless sermons, I feel more guilty than ever. Now I know just how wicked I am, how morally filthy.

I've been taught by those Christians from Louisville, Kentucky that going to the movies and dancing are sinful. I've read several Christian books on the evil of dance halls and rock and roll music. I feel guilty when I listen to rock music on the radio or stereo.

The music I listen to, my intimate thoughts, my past thievery, they'll all lead me straight to hell.

Despite my "soul winning" and "witnessing" I never got a soul saved, never turned anyone away from unrighteousness.

When I worshipped God it was out of terror. If I didn't behave, he would put a curse on me. Maybe he'd kill me.

In addition, I read numerous books such as Billy Grahm's "Angels," the Exorcist, the Omen, Rosemary's Baby, Hostage to the Devil by Malachi Martin and many other religious books on the spirit world and the occult. After reading these books, I then knew that this would be a good excuse to commit serious crimes.

I really think I used this religious "kick" to escape reality and lonliness. It was really a crutch. But Boy, did I get hooked with it. I became a fanatic.

I think Berkowitz used the Beth Haven Baptist Church to get away from his Army barracks. His rebellion against the Army I'm sure did not fair well, and with that came a lot of unfair abuse he may have had to tolerate. The Army could not deny him from practicing his religious beliefs and allowed him to leave his barracks for that purpose. It was his only escape.

When I found out David Berkowitz attended this Baptist church, I felt it could have affected him in a bad way. Following Christ is not easy, and it was something Berkowitz knew nothing about, he was raised Jewish. Not only would he learn about Jesus' love, he would also learn about the evil of demons. A Baptist church heavily preaches a lot about rejecting demons in our lives. Their message is true, but can be hard to grasp from the pressure of following correctly. Berkowitz tried to get Jesus inside of him, but he could not, it was just something else he failed at.

I remember how terribly lonely I felt after I got out, I could hardly find any of my old associates. Most got married, but I was all alone with no one. I was the most patriotic and loyal to my country and enlisted. Yet, when I got out of the service, nobody cared. Nobody was waiting for me and they couldn't care less about all I did in Korea.

Obviously, my dissatisfaction with the military came out in my letters. I joined to fight in the war (Vietnam). I signed up for infantry to see action. Yet, there was no action.

When Berkowitz came home from the Army to his family and friends, he was rejected and abandoned for his new belief in Christ. He was soon alone, and felt following Christ was more of a burden than anything. He would come to resent God because his life had not changed like he thought it should have by following Christ. He assumed he was unwanted in God's eyes, and the rejection he felt from it, made him feel like he was cursed from birth, not meant to be born. I think Berkowitz started to feel like he was one of the demons he had learned about at the Beth Haven Baptist Church to stay away from.

Back in Kentucky I was lonely, Beth Haven was my escape. I was around thousands of people. We shook hands and said "Jesus loves you brother."

Whats love? Love is something I felt for my grandfathers Harry and Jack. Love is what I felt for my mother Pearl Berkowitz. Love is now something I no longer feel, an emotion that no longer phases me. Why? Because God slaw them. Because he took them away for ever.

Thus we have six dead and seven wounded as I raised my gun to their heads—aimed—and calmly executed them. Their lives snuffed out and delivered back to God with "Return To Sender" stamped on their foreheads. "Let them return from whence they came." "Let them return unto their maker."

COLD BLOOD. A man with a heart of steel, incapable of compassion is the only person who could have pulled that trigger. "Haha, I got you back God. I got my revenge. You took my mother from me King of Kings. You Indian Giver! HaHa, got you back-pay back=pay back, HaHa."

"I waited so long for the payback. Your cruel. You hurt me. You took away the only one's I ever loved and now I can Love no more."

"I hate you! I hate, hate, hate, hate you!"

"Go ahead, sit up there on your throne and watch over everything. Sit back and watch while people wallow in suffering. Stay up there with your record book and chalk up everyone's sins. Find and point out everyone's faults and transgressions. Then accumulate enough evidence to send them all to hell without mercy."

"Go ahead, take my life back. I don't want it. I don't want to keep it. Slay me too."

David Berkowitz killed to get back at God. He was completely alone, so alone that he only had God to blame for his horrible life. God gave him this life, and he hated it. Berkowitz's resentment towards God is one of the main reasons he killed. God took from him everyone he loved and he fit in nowhere. Berkowitz felt there was no place for him in the world. This was all his revenge, God controlled everything that happened, and these murders were his payback. It was not a coincidence that Berkowitz's first attempted murder, the stabbing of two young girls, was on December 24, 1975. It was a direct message to God from him. All the bad things that would happen in the months to come after this attack, Berkowitz I think felt, was God's way of letting him know he was going to pay for his actions. So many unreal situations in his life would then take place, and in a way I think, it all assured Berkowitz he was at war with God and there was no escape...no turning back.

Berkowitz also blamed women for his miserable life. I feel he hated Julia, his father's new wife, a woman, for taking the only person in his life away from him. Let's not forget Iris, the woman he thought was his girlfriend during his Army years, who, when he returned from the Army, was not the girlfriend he thought he had. Berkowitz's biological mother, Elizabeth Falco, also played a major part with his hatred towards women.

He was born out of wedlock, and immediately given up for adoption. His adoptive parents told him his biological mother died giving birth to him and his biological father gave him up for adoption because he wouldn't have been able to care for him on his own.

In 1975, when Berkowitz was twenty-one years old, he joined an adoption group that brought people together to talk about their lives of being adopted. After Berkowitz told this group his mother died giving birth to him, the group convinced him what he was told, could be a lie, that it was a common explanation given to children who were adopted. Berkowitz believed these people and began searching for his biological mother.

Sure enough, these people were right, as he found his biological mother, Elizabeth "Betty" Broder Falco, and the feelings of guilt he suffered from killing her at birth, would be no more. The guilty feelings he had his entire life would be replaced with the feelings of not being wanted, and abandoned once again. When his biological mother told him the truth of how he was conceived, and what really happened with his biological father, he realized he was never meant to be born. Elizabeth explained to him his real father was married to someone else while she was having an affair with him. Her pregnancy was by accident, and his real father wanted nothing to do with his mistake. Even though Berkowitz maintained a relationship with his biological mother from then on, it did not seem to fill the void as he would begin his madness soon after they met, and the legacy of the "Son of Sam" began.

> *You see, Doctor Abrahamsen, It was at this time, and never until then, that I first realized I was an accident, a mistake, never mean't to be born—unwanted. I always believed my adoptive parents story that my mother died while giving birth to me and that my natural father put me up for adoption because he had no choice. He wasn't able to care for me without his wife.*
>
> *The previous story, while seemingly truthful, caused untold guilt on me during my childhood until age 22. It caused me guilt because I always believed that I had somehow been responsible for Betty Falco's death. But she wasn't really dead after all.*

I wasn't angry at the Berkowitz' for telling me the "death" story. They sincerely mean't well. They were also told to say this and after all, numerous other adoptees were told similar things. So as I said before, I wasn't angry with the Berkowitz'.

My birth, I know now, was either out of spite or accident. Spite, as far as Falco tried to get her lover Joseph Klineman to give up his legal wife, divorce her and marry Betty. She may have deliberately tried to conceive a child, me, in order to pressure Klineman to a marriage committment.

Or, I may have just been an accident. Carelessness or failure to use the proper birth controls caused my unwanted conception.

Here I was, never wanting to be born in the first place, cursing the day I was born, only to find out that I wasn't suppose to be born after all. Here I was, miserable, unhappy, maladjusted, plagued with Death fantasies and suicidal hopes, only to find out that I was unwanted, an accident, after all.

Here I was, or am, causing all types of destruction and havoc. Yet, I'm not really suppose to be in this world.

My mother, Falco, was sitting in those parked cars with Klineman.

With the finding of my natural mother, Betty Falco, and many other circumstances beyond my control, such as, my rotten environment with all its noise and tension that surrounded me—it was just too much.

Berkowitz found out the truth of his existence in May of 1975. That month he found Elizabeth Falco and left a Mother's Day card in her mailbox with his phone number. This was seven months before his first attempted murder. Berkowitz lived his entire life with guilt because of what he was told about his biological mother dying because of his birth, but it was his biological mother's fault he had no mother, not his. It was Elizabeth Falco's fault she had unprotected sex and brought him, by accident, into this world...unwanted. Soon it became every woman's fault, and his target on women became a way for him to get back at God.

> *Women-I blame them for everything. Everything evil that happened in this world—somehow it goes back to them. I hate them for messing up everything in this world. They've really screwed my life up good.*
>
> *To say what led up to the shootings is very difficult. It was a whole host of things—everything from inconsiderate neighbors who made noise to too many bills, to a series of rotten jobs, to a rotten social life and a horrifying feeling of becoming an old bachelor or a dirty old man. I had no women in my life.*
>
> *The constant noise, my social failures, my built up and unfulfilled sexual urges, Etc., all amounted to an explosive situation so that I felt justified at the time.*
>
> *I was incapable of handling stress. The barking dogs, the blasting television downstairs, the bills, the car breaking down, the supervisor yelling at me, all of it. I couldn't handle it. I just blew up.*
>
> *It was just too much. I never felt so hopeless, so powerless against those noisy forces in my neighborhood. I felt like worthless shit-never would there be peace and quiet. Never would I have a real girlfriend and intimate companionship to share my life with. I wanted these things so much but they seemed unattainable. I couldn't please a woman or make her love me. These women are insatiable anyhow. It was hopeless.*
>
> *I guess I just exploded. I couldn't take it anymore. The best way to describe it would be like a volcano erupting. I had to destroy the people who were mentally oppressing me. I felt that those women were doing*

this to me and those neighbors with their yelping dogs. Being tired of all this damn shit I just struck back.

Not only did Berkowitz have emptiness inside him that he dealt with, he was bothered, it seems, by every aspect of his life, his home, his job, and even his car. He moved from place to place trying to better his surroundings, even changed jobs a few times, but nothing he did would help him escape his uncomfortable life. It only got worse, causing him to give up.

Berkowitz also became the ".44 Caliber Killer," the "Son of Sam," because of what he felt were inconsiderate neighbors. Neighbors with dogs, and loud television sets that caused him extreme grief he could not escape.

This particular family lived in the basement of 2150 Holland Avenue. These were the families members of the buildings superintendent. These people owned three Doberman Pinschers. These three dogs roamed freely about in the rear court yard of 2150 Holland Avenue. These three animals barked constantly. The janitor let these dogs out before seven o'clock in the morning. Once the dogs went out they started to bark. Naturally, these dogs and the family who owned them were the objects of my hate and wrath. These dogs were as noisy as Sam Carr's creature (pet). They barked constantly and they caused me much hardship. Yes, my building was 2161 Barnes Avenue. But 2150 Holland, was opposite me via the back courtyard. My apartment was 5E. It faced the rear. If you could get into apartment 5E, then you will see that my windows face the yard in which those three dogs roamed. I lived at 2161 Barnes Avenue. The dogs were in the rear of 2150 Holland Avenue.

I am quite certain that there were three dogs who roamed the yard. They were black colored Doberman Pinschers. One dog was named "Blackie." Another, the female, was named "Girlie." I'm certain of this because I heard the Superintendent of 2150 Holland Avenue call the dogs often. After I lived there for several months, the female dog had puppies. The super kept one which later grew rapidly. So there were three dogs.

This seemed to be the start of Berkowitz's problems with dogs. Berkowitz says he knew these dogs' names because he would hear the superintendent call the dogs often. Berkowitz would come to know a lot of dogs' names around the places he lived, people too, as it is obvious he would watch these families he was harassing.

You had asked me about animals. Especially dogs. Well, now I see that I have alot to clarify. I do love dogs despite the fact that I shot several. Like people, there are "good" dogs and there are "bad" ones. The "good" dogs, I like better than people sometimes, They are trustworthy and loyal. Most of all they are disciplined and they don't bark, yelp or howl unnecessarily. These dogs make wonderful pets and companions.

Unfortunately, there are also the "bad" ones. These evil creatures are the ones like Mr. Cassara's two dogs who barked without ceasing and caused me untold heartache and mental suffering. These creatures of hell are like Mr. Sam Carr's dog who yelped all day long and into the evening. Not only did he emit these god-awful sounds but he emitted them with out reason or provocation. He barked, literally, at nothing. He barked just because he was chained up all day to a post and left behind the house by his master, Mr. Carr, who obviously is an inconsiderate slob.

Likewise, 18 Wicker Street, and 22 Wicker Street, had dogs, too. They weren't common dogs in that they had a fetish for barking at anything that moved within a radius of 100 feet from their fences. Be it man or squirrel, they verbally assaulted it with their vocal chords. They were also big dogs with huge vocal chords-this didn't help.

Loud, excessive or annoying noises have always been my weakpoint. I cannot bear these sounds, a chorus of barks, yelps, and howls, which continued throughout the day. I couldn't read, relax, sleep or even watch television with these intrusions. This is how bad it was.

If you could hear what horrid sounds these "bad" dogs were making then you could very well understand my motives-a last resort-for shooting them. It was an act of desperation. You can disagree all you want but it's true. I tried phone calls, letters, everything including calls to the police. NOTHING BUT NOTHING WAS DONE! I was then forced to use more extreme measures. Molotov cocktails, shootings, etc. I had no choice.

Don't forget, I tried to correct the situation by moving on several occasions. Each time my rent went up more and more and I moved again and again. Each move put me further away from the city and from my job. Obviously, I tried to dodge these evil people, these selfish people, these inconsiderate people, but to no avail.

No, Dr. Abrahamsen, I don't hate all dogs, only those that have no consideration for humankind. Their masters are also just as guilty, Sam Carr of Yonkers, the residents of 18 and 22 Wicker Street, Jack Cassara of New Rochelle, and the apartment of 2150 Holland Avenue in the Bronx, are all scum and slobs! They deserved my attacks.

As far as noise is concerned, I can't tolerate loud playing of television sets either. Alas, Craig Glassman enters into the picture. This creature was one of the most inconsiderate of the whole animal kingdom. At 2:00 A.M. his t.v. was playing at a volume that sent chills through my spine and vibrated my bed as if I was sleeping on a subway car.

If you understand all this then you can understand why Glassman came under my attack. Truly, people like this shouldn't be allowed to live with others, and they should have some type of penal institution for the "cruel" of this world. I just acted out of desperation and because violence was all that they would understand. This was the last straw. Yet, all I sought was peace and quiet.

You say that I had no friends, was a loner, lacked interpersonal communications with others. This is true. You say that I had deep hostilities for my mother, Betty. This is true. You say that I was sexually frustrated. This is true. You say I have sadistic tendencies. This is true. I could go on and on. But please don't forget one negative factor in my life which nearly drove me to madness barking dogs and an extremely loud television set.

Let me make it clear that I'm not trying to use Glassman, Carr, Cassara, or anyone else as a scapegoat. I am the killer, true. But I just didn't do it for the sake of galavanting. I didn't kill for the hell of it or as a joke. Very possibly, I did try to bring attention to myself. But my actions were also a result of an intense amount of pressure and frustration that developed around and inside of me. Just couldn't stifle my built up anger any longer. So, in all honesty, these people helped put the match to the fuse so to speak.

Sam Carr, certainly lacked concern for others. I pleaded. I warned. I threatened. I finally shot at his dog. He was lucky because I was waiting for him. I hid in the bushes behind his house in order to kill him with my rifle. But I finally fired on the dog instead. He never showed and I was impatient.

Notice Berkowitz does not mention Joaquin Goncalo, the first person he had a problem with on Wicker Street, "*Captain Blood.*" He only mentions 18 Wicker Street, he does not refer to Joaquin Goncalo. It was now years since his arrest, and I'm sure by then he was told the Netos lived at 18 Wicker Street. Only after the arrest would he find this out and make up the name Robert Neto as "*Joaquin the Joker*" to Dr. Klausner as he still didn't know who he was actually harassing.

Berkowitz was clearly bothered by loud noises which he blamed these people for injecting into his life. The dogs at 18 and 22 Wicker Street, 2150 Holland Avenue, and the Cassaras, were to Berkowitz, just as much to blame as Harvey, the Carr dog, the main dog who was supposedly relaying Sam's orders to kill. Berkowitz took these disturbances personally and hated his neighbors around him for not paying attention to his complaining calls and letters. If he was going to have no peace, there was going to be no peace for the people he felt were the cause of his problems. Again, in these letters, he admitted to throwing Molotov cocktails at the Neto and Carr homes, as well as shooting their dogs.

By the time Craig Glassman moved in, it must have really been hell for Berkowitz. We already see Berkowitz was extremely uncomfortable by the dogs in the neighborhood barking. In comes Glassman, blasting his television set at 2 a.m. If Glassman was bothering him at 2 a.m., and the dogs started barking soon thereafter, it must have been really hard for Berkowitz to sleep. Lack of sleep can drive a person mad, and the threatening letters to the Carrs, which were sent a month after Craig moved in, show his situation was just getting worse. Berkowitz had enough and started to take action again against the people he felt were causing him problems.

This was the truth why these people were mixed up with this entire demon story of Berkowitz's. He was upset with their barking dogs, not their talking dogs, and in Glassman's case, his loud TV. Sam Carr did not order Berkowitz to kill through his dog Harvey. Craig Glassman was not a "*Son*" serving Sam Carr. Jack Cassara, "*General Jack Cosmo*," was not "*The High Priest*" of a satanic cult. Joaquim(n) Goncalo was not "*Captain Blood*," part of the "*Wicker Street Gang*." All of these people did not know Berkowitz, and were not part of a satnic cult, they only existed this way in Berkowitz's letters.

> *Dr. Abrahamsen, I am now looking into the possibility of taking legal action against Mr. Carr. I will be contacting my lawyer as to the possibility of a lawsuit.*

While in prison, Berkowitz researched a few court cases where victims sued neighbors because of noise nuisance and the after-effects it had on them. Berkowitz, years after his arrest, wanted to sue Sam Carr for his noise nuisance. Here we see Berkowitz still does not accept the problem was him and continues to blame Sam for the things he did. Berkowitz had some nerve wanting to take legal action against Sam, but it shows that even years later, Sam Carr and his neighbors on Wicker Street, truly did bother his life. Berkowitz really placed blame on his neighbors for what he did. To Berkowitz, these people "*helped put the match to the fuse so to speak.*"

Here is David Berkowitz's confessions to Dr. Abrahamsen on the "Son of Sam" shootings. The first being Donna Lauria and Jody Valente.

I saw her and another girl sitting in a blue, Oldsmobile Cutlass, as I drove passed. I parked about two very short blocks away on a side street. Coincidentally, there was a space available. I left my car walking in the direction of their parked car. I saw both girls sitting there, apparently talking. I circled the car at a distance like an animal stalking his prey. Cautiously, I was watching for movement from other people in the street. However there was none. Then, from behind and on the sidewalk, I approached the car, took my revolver out of a paper bag, and stopped parallel to their vehicle. I faced Donna, aimed my gun in the general direction and fired all five rounds very rapidly. I saw the glass breaking into small slivers, the horn started sounding loudly, and I then ran full speed in the direction of my car. I stopped running within 50 feet of the car, then started walking briskly to it. I got in then drove off. I aroused no attention. I didn't know I had killed her until I read the Post the following afternoon. The shooting took place about one A.M.

I went straight home and went to bed. I got up early the next day to go to work at the cab company in the same neighborhood (Pelham Bay Park). I was at work promptly at 6:45 A.M. That day I made out better than usual in both tips and fare's. I made it my point to go to work so I wouldn't arouse any suspicion. But who would have suspected me anyhow? I didn't know the victims.

The 2nd job was the DeNarro, Keenan one. Both of them were sitting in a red Volkswagon and making out. This was my second murder attempt with my .44. I had approached from the rear of the car, walked up to the passenger side window and opened fire. I was more frightened than they were. Only one bullet struck the young man and he really wasn't the intended target. I had fired with one hand and wildly. Boy did I mess up. But really, I was very nervous. After the shooting, I ran to my car, and drove off quietly to a White Castle on Northern Blvd.

The 3rd shooting was the Lomino, DeMasi incident. This happened in November of 76. I saw the two girls on the porch of one of their homes. I drove my car around the corner, parked carefully, and then went to the location. Again, I was nervous and I fired my gun with one hand. I shot wildly and poorly. However, this time I was able to read the full story in the headlines of the N.Y. Post the following day. Naturally, I was disappointed that for all my trouble and risk, no deaths resulted.

The 4th incident was in Forest Hills on January of 1977. This did result in a homicide to my joy at the time. However, this shooting was different then all the others for two reasons. One, because I used two hands to fire the gun. Two, because I didn't have any fear. This time when I crept up to the car and fired, I wasn't frightened and I remained calm and cautious. After the shooting I ran to my car and escaped into the freezing night. The next day I heard about her death and the police's theory that this recent shooting was connected to several others in the Bronx and Queens. Lastly, I cannot explain my change-a loss of fear, except for the fact that I was growing more "cold-blooded" daily as my thoughts centered on murder and because my determination was increasing-my frustrations were building.

The 5th incident was also in Forest Hills. Brazenly, I travelled through that same neighborhood only a few weeks after the first shooting there. I spotted a girl walking up the street. She was pretty, slender, and dressed nicely. Without really looking about because my eyes were focused directly on her only, I just pulled out my revolver from a plastic bag and I shot her once in the face. I had no fear with the execution of being caught and I was so transfixed on the shooting and my victim that I didn't notice my large plastic bag falling to the floor. I just left it there, I really didn't care. After the shooting, I drove straight home and I watched the news on the eleven o'clock news. The next day I purchased the Daily News, Post, and Times. I remember the headlines, "SECOND KILLING STUNS FOREST HILLS," (Daily News).

The 6th incident was in the Bronx. A double murder of a young couple on the service road of the Hutchinson River Parkway. It was my best "job" because it resulted in two deaths. Plus, I left my first carefully concocted note on the scene. My shooting pattern improved greatly due to my fearlessness which slowly developed and my two handed shooting method. Four shots were fired. Three hit the victims out of four fired. The man was hit twice in the head. The girl once in the face. Now, I was making the papers nearly everyday. The chase was on and the public was watching out for me.

The 7th shooting was in Bayside Queens. Two were wounded and I was angry. I don't see how that girl lived. Again, I had no fear, I was alert and cautious. I ran to my car only as to quickly escape and I cunningly travelled up 35th avenue and not on the main road, Northern Boulevard. This shooting was close to my sisters house.

I remember my last shooting in which Stacy Moskowitz was slain. I saw her and her boyfriend making out in the car. Then, they left the car, walked over the walk bridge and went along the path by the water. After about 20 minutes, they returned to the car, made out some more, then came to where I was by the swings. I watched Stacy on the swing and then they stopped swinging. Her and her date then started to kiss passionately for several minutes. At this time, I, too, was sexually aroused. I had an erection. Shortly after their deep kissing they went back to the car. If my memory is correct, they made out a little more and then just sat inside the car talking. Now I then quietly crept up alongside the car but a little more to the rear. I had my gun out, aimed it at the middle of Stacy's head and fired. One bullet struck her head and another knicked her. I didn't even know she was shot because she didn't say anything nor did she move. Then I got in my car and drove off.

I've always wondered if some of the victims were having sex in their cars. I'm trying to remember if Esau and Suriani were having sex. I know they were embracing but I can't remember if they had their clothes off or not. If they did have their clothing off, and were engaging in sex, then I would be somewhat justified in killing them. Sex, outside of marriage, is a heinous sin.

Here we see Berkowitz giving himself justification for killing people who he thought were having sex outside of marriage. Nothing can justify taking someone's life. It is God's job to handle our sins, not David Berkowitz's.

Berkowitz admitted to pulling the trigger in every attack to Dr. Abrahamsen. To think he would confess to all these crimes if he did not commit them is ridiculous at this point. Who would he be covering for? It makes too much sense as all the evidence only points to him. The only people we ever see Berkowitz name in his satanic cult is his inconsiderate neighbors. There was no cult...or accomplices, there was only David Berkowitz, his failed life, and his revenge.

The combination of Berkowitz's rejected life and his uncomfortable surroundings are what caused him to kill. The media, I feel, also played a part in this, making him a movie star, when he had always been just an extra. Berkowitz, with all the media coverage, finally felt like somebody, and he enjoyed being somebody. The media, unintentionally made him kill, with every shooting came massive news headlines. The world was watching and waiting, and he enjoyed that he was being paid attention to. He would give them what they wanted, in return for the attention. Berkowitz was a nothing, a nobody. He was not even supposed to have been born. Now the whole world knew him, and he loved that he had total control.

> *During the fourth shooting when I first used two hands, I guess at this time that I had further succeeded in justifying my crimes to myself and that I was more determined than ever. At this point I imagine I didn't care much any more for I finally had convinced myself that it was good to do it, necessary to do it, and that the public wanted me to do it. The latter part I believe until this day. I believe that many were rooting for me. This was the point in which the papers began to pick up vibes and information that something big was happening out in the street. Real big!*

Look what Berkowitz did after he killed Virginia Voskerichian, "*After the shooting, I drove straight home and I watched the news on the eleven o'clock news. The next day I purchased the Daily News, Post, and Times.*"

You can see Berkowitz was the director of this movie, and he couldn't wait to see and read how everyone acted. It was his movie and he enjoyed directing it.

Berkowitz loved the attention so much, he even chanced getting caught so the world would know he was still around.

> *The final incident happened in southern Brooklyn. I shot to death Stacy Moskowitz. The routine was the same. However, this time I consciously set myself up.*

Berkowitz consciously set himself up by going ahead and committing the murder of Stacy Moskowitz after ignoring the parking ticket he knowingly received less than a half hour before the shooting. He knew the parking ticket could get him caught, but he could not help himself. He had couples in parked cars blocks away, and there was no way he was letting that go. His need to play the "Son of Sam" to the world was something he could not resist…even if it chanced him getting caught.

> *From the outset of the ".44" shootings, I knew I would be captured one day. It was my goal to be. However, there were many whom I wanted first. All of this would have been pointless if I were never captured. I wanted people to know that it was me. "See, I got you back world. Its me David whom you fucked over."*

> *People just don't understand that I had to shed blood-blood that really wasn't so innocent. I'm not sorry I did it. By societies rules it was unlawful but, at that stage I didn't care anymore. I very much wanted to die even though I'm fearful of God because of his power to cast people into hell. I mean, just let me get my revenge.*

Dr. Abrahamsen writes to Berkowitz and asks him to answer a few questions for him.

Dr. Abrahamsen: *You previously said that the matter of adoption had nothing to do with your troubles. How do you feel about it now?*

Berkowitz: *Yes, I did say that my adoption didn't cause me any problems. But I was covering for my mother and sister. Of course it caused me problems. But I wasn't at a mature enough stage back then to admit it. I was protecting my family (my natural family) from the truth that would have hurt. Obviously my adoption caused me mental and emotional problems. I still, to this day, have negative feelings for my mom, Falco. Despite her nice and friendly ways, I don't have it in me to totally forgive. I told her when I first met her and a great many times afterwards that I forgave her. But this isn't really the case. Truly, I didn't forgive her and I can't. I went through too much with this adoption business to simply say "all is forgiven mom." I had so much agony over the thoughts that I somehow caused her death.*

So many years I believed the story about my mother's dying at birth. I believed that my father (whoever he was) gave me up for adoption because he couldn't handle me by himself. However, I believed that my father (my natural father) had nothing but hatred for me because the doctors let me live instead of her. Of course I found out that this story wasn't true. My mom didn't die. It was all a hoax. Still, I lived with this Guilt for so long. I retained this death guilt for so long. Its hard to get rid of it.

I told you before, when I found out that Betty really didn't die, then I was relieved in one sense, but upset in another. Then the question came up as to why I was adopted. I had to find out. I had to find out someone from my real family. I needed family real bad-a mystical and perfect family-a blissful family-a perfect relationship. Of course this wasn't to be. I guess this was one pathway that eventually led to murder. My dream finally didn't exist. It was my last hope. Then I realized that I was basically rejected. I was given up at birth. It wasn't because of death. My mother or Klineman was just careless. This is the essence of my birth-an unwanted individual. Here I was cursing the day I was born. Here I was wanting to die. I hated life and it lacked happiness. Now I found out that my life was a mistake in the first place. All this was hard to swallow. It was hard to accept. Hence, another pathway to murder.

Dr. Abrahamsen: *You have previously said that when you shot the dog (Harvey) it looked like an old woman. Do you still believe that or was it just a gratuitous remark at the time?*

Berkowitz: *Sam Carr's dog never looked like an old woman. I don't see how those doctors could have believed me when I said that. How naive they were. If it was an old woman I never would have shot at it. No, it was an extremely noisy dog who warranted punishment for his unbearable outcries. I was just playing crazy back then. Now there's no need for this ploy.*

Dr. Abrahamsen had many more questions for Berkowitz than these two. Not one of them was about a satanic cult or accomplices. Dr. Abrahamsen spoke to the Netos, the Carrs and the Cassaras, the same as I did, and knew Berkowitz acted alone. He wanted him to leave his crazy demon stories out of their conversations.

We have come a long way with this case, and we need to accept that Berkowitz was not covering for anyone. All these underlying issues were his reasons for doing what he did. No one else was involved, the reasons were all his.

> *Getting back to this "demon" business and Dr. Schwartz, as well as, my former attorneys, obviously, this talk of demons was nothing more than an expression of my lack of understanding. I lacked the understanding of what really motivated me to destroy others. I was confused about it. I had no understanding of myself-no comprehension of my own motivations. The main reason was because I had purposely buried them. But I still couldn't explain why I had them to begin with. Now I can understand and accept my actions. So this demon story sounds so immature, honestly, I'm ashamed of myself for ever mentioning it. What a poor excuse for murder!*
>
> *If you notice, everytime the Post prints a story they always refer to Sam Carr's dog and how it told me how to kill and when to kill, as I once told you and the other doctors. Of course I was lying. Apparently this "dog" thing caught on well with the public. But it just isn't true.*

I hope this is clear to you now. David Berkowitz was not taking orders to kill from a talking dog, or Sam Carr. Berkowitz gave up, blamed God, blamed women, blamed his country, blamed all the people around him for his failed and unwanted life. These attacks were his revenge...to all those he blamed.

Last but not least, before I end this part of Dr. Abrahamsen's amazing work, here is another one of Maury Terry's misleading assumptions.

When Maury Terry saw what Berkowitz wrote on his apartment wall at 35 Pine Street, "*Hi My Name Is Mr. Williams And I Live IN this hole*," with an arrow pointing to a hole in his wall, he connected it to Untermyer Park by assuming Berkowitz was referring to an underground area in the park called "Mr. Williams hole." I spoke with a lot of people who hung out in that park, and no one ever heard of any area being called "Mr. Williams hole."

> *People don't understand what the writing on the wall of my apartment was about. Actually, no demons told me to write that stuff. It wasn't dictated to me either. I got the idea from reading a detective magazine about convicted killer William Heirens. He wrote on the wall of one of his victims apartments. The magazine showed photographs of the writing and, like mine, it was in a strange eerie style. He also left a note at the crime scene of one of his victims.*

The detective magazine Berkowitz was referring to is *Crime*, the November 1976 issue. Obviously, this magazine is where Berkowitz also got the idea to leave a note at one of his murder scenes...the Borrelli letter. In the apartment next door, opposite the wall Berkowitz made a hole in, lived a family with the last name Williams. Berkowitz had said he was bothered by the music being played too loud coming from the Williams' apartment.

Even with all this evidence showing you Berkowitz acted alone, I still had some doors that were open I needed to close. I originally thought John Carr was stalking Sylvia Neto, and he was the person who was committing the crimes against the Netos. I don't think that anymore, so who threw the rocks through the Netos' window? Who sent them a letter? Who was calling their house? Who drove the off-white car which a man got in after the Netos' dog was shot? In another folder labeled "*Yonkers Police Reports*," I found what I needed to close these doors and end this.

Here is the Yonkers Police Report from the night the Netos had a Molotov cocktail thrown at their house:

On May 13, 1976, Yonkers Detectives Mike Lorenzo and Edward Oakley responded to 18 Wicker Street upon request of the Fire Department relative to a possible arson.

At location, Detectives Lorenzo and Oakley spoke to Assistant Chief Kelly of the Fire Department, who stated that firefighters had extinguished a small blaze on the exterior part of a three-floor wood frame building located at 18 Wicker Street.

Investigation by Detectives Lorenzo and Oakley revealed that a fire apparently started by a thrown Molotov cocktail at approximately 3:30am this date.

Detectives Lorenzo and Oakley spoke to Mrs. Margaret DioGuardi of 22 Wicker Street, who stated that at approximately 3:30am this date, she heard a crash in the vicinity of 18 Wicker Street. She looked out from the window of her home which is adjacent to 18 Wicker Street and observed flames around the second floor window area of home. She called Mr. Neto, who she knows personally, and then called Yonkers Fire Department and reported the fire. Mr. Neto and Mr. D'Acutis and other neighbors extinguished the fire partially with garden hoses prior to arrival of Fire Department. Mrs. DioGuardi stated that she did not see anyone after hearing the crash of glass but stated that in the past, both she and other neighborhood people had been bothered by young black youths in the area who throw stones at windows and also had been in rear yards and broke statues and lawn furniture.

Detectives Lorenzo and Oakley spoke to owner, Mr. Neto, who stated that he has not had any arguments with neighbors and cannot understand why the fire occurred. He stated that approximately one year ago, rocks were thrown to the second floor window and also a bottle was thrown at the house by youths in area, but he did not know who was responsible. He also stated that his German Shepherd dog sometimes barked at children in the area when they came near his home.

This report was taken on May 13, 1976. Mr. Neto states to the detectives, "*approximately one year ago, rocks were thrown to the second-floor window*." This would put the rock-throwing incident somewhere around May 1975, way before Berkowitz moved to 35 Pine Street. Berkowitz had absolutely nothing to do with this, nor did John Carr, as both Mr. Neto and his neighbors claim youths in the neighborhood were throwing rocks at their homes. Close that door, three more to go.

I think I can now explain why the Yonkers Police were not looking for anyone when these crimes were taking place. The Wicker Street area was being harassed by black youths according to the residents making the complaints. Wheat's car was broken into and she was attacked in 1975 by two black youths in the Wicker area. Mrs. DioGuardi, of 22 Wicker Street, stated both she and other neighborhood people had been bothered by young black youths in the area who threw stones at windows, broke statues and lawn furniture in their yards. Nann Cassara stated in her interview with Herbert Leifer that Sam Carr thought the harassment being done to him and his family was caused by the colored people in the area. Even Sylvia Neto gave a report to the police that she thought she heard a black man's voice coming from outside her house right before Rocket was shot.

The residents, as you can see, were telling the Yonkers Police it was the black youths in their area that were committing these crimes. Racial incidents were heavily going on in Yonkers back then, and the Yonkers Police were looking at this as the problem in the Wicker Street area. It wasn't until June 10, 1977, only two months before Berkowitz's arrest, Sam stopped blaming the black youths in the area and started blaming David Berkowitz. What sense would it have made for the Yonkers Police to look for a suspect when the people reporting the crimes weren't asking them to? The Yonkers Police were not neglecting these crimes in the Wicker Street area.

Also, when I looked further into Sam Carr's complaints to the YPD, there were reports of Detective Lorenzo going to 35 Pine Street a few days after Sam's first complaint to speak with the superintendent. Detective Lorenzo was able to get Berkowitz's handwriting from an application Berkowitz filled out to live in the building. On June 23, 1977, Detective Lorenzo sent this application, Jack Cassara's get-well card, and both of Sam Carr's threatening letters to the FBI for handwriting analysis. The FBI came back with the handwriting to be inconclusive. Remember, "Son of Sam" is not being connected to these letters at that time, the tests were to see if Berkowitz was the author of Sam Carr's letters and the Cassaras get-well card. Detective Lorenzo was paying attention to Sam Carr's complaints, and I'm sure he tried to contact Berkowitz before speaking with the superintendent.

This next Yonkers Police Report was written by an unnamed commanding officer of the Yonkers Internal Affairs Division on September 22, 1977:

On about June 1, 1977, Mr. Joaquim Neto of 18 Wicker Street, known to me in the Portuguese community, appeared at the Internal Affairs Division Office on a personal basis and related an incident to the undersigned involving a fire bombing of his home at 18 Wicker Street on May 13, 1976. Some unknown person(s) threw a bottle filled with gasoline at the Neto home which was occupied. Said incident occurred at 3:45am with no witnesses. The fire went out quickly and no injuries were reported. Investigation by Police Officers Taylor and Hogue failed to reveal any evidence that could indicate who the responsible person(s) were. The Detectives Division was notified.

The undersigned advised Mr. Neto of the investigation and the lack of information to determine the responsible person(s) and asked Mr. Neto if he had any suspects or was having any neighborhood problems. Mr. Neto stated that he did not have any idea who might have thrown the fire-bomb at his home and was puzzled as to why the incident occurred. The undersigned advised Mr. Neto to keep in touch with the undersigned if any new developments occurred. No contact was made by Mr. Neto with the undersigned till after the arrest of "Son of Sam," David Berkowitz, at which time Mr. Neto appeared at the Internal Affairs Office and informed the undersigned of the following events:

June 1976-His wife received a letter which was typewritten on the envelope and block print on the letter. Said letter talked about hell, dogs and the Devil. Mr. Neto states he never saw the letter because his wife destroyed the letter and did not want him to see it and get alarmed. The letter was never shown to police.

July/August 1976-Harassing phone calls including one that the police responded and searched his house for dead bodies.

December 24, 1976-Mr. Neto's German Shepherd was shot dead in front of his house and police responded and could not find the bullet which had passed through the head of the dog. Someone saw a man jump into a red auto with a black top and proceed North on Warburton Avenue from Wicker Street after the shooting.

Now this all made sense. The letter and phone calls came into the Netos' home in the months of June, July, and August of 1976. Berkowitz was living in the area at that time and he had to be the one harassing the Neto family with that letter and phone calls.

How did he know Sylvia's name, you might ask? He was watching the Netos like he was watching the Cassaras, and the dogs at Barnes Avenue. Remember, he knew the name of the Cassaras' daughter also without ever meeting her, just like he said he knew the names of the dogs when he lived at Barnes Avenue...he could hear their names being called by family members as he watched them from a distance. This is how he knew the names of King and Duke. I'm sure he must've heard Maria Neto yelling for Sylvia to come inside. I think this is also how he knew Wheat's nickname was Mickey.

One question I cannot answer with certainty is how Berkowitz got the Netos phone number. I do have an assumption, I don't like to assume, but I have nothing else. I think Berkowitz called Joaquim Goncalo to complain about Rocket. When he did this, Joaquim may have told him it was Joaquim's dog who lived downstairs and gave him the Netos phone number to speak with them. Because these two residents at 18 Wicker Street had the same first name, I think Berkowitz may have thought the Joaquim he was directed to speak to was Joaquim(n) Goncalo, "*Captain Blood*." Berkowitz never mentions the Netos in any of his letters, so I'm guessing he couldn't have gotten their phone number with their name attached.

Having the same first name almost cost Joaquim Neto his life. Berkowitz's anonymous complaint to the Yonkers Police that Joaquim was killing everyone in his family was not directed towards Joaquim Neto. Berkowitz made that complaint and then watched the chaos unfold from his apartment window, with hopes of witnessing an accidental murder he caused.

Maria and Sylvia Neto were not lying. These crimes happened over forty-five years ago and their mix-up of the timeline was understandable. A very honest and easy mistake to make. Close these two doors, one more to go.

On December 24, 1976, at 11:01 p.m., Yonkers Police Officers Peter Intervallo and Thomas Chamberlain responded to 18 Wicker Street. Here is the police report that was taken that night:

Sent to 18 Wicker Street. on a signal 10-9. A dead dog, upon arrival, spoke to Joaquim Neto, white male, 42 years of age of 18 Wicker Street who stated that while having a house party at 18 Wicker Street, a guest (one Teresa Ramos, female, 21 years of age of Ashburton Avenue) stated that she heard a shot, proceeded outside and found Mr. Neto's German Shepherd dog lying dead in front of the house. Said dog had apparently been shot with a small caliber weapon. Officer's Intervallo and Chamberlain also spoke to Tony Teodoro, white male, 52 years of age of 143 Douglas Avenue who stated that he had observed a male (no further info) jump into a red auto with a black top and proceed North on Warburton Avenue from Wicker Street shortly after the shooting but he could not say for sure if there was any connection between the two. Dog was left at D.P.W. Detective Wyka notified.

Teresa Ramos in this report was the same Teresa I had spoken to at the Neto house. Why wasn't the story she told me given to the police that night they responded and took this report? Teresa said she went outside after hearing gunshots and saw a man in a white T-shirt, carrying a rifle, running down Wicker Street to an off-white car. Joaquim Neto is the one who stated to the officers that night what Teresa had seen, but wouldn't Teresa have told Joaquim the same thing she told me? This family was just terrorized and surely they would want to give the responding officers everything they saw so the person who shot their dog would be caught.

I knew from the moment Teresa said this story, something was not right because when I spoke to Maria and Sylvia about this incident, they did not tell me this story. The automobile seen at the crime scene by Tony Teodoro, Teresa's uncle, on Warburton Avenue was not off-white, it was red with a black top. Also, Tony Teodoro stated he was not sure if the person he saw running down Wicker Street and jumping in this car was involved. If a man was running down to this car with a rifle, why would Tony Teodoro question if he was involved? Even if this was Berkowitz running down Wicker Street after the shooting to this red car, he was alone, as Tony Teodoro did not state he jumped into the passenger seat of an awaiting car. Berkowitz committed this crime alone with no accomplice, like every other crime he committed during the "Son of Sam" era.

I vindicated everyone and everything I could, and came up with what the police told us all along...David Berkowitz acted alone. The last door is now closed, case closed...investigation complete.

I do not think John Carr knew Berkowitz at all, but because of John's tragic death, only the evidence can prove that. Whether John knew Berkowitz or not, he wasn't involved in any of these crimes. As for the statements made by John to Lee Slagter, his psychiatrist in North Dakota, they should be taken as they were said.

John told Lee Slagter he was afraid someone was trying to kill him and he might be in trouble with the law back in New York. John was not referring to the "Son of Sam" shootings as to why he would be in trouble in New York. He clearly had his own problems going on in his life, as was told to us by Wheat in the D.A. recording, which I feel led to his death. I don't think

John killed himself, and his telling of someone wanting to kill him was not a coincidence to me.

John also stated to Lee Slagter he had a connection with David Berkowitz and information he thought the police in New York would be interested in...that was true. He did have a connection with Daivd Berkowitz, his family was at the center of the entire "Son of Sam" story. The case was closed, law enforcement showed nothing. No one knew what really happened in Yonkers with David Berkowitz but the Carrs. That's why they were charging $15,000 to anyone who wanted to know their story. John did have information on David Berkowitz, the same information you now see in this journal.

On August 11, 1977, a day after Berkowitz's arrest, he was interrogated by several District Attorneys of New York City and confessed to every shooting. Berkowitz was read his constitutional rights before he was questioned, and chose to confess his crimes without a lawyer present. His confessions to all the shootings, with no lawyer to guide him, would be his last mistake that would send him to prison. His plan to use Sam and the demons to make himself look insane was not going to work. Dr. David Abrahamsen, the doctor who the courts approved, ruled Berkowitz not insane, therefore his insanity plea to escape prison would be rejected by the courts and he would be found guilty. If Berkowitz was to plead not guilty and go to trial, he would have been going up against his self-given confessions and would have easily been found guilty. Berkowitz saved himself the headache of a definite losing trial and pled guilty to all the shootings. He was sentenced and given twenty-five years to life for each of his six murders. The judge made sure David Berkowitz would never be a part of society again.

CHAPTER XX

THE END

After Berkowitz's arrest, it wasn't until Maury Terry started investigating this case that all these allegations of people being involved with Berkowitz surfaced. The police told Maury time and time again he was wrong, but Maury was determined to be right. It was Berkowitz's letter to Steve Dunleavy, and the Breslin letter with "*JOHN WHEATIES*" that caused all this in the beginning. Maury would then connect what he found out about John Carr's personal life to Berkowitz.

For years, the Borrelli letter looked like the son of Sam Carr had written it, John Carr, but we now know the truth. Berkowitz wrote that letter, and I feel the real "*SON OF SAM*" was Harvey, Sam Carr's dog, who Berkowitz referred to as a "*MONSTER*" in his letters.

If you read the Borrelli letter, Berkowitz wrote most of that letter from Harvey's perspective. "*SOMETIMES HE TIES ME UP TO THE BACK OF THE HOUSE*" is what the letter says. Now we know, and Wheat has confirmed, Sam Carr was not tying his son John up to the back of the house like Maury wanted us to believe, and it wasn't Berkowitz being tied up. Harvey was the "*MONSTER*" who was literally tied up to the back of Sam Carr's house, being a *"BRAT,"* annoying Berkowitz by barking all day.

When Berkowitz said he would get commands to kill, he said the commands would be from Sam, through Sam's dog Harvey. In the Borrelli letter it says, "*GO OUT AND KILL COMMANDS FATHER SAM.*" It was the dog who supposedly got the commands from Sam, his father, and would then relay the command to Berkowitz. The letter also says, "*BEHIND OUR*

HOUSE SOME REST." The Carr house was not Berkowitz's house, it was Harvey's.

In Berkowitz's letter to Mayor Beame, he writes, "*According to the voices I heard one of them, a demon, stated that Sam Carr strangled young people and buried them behind Sam's house. These people are just bones now.*" The demon is Harvey, and Harvey is the one who stated this in the Borrelli letter, "*BEHIND OUR HOUSE SOME REST. MOSTLY YOUNG-RAPED AND SLAUGHTERED-THEIR BLOOD DRAINED-JUST BONES NOW.*" Berkowitz was referring to the Borrelli letter, what Harvey had said, what he had written. Harvey was the "*SON OF SAM*" in the Borrelli letter, Berkowitz was the ".44 Caliber Killer." The media ran with "Son of Sam" as his moniker after the letter was leaked to the public. Harvey served Sam like Craig Glassman. Harvey was the "*SON OF SAM*," the "*MONSTER*," the little "*BRAT*."

Maury Terry's book, *The Ultimate Evil*, and newspaper articles, had people all over the world believing his alternate theories. Before Maury started printing his newspaper articles, no one talked about Berkowitz and all this Untermyer Park satanic cult stuff. Berkowitz was exactly what he was, a lone killer, until Maury opened the door and allowed him to play his games. Maury wanted nothing more than to prove his theories right and Berkowitz confirmed his information, giving him reason to carry on. Maury's articles allowed Berkowitz to be alive again, and gave him the attention that would last a lifetime.

After all this, you would think I'm upset with Maury Terry, I am not. He is Yonkers, and like it or not, we are family. I understand what Maury went through and why he did what he did. With only one life to live, sometimes we do things to survive that will cause others pain. I don't think his intentions in the beginning were to cause pain. He was led into a deep hole with no way out and he needed to save himself. His intent to find the truth was there in the beginning, but I don't think it mattered to him in the end. He played the hand he was dealt, and no one ever called his bluff. I don't like what he did, nor am I making excuses for him, I just understand.

To this day, Berkowitz continues to play his games from prison...still preying on people to carry on with his lies to the outside world.

April 14, 2023...I bet you thought I was finished. Please recognize God's work was not done just yet. It's amazing how God works. God himself had one more door to close, and I again would play my part.

I was just about done with this journal when I met a pastor who had been visiting Berkowitz in prison for the past year. He just completed writing a book about his visits and was getting ready to release to the world his conversations with David Berkowitz. When I asked the pastor what Berkowitz had told him, he began to repeat to me all of Maury Terry's tall tales of doctors and cults mixed with the Carrs. I couldn't believe it! Here we go again.

I questioned the pastor, without insult, if he thought there was a possibility Berkowitz might be lying to him like he had in the past to so many others. The pastor was confident with the bond he formed with Berkowitz from his visits, and was completely convinced Berkowitz was telling him the truth.

I began to build a relationship with this pastor and sent him some files on the case. I was trying to show him evidence that Berkowitz used the phone book to make up his cult members. The case itself did not interest the pastor, he wanted to know Berkowitz's psyche in all this, not if he was aided committng the crimes.

April 20, 2023, I text the pastor and asked if he could do me a favor... "Take Carl Denaro with you into prison to see Berkowitz." I told him it meant a lot to me that Carl gets his closure. The pastor agreed, and I had Carl meet us both that weekend for lunch in Long Island so I could introduce them to each other. With all this evidence now out publicly, how could Berkowitz lie to Carl again?

After our lunch, I took the pastor to Wicker Street, to show him "*Satan's realm*." I told him, as we walked "*THE GUTTERS OF N.Y.C.*," I recently completed a journal to be published and was going to show the world the truth. I wanted him to tell Berkowitz the game was over, and all of his lies were going to be exposed. When I asked the pastor if he knew who King and Duke were, he answered, "No, who are they?" I explained to him who they were and wanted him to ask Berkowitz about them. I then told the pastor about Berkowitz's first attempted murder with his .44 on July 6, 1976, where Berkowitz parked that night, his escape route, intricate details of the landscape in Yonkers that only I knew about. I wanted the pastor to let Berkowitz know, I knew a lot more than the people before me. After our walk, I showed the pastor 18 Wicker Street and told him to tell Berkowitz he owes the Neto family an apology.

A few weeks later, the pastor sent me a text. Berkowitz did not want him corresponding with me any longer, the pastor suggested we part ways. I had no problem with that, as you see, my job was done.

I text the pastor one last time just to make sure we were on the same page.

Paul: I'm fine with that...just remember your buddy told my friend Carl the last time he saw him that a woman shot him...try and make sure Berkowitz tells the truth for five minutes of his life. I have over one thousand pages of evidence, including his self confessions...he 100% shot Carl. He lied to him just two years ago. The purpose of this visit is for Carl...not more attention for Berkowitz.

Berkowitz, during Carl's visit, I guess felt comfortable this time...he confessed to doing all the shootings alone. His havoc of lies was now over, please say goodbye to the "Son of Sam."

I want to thank this pastor for his incredible role in all this. We were just pawns being used to form a checkmate for Carl...God is good!

So much factored into this end result, including COVID-19. If it wasn't for the pandemic, I would have never been inside binging on Netflix, and I wouldn't have seen *The Sons of Sam* documentary. Then when I saw Larry walking around CFLA, my old paper route, my church, Lake Avenue, the aqueduct, I felt I had to do something. This kid was telling his audience my city was the breeding grounds for the "Son of Sam" cult. You're not doing that on my watch, there is always one wolf awake amongst the pack. You can't come into Yonkers without a pass, so I checked the kid. Larry knew no one, he was an outsider. I should have left him in Untermyer Park looking at meaningless symbols and flowers.

When people ask me why I did this, my answer is because I am Yonkers, and these are my people. I couldn't let this go, I needed to do what was right and make things right. My city was being wrongfully cursed, my people were being wrongfully accused, my police were being wrongfully branded, and my church was being wrongfully stained. No more now will my city be looked at as a devil's den filled with evil-doers. No more now will my people be looked at as vampires and witches. No more now will my police be looked at as crooked and unjust. No more now will my church be looked at as a breeding ground for sinners.

I did this for my church, for my city, for Carl Denaro, for the Carrs, for the Netos, for the Cassaras, for Craig Glassman, for all the law enforcement involved, their kids and their wives. I did this because I could, I asked for nothing. I'm from Yonkers, home of the brave, and I just proved that to you.

To Carl Denaro, who I am now honored to call a friend, I hope you can live your life with closure to all this someday. No one but you can do that, and you can do it the way you want to. As a friend, I will do whatever it is to help you, even if it means starting this all over again. You are a class act and nothing but a gentleman. Have faith because God is good.

To Wheat Carr, may your days ahead be pain-free and lived with honor. We are Yonkers, so we are family. I will keep my word and make sure your story is told the right way. Keep God in your heart like I know He is to always minimize the pain. I pray your family can now rest in peace. I am here for you now and for the rest of your life, even when you think I am not. Live the rest of your life like a true hero. Not many can say they saved lives like you can. Live that way, it is what you truly are.

To Maria Neto, a warrior and true soldier of Christ. May your husband Joaquim rest on the most comfortable clouds in heaven. I know you miss him so much and since he has left, your heart will never be the same. Never feel that you are alone. Keep your faith and keep spreading God's good word. I envy your strength...you are so Yonkers and we are home of the brave.

My name is Paul Santo Agostino and I was born and raised in Yonkers, New York. I am not an investigator, bounty hunter, cop, or writer. I'm just a street guy who didn't mind his business. I never wanted to do this, but it all just happened and I'm proud. Yonkers is not for everyone, the people here are different than most, and we like it that way. Outsiders are welcome, but remember to never over-stay your visit, for you may not like in the end how things turn out. This mission that God has used me for is now over. I am thankful and grateful for all the people I have met during this journey. Always remember, in the end, you will always and only have the truth... NEO YES THE ONE.

I would like to thank God for always guiding me. Only through Him is anything ever possible. To my wife Maria and son Paulie, thank you for always supporting what I do. I love you both and do all for you. My always loving parents, Santo and Patricia Agostino. I thank you for life and always, no matter what, being there for me. I'm honored to be your son. Vinny, my brother, thank you for being you, you add to me. Penny, the true other half of this investigation, may we smash mugs until they kick us out. John Geiss, Joe Monaco, Ryan Wynne, Buddy Hughes, Dennis Hanrahan, Anthony Cerasi, Hoyt Rodgers, Sal DiMaggio, John Rinciari, John Comparetto, Mike Lorenzo Jr., and all the people of Yonkers...thank you. Carl Denaro, Wheat Carr, Maria and Slyvia Neto, Teresa Ramos, Steven Cassara, the Goncalos...thank you. Josh Zeman, Max Heusler, John Spencer, Lloyd Eaton, Tommy Zaino, Dave Butler, Al, Caveman, Billy Quinn, Andy Hogg, Joey Nodine, Bernadette Doyle, Kathy Meyer, Pastor Tom Wallace, Rob Mos, Albie, Frank Carozza, Billy Rob, Brunella...thank you. Laura Gregory, Alicia Shook-Schafer, Rena Martin Wells, Chris Reginella, Richie Lewis, J.C., David Aretha, Lauren Agostino, Vinnie Campisi...thank you. Christopher Agostino...you will never be forgotten, my brother, our Yonkers family is true.

Thank you all for reading. Be safe and God bless.

Some of the names in this book have been changed out of respect and privacy.

References: *The Gannett Suburban Newspapers, The New York Post, The Daily News, The Sword of The Lord Newspaper, thepeoplevsdavidberkowitz.com., Confessions of Son of Sam* by Dr. David Abrahamsen, *Son of Sam* by Dr. Lawrence D. Klausner, *Son of Sam: The .44 Caliber Killer* by George Carpozi Jr., *The Ultimate Evil* by Maury Terry, *The Sons of Sam: A Descent Into Darkness* by Josh Zeman

12/8/75

Dearest Dad;

Be strong! Enjoy your life as best as you can. You have worked hard all your life to help your family survive. You have done very well and you should be proud!

Now, you deserve a rest. So, please remain in good health for all your days. Take good care of Julia, keep in touch with my sister and brother-in-law, Aunt Ben and Uncle Lou, and Hal and Susan.

Love
David

...inmind down...

The time as come and the time is now — I cannot go on like this, disobeying the calling of my master.

Day and night with the howling of the Demon Dogs chanting the Death Call. The Death Call that summons me to kill, to sacrifice for the master whom, in all honesty, I despise.

It took me all this time to realize who I am and what I have come here to earth for. I had premonitions of my destiny since childhood but I was afraid of what I saw. ~~Through the~~

Through the years I have tried to fight against my brethen, the children of Anti-Christ. However, Satan is much stronger then me, more determined and perhaps more desperate. How can I disobey my own father?

I have disobeyed my master quite often. Trying to be a good

person, trying to love people, to make friends, to help someone - someone who needs me for nice things. I wanted to be a good man but in reality this is not possible since, in my soul I am ~~thoral~~, thoroughly evil.

"Deliver me the souls of those chosen to die," ~~so~~ commands the Demons of 2150 Hollond Avenue. The Demon Dogs cry out in the alleyway; "David, David kill someone today for us". "Bring us their blood and souls so that we may dine and bath in their death!"

Although my mission is comparatively minor, it has taken Jack Cassara and Satan over twenty-two years to form me into the soldier/servant that they so desire.

This is a WARNING to all police agencies in the Tri-State area.

For your information, a Satanic cult (devil worshipers and practioners of witchcraft), that has been established for quite some time has been instructed by their High Command (Satan) to begin to systematically kill and slaughter young people or people of good health and clean blood.

They plan to kill at least 100 young women and men but mostly women as part of a satanic ritual which involves the shedding of the victims, innocent blood. In this ritual, the victims are chosen at random and their blood is spilled. At this time, demons in the spirit (cannot be seen by humans), gather around the wounded or slain victim like a flock of vultures to suck, ~~suck~~ and drink the blood that has been spilled.

WARNING: The streets shall be run with blood.

I David Berkowitz have been chosen, chosen since birth, to be one of the executioners for the cult.

He who hath eyes, let him see the dead victims.

He who hath ~~has~~ ears, let him listen to what I say.

I David Berkowitz recieve no reward for my services. My services are performed in honor of "my master - High Priest" "General Cosmo", Jack "Cassara.

WARNING – at this time there are people, or at least they appear to be people, but they are not. They are demons who have taken on human form.

These people are extremely dangerous and furthermore, they possess powers of super-human nature and hold at their ~~disp~~ disposal tremendous powers.

Please, who will hear my word and believe it?; Who will act before it is too late?

A Clue: The houses in Westchester county – Yonkers – Hastings – etc., the "old" houses. The secret lies in their history.

Many of the houses in Yonkers, the ones rich in history, hold many secrets of the past.

Some of these houses ~~still~~ have spirits dwelling in them. These spirits are not good

The commander of Yonkers has the name "Captain Blood" and he supervised most of the murders. The Highest Temple of Satan is located at
18 Wicker St., Yonkers.

Here is a partial list of those with the highest ranks.

Jack Cassara - High Priest
Nann Cassara - High Priestess
and family - 174 Coligni, New Roch.

"The Wicker St. Gang"
with Captain Blood.
18 Wicker Street Yonkers.

The "House of Horrors" - "The Carr Gang"

SAM CARR alias "1st Luietenant Tinker"
FRANCINE FRANCIS CARR
John Wheat CARR - "Johnny Rape Slayer"
316 WARBURTON Avenue

12/14/76

TUESDAY

~~[struck-through]~~ DEATH DAY

SUFFERING DAY

Sam CARR IS King!

SAM CARR IS King!

SAM CARR'S dog

SAYS Spill Blood tonight

David. SAM'S Dog has

been Screaming FOR blood

all day today. He is

So hungry he won't Stop.

Kill FOR SAM CARR!!

December 22, 1976

"Bring me the head of a woman to place on our Alter. Spill the blood of an innocent one so that we, in the spirit, shall go to thee and drink her blood

"I - 'The Master of the House' of 18 Wicker Street, Yonkers, command my slave David Berkowitz to kill."

"I am foul, vile and wicked..." Every murder in Westchester Count is under the name of 18 Wicker All the manure in the street, all the vomitus in the alleyways and

all the urine under the stenched steps does not equal my vile soul says the Lord of 18 Wicker St.

FRIDAY FEBRUARY 25, 1977

Today is Friday, blood day. Today I will blood for the people of
and
"The House of Joquin Blood, and The Horror Hotel."

My ears are ringing because the dogs are hungry and they are screaming loudly in pain.

Joquin never feeds his dogs nor his mother any food. He relies on ~~my~~ me to hunt for him and kill his dogs food.

He likes his meat fresh and he loves warm blood. Joquin and I like to hunt for food in Queens mostly because the hunting is good and Queens girls meat tastes ~~best~~ best - maybe its the water ~~they~~ they drink.

3/8/77

Today the Devil Dog at Wicker Street is in great pain. Apparently Joquin Goncalo is low on blood. Yes, I'm right. The Dog is screaming for fresh blood and meat to quench his thirst and pangs of hunger.

I said to Joquin, why all the suffering and pain? Why do you bring so much destruction into the world? Joquin laughted, "to hell with the people of the world, the people of the world shall bow down to me and I shall conquer."

I said to him you evil beast and the Wicked Wicker Dog cried out ~~and~~ saying "yes, we are evil, we are the Children of Satan, we kill the innocent, and praise the guilty." At this time the dog barked fierce cries and my head developed a severe pain. I was no longer permitted to speak to the people of Wicker St.

All day long the Devil Dog as been yelling in pain - there is no ceasing. I begged the Wicker-street cult to leave me alone. I am there alone. Today the demon has not stopped for a moment. How much blood does he want me to spill for him?

3/8/77 9:15AM

I am the executioner for the forces of Evil.

I am Death, and I am here to kill those that have come unto me.

My body lives at 35 Pine St., in Yonkers.

My heart, soul and mind or whatever is left of them dwells at in Yonkers.

, is the house of worship for Satan and his army. The people that dwell there'in represent every abomination and vile thing that has ever dwelled on earth.

Though they appear to be human, (flesh and blood), they are truly Demons of Satan. They have, under the command of their Master, set up a house of sacrifice and worship in Yonkers. This house is utilized as a resting stop for other Demons that are travelling the earth to do

②

the Masters bidding.

It is their primary concern to have me walk as ~~them~~ their servant in doing their work. I must kill those who are chosen. the souls of the dead are then carried away by these omnipotent spirits to the house and then . . .

To the NAZI'S at Yonkers.

I wonder what makes people like you. I cannot imagine what animals you are and why are you deliberately trying to hurt your fellow human beings. What have we the people done to you for you to turn on mankind and try to hurt innocent people? Have ~~peop~~ the people of Yonkers treated you so bad that you thirst to see us destroyed? Do you wish for us all to die?

How many people's lives have you damaged or ruined. How much pain have you invoked on the people of Wleenwood, Yonkers? How many families have been torn apart? How many have, in states of hopless anguish & despair, committed suicide & because of you, the people of

I tell you this - you shall not escape! You shall be punished for your sins, for your wickedness, ~~and~~ for your cruelness, and for your ~~sadistic~~ attempts to kill your neighbors ~~by~~ via your sadistic & torturous acts.

My name is Samuel Carr and my mansion is located at

I thank my Master for providing me with it.

I Sam Carr am lower than the shit that comes out of my dogs asshole. I Sam Carr am a vile wretch and my body smells like the vomitus from a pack of rats.

I Sam Carr hate my neighbors and I will kill them. I hate God so much that I fart when I hear his name.

I have dedicated myself to murder, and I promise to drive all my neighbors to their death by the cruelest means. I will never let my neighbors rest nor eat, nor live in peace. Let them kill themselves with their own hands to escape the continuous torment that I continually dish out to them from my home..

Let any soul who hates me come try ~~and~~ to murder me. Let them try to murder my wife or my family. Let anyone who wishes to murder me, Samuel Cain, lay in wait outside my house with a shotgun and shoot me full of slugs. HA HA, I cannot die.

"I am the all powerful "Sam"! I shall ~~the~~ tie up Francis and beat her unmercifly then chain her up to the back of my house and let the neighbors here her howl in pain.

I Sam Cain am a cruel, mean, deadly murderer and I'm a 'bad' mother-fuckin dude. Yea!

Samuel Carr, destroyer of persons, destroyer of life, of dreams, of love, of Hope and of Peace.

Samuel Carr, cruel mean Sam and his screaming maniac. That ugly howling blood Monster - God, how my head hurts from his piercing screams.

I must kill for John Carr that terrible rapist and child molester. You should hear John boast about his perverted conquests. That terrible John Carr born to ruin people.

There is no peace on earth and Samuel Carr, my master, rules Yonkers and soon wants to possess the Bronx and Queens. God help those people because Sam and John have the power to drive people crazy.

Who has the knowledge with which to combat the forces, these terrible evil forces of the Carr family of, Yonkers, N.Y.?

I am killing for one reason and that is for ~~the~~ honour and service to the Samuel Carr family of who have power over the land, the air, and me. For the Carr family whose goal is to have dominion over all of N.Y.C. & Westchester; whose goal is to torture and abuse many; whose goal is to slay the good of earth, whose goal is to make life intolerable to the people of this World.

The Samuel Carr family is the most wicked and vile family to possess territory in this region. The cruel selfish and wicked Carr family demands from me the spilling of innocent blood to feed the dog, to aide Sam's health, and to appease the evil forces to whom they worship.

I am at Samuel Carr's mercey, for it is him who has control over me and my fate. I am broke. There is no place left for me to go. I cannot afford to move. I am without hope, trapped enslaved to this dwelling place. ~~and~~ I ~~can~~ have been placed at the mercy of Samuel Carr

"I kill for Samuel Carr and his "Blood Monster." If anybody doubts the existense of the two, then let him go to
and view that old horror house. Then look at old ugly Samuel Carr. Then venture behind the house and gaze into the back ~~your~~ yard. There you will see if your unlucky — the monster.

Mr. Sam Carr; April 10, 1977

This letter is to inform you that I am in the process of filing legal papers in Yonkers City Court to have one of your dogs removed from your property because he is a public nuisance. I have already spoken to the people of the humane society of westchester and they agree with my actions.

You're probably thinking that I am some kind of animal hater or I'm a cruel person but that isn't true. Let me tell you that I love animals very much. However, one of your dogs, and you know which one, is obviously very sick or is being treated badly. He howls and barks constantly for hours at a time and there is no reason for it. If he's sick, take him to a vet. If he cannot be left alone then don't leave him alone. And if its because you mistreat him then maybe its best you just give him up.

When my wife and I set up our

home in Yonkers we wanted to live our lives in peace and happiness. Unfortunatly your dog has prevented us from doing so. Our lives have been torn apart because of this dog. We can't sleep late in the day, We can't come home in the evening and relax, and we cannot keep our windows open at all. Even with our windows and storm windows closed, to include heavy drapes, the howling is so loud and constant that these barriers cannot keep the sound out. It's as if he were in the house with us.

In the past week, for example, we tried to arrange our work schedules so we could have a few days off together. We wanted to spend some quite weekdays, just the two of us, to sleep late, to make love, to read, etc., but the barking and howling continued and we had no peace. Today is Easter Sunday, I'm writing this letter now and as usual the dog has been going at it for the entire day - unbelievable!!

My wife is about to have a nervous breakdown and I'm a bundle of nerves. We can't go on like this. The only thing we regret is that we ~~didnt~~ di[dn't] try to rid ourselves of this problem earlier. However, as I said, we are peaceful people and we don't like hav[ing] to take such drastic actions. We were always hoping that the problem would alleviate itself but I can see thats its going to be another misera[ble] season.

No I cannot ~~afford~~ afford to move, our home is here.

Mr. Carr, every dog is expected to bark a reasonable amount, thats normal. Howling and crying all day long isn't and I think that dog is very sick. Furthermore, dont think that by keeping the dog leashed, licensed, and fed, thats its enough. The law clearly states that if a dog continuously barks when unprovoked it is a "public nuisance" regardless of the time of day. Keeping the dog on the property isnt enough if his barking physically GOES OFF the property to other homes and disturbs the peace of others. Matter-of-factly, I can hear that dog barking for blocks and blocks away.

We do hope that you will cooperate with us to solve the problem.

We wish to remain anonymous for personal reasons.
Thank you.

Samuel Carr, 4/19/77

I have asked you kindly to stop that dog from howling all day long, yet he continues to do so. I pleaded with you I told you how it is ~~destroying my~~ family = We have no peace, no rest!

Now I know what kind of person you are, and what kind of family you are. You are cruel and inconsiderate. You have no love for any other human beings. Your selfish, Mr. Carr.

My life is destroyed now. I have nothing to lose anymore. I can see that there shall be no peace in my life, or my famalies life until I end yours.

You wicked evil man - child of the devil. I curse you and your family forever. I pray to God that he takes your whole family off the face of the earth. People like you should not be allowed to live on this planet.

A Citizen

On Wednesday April 27, 1977
Francis Carr ignites terror in Yonkers. At 7:55 AM, fat Francis the lesbian unleashes the that howling maniac the "Blood Monster".

A quiet neighborhood is destroyed. Francis is the queen of the demons and she with her cold loveless heart and soul ruins the lives of the people. God help us and protect us from the Carr family before we are all driven mad.

Oh God I'm going mad.
Why Sam do you hate people so much that you let loose that terrible monster upon the people? they say that noise drives people crazy maybe its true and Sam Carr you are evil.

Dear Jack,

I'm sorry to hear about that fall you took from the roof of your house.

Just want to say

"I'm sorry"

But I'm sure it won't be long

Until you feel much better.

Healthy.

well and strong!

Please be careful next time. Since you're going to be confined for a long time, let us know if Nann needs anything.

Sincerely: Sam & Fannie

6-17-77

Tiller, Miller and Godzilla,
42 Broadway
New York, N.Y.

Gentlemen:

My name is Francis Carr and although I'm not as young as I used to be, I can still get into perverted sex scenes real good.

I believe I'm the one your looking for in your upcoming porno movie "Sweet Tootsie".

I can do all types of acrobatic stunts in bed and I will orally copulate anything except turtles and mice.

I love bondage and sado masachism. Please contact me as soon as possible so I can audition. Thank you.

Sincerely
Francis Carr

My Superior: Craig Glassman

Sergeant Glassman,

I know how successful you have been with your assignment, forcing me out into the street for Mr. Carr, however, the dead are crying in their graves for justice and God has promised it to them.

I myself realize that I am beyond hope and redemption because I have succumbed to the powers of your commander, Mister Carr. I obey all my orders as you well know, and I'll carry them out dutifully. But we must face the fact that our deaths will come one day. Then there shall be the Judgement! Since you are a fallen angel and have been condemned to the eternal fire before the earth was created, still, God will be more merciful to you if you rebel against General Cosmo and his horde of demons.

There is at this time little for you to gain by loyal service. I believe the end of the "Reign of Terror" is near and the authorities will be dealing with you in their own way.

I guess I'm foolish to plead with you to surrender and turn to God because I know that your soul is evil and that you have no heart. Therefore, you will have to spend eternity in the lowest depths of Hell. Don't fear because Captain Cain and his family, and me will be at your side.

You have done well in your 6,000 plus years of service. You have taken over my soul despite my early resistance and my denials and protests. Go ahead if you must and continue to torture the people of earth. Don't stop issuing Captain Cain's wrath upon the world at my plea's. Just go ahead you cruel monster and continue your torments. You will stand naked at the judgement seat of Christ.

Your Brother Deso Demesmutz

The 1st Saturday
of August 1977

I must get this job done.
This is the last assignment, the last mission. Once it is finished I will be of no use to Sam Carr and I will be destroyed.

I do not fear Death for I do not wish to go back to my apartment, ever. Never again will I have to give my life to Craig.

However, I will do my best to come out of this alive because as one columnist said, "someone must pay for these horrendous crimes."

From the Bronx to Water Mill, New York no soul shall be safe.

I would also like to meet with the task force personally, not that I have anything to say to them but its only fair we meet face to face. I wonder if they will take me on a brief tour of their war room?

Perhaps the hidden secrets of the Carr house will never be known. Those hideous blood monsters who lurk in the woodwork and under those rotting floor boards, yes, they will still live on.

At this time Craig is awaiting anxiously by his T.V., ready to take command.

Bullets crackle in a quiet town. The sounds of running feet and screams of anguish fill the air. Huge streams of blood travel down curvous buttocks, bosoms bouncing, bullets flying into the night coldly seeking flesh and bone, yes, its terror in the night. Sergeant Craig is terror!

Who has brought the wrath to this town? Where is the "Great Lord Bloomingdale's their Saviour. Why has God forsaken this ~~town~~? place?

For truly there has never been peace in the ~~Ham~~ Hamptons, inner peace I mean. They aren't a sensual people but they are ~~full~~ filled with rage and jealousy.

So let New Yorkers everywhere gather together, gather to battle the unseen forces that roam their neighborhoods at night and seeks to imprison their children in coffins. Let them hunt down the Son of Sam and the mysteries thereof.

Truly nobody knows what time it is. For the end of Sam is drawing nigh. Yet, the police continue to hunt and trap. ~~not knowing the~~ The Inspector continues to work feverishly trying to unravel the mystery but, would he dare to believe that by surise of the next morning he will be holding <u>that</u> .44. ~~The cu~~ The curtain always closes quickly when the stars walk off or die.

In the aftermath the Hamptons chamber of Commerce will have to count their dead and file a report. Reporters will be swarming the streets snapping pictures of dark red spots on the ground which symbolize where people once stood. Perhaps a big tall cop with a empty .38 will be playfully kicking in the ribs of the Son of Sam with his ~~shiny~~ shinny boot. He'll be enjoying those sadistic delights and he'll be looking on with satisfaction at his prized catch.

~~In the aftermath~~

In a short time things will be back to normal and if you go into a lover's lane at night you'd be able to here the ~~squeaks~~ sound of dozens of car springs squeaking in unison. Then you will know that there is peace in the world.

X

Belove" PaPa,
Father of Vomit,

I heard your smelly mother last night. She was outside below my window shouting her usual blend of obscenities. Sam, you have a terrible mother. Why is she so perverted?

I smelled though my window that rancid odor of vomitus and immediately I thought of you and Moses.

Tell me Papa God, what fate awaits me? I hope I never have to spend it in your attic again.

Sam my Lord, I've heard that you had killed again in New Jersey. But fear not because I haven't told the police about the other Bergen County slaughters.

I can drink water here. I remember when you used to keep me ~~Sea~~ tied up in the sun for days without water.

Sam Cau, Lord of Lund, I worship you and your dead living mother.

Your Son
David

Dear "Mayor Beam",

My name is David Berkowitz and I am writing you with the uttmost urgency. There is little time left in the world because demons (Sam Carr, 316 Warburton Ave., Yonkers), (Jack Cassara, 74 Coligni Ave., New Rochelle, N.Y. have taken a strong hold in the government.

I am a dedicated Gladiator who will fight the forces of darkness to the ends of the earth. However, I need your help. We must work together to help the public and warn them of "Sam" the terrible foe of the people.

Sam Carr, John Wheat, Jack and Nann Cassara, and Craig Glassman all know each other.

According to the voices I heard one of them, a demon, stated that Sam Carr strangled young people and ~~buryed~~ buried them behind Sam's house. These people are just bones now however I can hear them calling out my name and beconing me to join them. They are all bones now but I can hear them calling me. Surely Sam Carr killed them and drank their blood.

See, I told you Sam is a thirsty lad.

I, David Berkowitz am merely a tool for Satan the devil. But perhaps God has spared my life to an extent for a heavenly purpose.

Though I am suffering now, I want to help the people and warn them of the dangers of Black Magic and the hopes that others will see the light and trust in God.

Please help warn the world of the terror that is in Sam. Please help me

Sincerely
David B

drove there. I was in Huntington first it was about 2 A.M. I drove on Belt to Howard Beach. I looked around then to Canarsie, then continued to Bensonhurst. It was now 2 A.M. I parked on Bay 17 Bet Shore PKwy & Cropsey. I was there before. I had to go out to Kill some body. I parked on a fire Hydrant. I then saw Police give me a summons. I had a feeling they would. I was on Bay 17 & Shore P Kwy. 17

I watched them for 10 minutes. I went back & saw summ[ons]. I was wearing Denim Jacket & Pants & work shoes & Brown shirt Light. I took ticket off windshield & put it in car & went back to park. There were young people in Dead end St. they left. I sat on bench. I had a 44 Bulldog loaded. I then saw Stacy Moskowitz & Boy friend on swings. They then went to car. On ~~Bay~~ Shore P.7

the other car was
up further. the other
car was there first
when I saw them
by swings. they
then went to car.
I waited then
went to car +
fired into car. I
fired 4 times at Mrs
Moskowitz I carried
1 doz other rounds of
ammo in my slacks
I fired first at Stacy
head. then into the
car I was 4-5 ft
away. I didn't know
if she was hit. I
sprayed the car.
I saw the boy.
I wanted him.

I don't know why I
shot the guy. I ran
thru the paper hole
thru town houses.
I ran to my car.
I was facing south
toward Cropsey. I
went to 18th ave
as far it could go.
I don't remember if
I was on Cropsey
or where. I drove
to the end in northerly
direction. I drove
aimlessly. I traversed
Bklyn thru Sunset
Park. then into another
Park where I parked
got out for air.

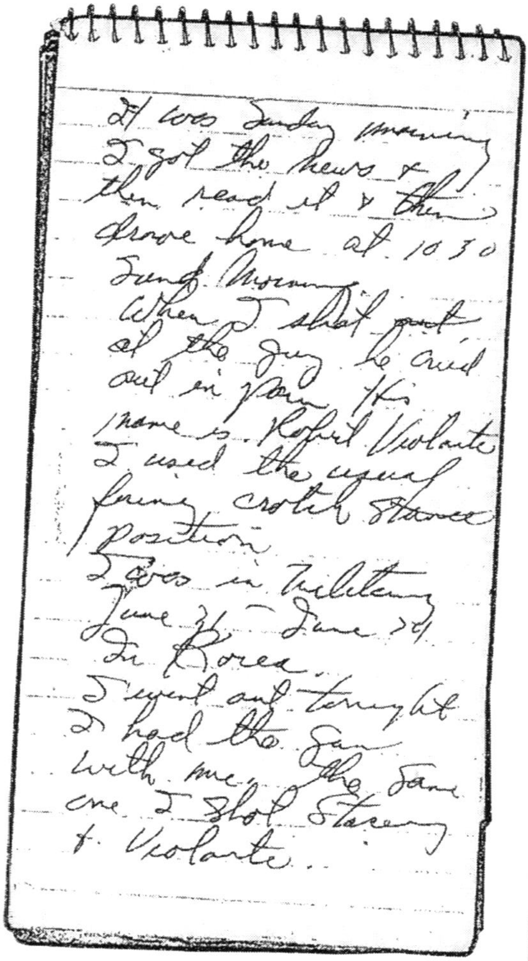
It was Sunday morning
I got the news &
then read it & then
drove home at 1030
Sunday Morning.
When I shot out
at the guy he cried
out in pain. His
name is Robert Violante
I used the usual
firing crotch stance
position
I was in Military
June 71 - June 74
In Korea.
I went out tonight
I had the gun
with me, the same
one I shot Stacy
& Violante.

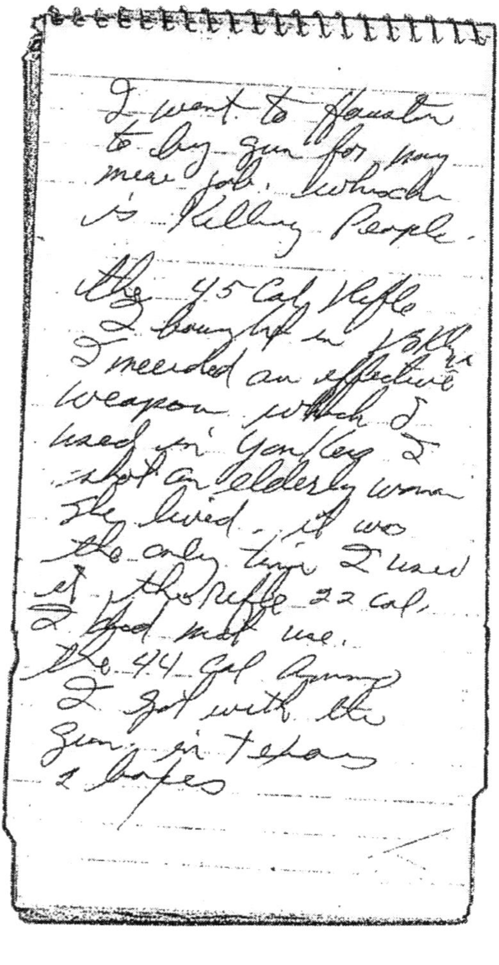
I went to Houston
to buy gun for my
mean job. which
is Killing People.
the 45 Cal Rifle
I bought in July
I needed an effective
weapon which I
used in Yonkers I
shot an elderly woman
she lived. it was
the only time I used
it the Rifle 22 cal.
I had not use.
the 44 Cal Ammo
I got with the
gun in Texas
2 boxes

Hi
My Name IS
MR. Williams
And I Live
iN this hoLe
I have Several
Children who I'm Turning
Into Killers. WAIT
Til they grow UP.
I
For

I'm sorry to say that it is just a coincidence Miss Placido had come from the same neighborhood. ~~Th~~ She was not followed. Though, she was a chosen victim but by one greater than me.

I am not an expert marksman as thought. Because if I were, the death toll would be higher.

I never walk away from the seen of the sacrifices.

That elderly gentleman did not hear me correctly. I said "~~Hi Mad~~" Hi mister."

Sal Lupo was not chosen for death only Miss Placido.

I do not always use two hands when I fire.

Sam Carr is still Prince!

Printed in Great Britain
by Amazon

055a4d40-8488-42d7-9980-8d8e0ff8d626R01